CHRIST, THE CHRISTIAN
AND THE CHURCH

TO

ERIC SYMES ABBOTT

IN GRATITUDE

ERICO ERICUS
VICE-CUSTOS TRANSLATUS
CUSTODI TRANSLATO

CHRIST, THE CHRISTIAN AND THE CHURCH

A STUDY OF THE INCARNATION AND ITS CONSEQUENCES

By

E. L. MASCALL

Student of Christ Church, Oxford
University Lecturer in the Philosophy of Religion
Priest of the Oratory of the Good Shepherd

O admirabile commercium:
Creator generis humani,
animatum corpus sumens,
de Virgine nasci dignatus
est: et procedens homo
sine semine, largitus est
nobis suam Deitatem

1724

LONGMANS, GREEN AND CO
LONDON ◇ NEW YORK ◇ TORONTO

LONGMANS, GREEN AND CO LTD
6 & 7 CLIFFORD STREET LONDON W I
BOSTON HOUSE STRAND STREET CAPE TOWN
531 LITTLE COLLINS STREET MELBOURNE

LONGMANS, GREEN AND CO INC
55 FIFTH AVENUE NEW YORK 3

LONGMANS, GREEN AND CO
20 CRANFIELD ROAD TORONTO 16

ORIENT LONGMANS LTD
CALCUTTA BOMBAY MADRAS
DELHI VIJAYAWADA DACCA

First Published 1946
Second Impression by Photolithography 1955
Third Impression by Photolithography 1957

By the same author :
He Who Is.   A Study in Traditional Theism
Corpus Christi
Existence and Analogy
Christian Theology and Natural Science
Via Media

MADE AND PRINTED BY OFFSET IN GREAT BRITAIN BY
WILLIAM CLOWES AND SONS, LIMITED, LONDON AND BECCLES

PREFACE

I HAVE attempted in this book to exhibit the Incarnation of the Son of God as the foundation and the unifying principle of the life and thought of both the individual Christian and the Church of which he is a member. That in Jesus of Nazareth human nature is permanently and inseparably united to the Person of the Eternal Word, that by baptism men and women are re-created by incorporation into the human nature of Jesus and receive thereby a real communication of the benefits of his Passion, that sanctification is the progressive realization in the moral realm of the change that was made in the ontological realm by baptism, that incorporation into Christ is incorporation into the Church, since the Church is in its essence simply the human nature of Christ made appropriable by men, that all the thought, prayer and activity of Christians, in so far as it is brought within the sphere of redemption, is the act of Christ himself in and through the Church which is his Body—these are the ideas that I have tried to expound; and the thread that unites them all is the doctrine of the permanence of the manhood of the glorified and ascended Christ.

The bare outlines of this theme could easily be sketched in forty or fifty pages. On the other hand, a complete and systematic exposition of the doctrine of the Incarnation and its consequences would far outstrip the limits of a single volume. The task that I have tried to perform lies between these extremes. I was led to write this book by the conviction that there are a number of living theological problems of the present day upon which the central principle of the permanence of Christ's manhood is capable of throwing considerable light. I have therefore discussed in some detail such of these problems as I felt capable of attacking at all, while giving to the rest of the theme only such consideration as was necessary to impart coherence and continuity. Where I felt that I had something to say that might clear up an obscurity I have said it at some length, even at the risk of digression from the main theme, but where I felt I had no special contribution to make I have tried to refrain from making it. It is well, I think, to state this plainly lest anyone should suppose, for example, that I am

under the delusion that the fourth chapter contains an adequate
exposition of the Atonement or that the seventh purports to be a
definitive pronouncement upon the many vexed questions now
under discussion by patristic scholars as to the precise nature of
the various orders of the Ministry and their functions in the
primitive Church.

It was obviously necessary to begin by expounding the doctrine
of the Incarnation itself, as the foundation for the rest of the book.
In doing this, I have made use of two comparisons which have
received little attention in recent years, but which, as regards both
the respects in which they are applicable and those in which they
are not, are, I believe, extremely illuminating; I mean the comparison of the union of Godhead and manhood in Christ with the
union of body and soul in man, and the comparison of the relation
of incarnation with that of creation. I have traced out the line
of Christological thought which passes from Gore through Weston
to Dr. Relton, and I have ventured to suggest that, in spite of the
great services that they rendered to Christology, these three
distinguished writers were unduly influenced by two contemporary emphases of thought. One of these was an anthropocentric
tendency, which led to the neglect of the warning given by
Quicunque vult that the Incarnation must be viewed as the taking up
of manhood into God and not as the conversion of Godhead into
flesh. The other was a desire to substitute psychological categories
for ontological ones, which in effect involved the reversal of the
attitude taken up by the Church in the fifth century in the adoption of the person-nature terminology at Chalcedon. But I am far
from suggesting that psychological considerations have no place
in a discussion of the Incarnation, and I have in fact tried to show
that a deeper consideration of psychology than has sometimes
been given leads to a more satisfactory doctrine of our Lord's
human knowledge. I would add that the appearance of such a
work as Dr. A. M. Farrer's *Finite and Infinite* should be sufficient
to dispose of the common assumption that the notions of being and
substance are altogether obsolete.

In the subsequent chapters, which are concerned with some of
the consequences of the Incarnation, I have argued that many of
the antitheses with which contemporary theology bristles are as a
matter of fact false ones. It would, of course, be ridiculous to
suggest that all the theological controversies of the present day are
merely the outcome of superficial misunderstandings and that no

real issues are at stake. But I am entirely at one with Canon Balmforth in the strictures which he has passed upon what he describes[1] as "that plaguey 'either-or' delusion," with which both dogmatic and ascetic theology to-day seem to be obsessed. Indeed what has chiefly convinced me of the supreme significance of the doctrine of the permanence of Christ's manhood as the central principle of Christian theology has been the extent to which that doctrine has made it possible to get beneath—or should one rather say "above"?—the either-or level, and to see the two contrasted elements as mutually involved in a synthesis in which one can say "both-and." (Need I add that I am not a Hegelian?) And if this book has been worth writing at all, it is, I dare to hope, because it points the way, in several important matters, to the possibility of such a synthesis. As instances of this I would draw attention to the following:

(a) The contrast between "imputation" and "impartation" (Chapter V).

(b) The contrast between "realized" and "futurist" eschatology (Chapter VI).

(c) The contrast between the idea of the Church as the ark of salvation and the universality of grace (Chapter VIII).

(d) The contrast between the Eucharist as the re-presentation of Calvary and as the participation in the worship of heaven (Chapters IX to XI).

(e) The contrast between personal devotion and the liturgical and corporate life of the Church (Chapters VIII and XII).

(f) The contrast between "faith" and "mysticism" (Chapter XII).

(g) The contrast between "rational theology" and "revelation" (Chapter XIII).

And in trying to reconcile these contrasts I have been led into several discussions which may perhaps be of independent value. I would instance the following:

(i) The remarks upon the participation of the Christian in the eternity of God, arising out of the problem of eschatology (Chapter VI).

(ii) The development of the doctrine of sacramental re-presentation, which was found to be necessary, as supplementary to

[1] In *Christendom*, March 1941, p. 61.

Dr. Hicks's refusal to equate sacrifice with death, for the formulation of a sound Eucharistic theology (Chapter X).

(iii) The affirmation that the participation in the life of God which is supremely manifested in the mystical union must be seen as directly connected with the Christian's adoption into the sonship of Christ, a point which has been insufficiently emphasized by Catholic mystical theologians, who have thus exposed themselves to attacks from both neo-Protestants and certain representatives of the "liturgical" school.

It will be clear how great are my debts to other writers; the references in the footnotes and the bibliography which I have appended will be sufficient evidence of this. The quotations which I have given from the fifth book of the *Ecclesiastical Polity* will, I think, show how much of what I have said which may seem to run counter to certain tendencies in recent theology is to be found in the thought of "that learned and judicious divine, Mr. Richard Hooker." And I cannot but regret that the books which Robert Wilberforce wrote in his Anglican days have been allowed to lapse into obscurity; they contain in germ most of what has been written in recent years by such authors as Abbot Vonier on the Eucharist and Mersch and de Lubac on the Mystical Body of Christ. If I have made but few quotations from Fr. Lionel Thornton's great work, *The Common Life in the Body of Christ*, it is because if I had done more it would have been virtually impossible to stop. It does in fact provide the Biblical foundation for most of the latter part of my book. There are two further works which, though they came into my hands when my manuscript was practically complete, I feel bound to mention for their bearing on my subject, although I have made no positive use of them. The first of these is *The Christian Sacrifice*, by Canon Eugène Masure; its author says so many things that I have tried to say, and says them with so much more profundity and eloquence than I could ever hope to command, that it would be ungenerous of me not to express my gratitude and admiration for his inspiring and irenical treatise. The other book is Dom Gregory Dix's *The Shape of the Liturgy*, in which there are developed, with a wealth of patristic erudition and with many piquant and illuminating reflections upon the Church's life and worship both past and present, the conceptions which this learned Benedictine briefly expounded in his essay in *The Parish Communion*. It is obviously impossible to

anticipate the judgment that liturgical scholars will pass upon its
more provocative conclusions, but it is, I think, safe to say that no
other book in the English tongue has so successfully and vividly
shown the organic connection between the life which the Church
lives and the liturgy by which she lives it. I am glad—and, I would
add, relieved—to find that on the points where Dom Dix's book
and the present work make contact, my argument is strengthened
and not refuted by his scholarship.

If it be true that *Qui s'excuse s'accuse*, I must by now have sufficiently laid myself open to condemnation. And anyone who tries
to reconcile differences must always expect to find that he has
unwittingly "launched his olive-branch from a catapult." Nevertheless, I believe that *Beati pacifici* is a pronouncement that applies
to the realm of thought as well as to that of practical affairs. I
can only repeat that I offer this book in the hope that it may throw
some light upon points that are obscure in the theological controversies of the present day, and that it may exhibit in some small
degree the architectonic and synthetic power of the central truth
of the Christian Faith, that of the assumption of human nature
by the coeternal and consubstantial Son of God.

In concluding this preface I will add only the following words
of Duns Scotus:

"In choosing or rejecting an opinion, a man ought not to be led
by love or hatred for its holder, but rather by the truth itself; and
therefore we ought to love both sides, those whose opinion we reject
not less than those whose opinion we follow, since both of them help
in the discovery of the truth; and therefore it is right to say
Thank you to all."

My thanks are due to the following friends who read this book
in manuscript and made many valuable comments: the Rev.
Canon H. Balmforth, Principal of Ely Theological College; the
Rev. C. D. Waddams, Fellow and Chaplain of St. Catharine's
College, Cambridge; the Rev. G. B. Bentley, Provost and Priest-
Vicar of Lincoln Cathedral; and the Rev. P. M. S. Allen, Chaplain
of Scholae Cancellarii, Lincoln. None of them, however, is to be
held responsible for any of the opinions which I have expressed.
I must also thank the Rev. R. H. Daubney, who kindly undertook
the wearisome task of reading the proofs.

For permission to make quotations from the following works I am grateful to the publishers mentioned: *The Works of Richard Hooker*, arranged by John Keble, and an article in the *Journal of Theological Studies* by Sir Edwyn Hoskyns, the Delegates of the Clarendon Press, Oxford; Bishop Gore's *Dissertations, Belief in God*, and *Belief in Christ*, Messrs. John Murray; Fr. Thornton's *Common Life in the Body of Christ*, the Dacre Press; Dr. Relton's *Study in Christology*, the Abbé Bremond's *Literary History of Religious Thought in France*, Sir Edwyn Hoskyns's *Cambridge Sermons*, and *The Parish Communion*, the Society for Promoting Christian Knowledge; M. Maritain's *Degrees of Knowledge*, Fr. Bulgakov's *Orthodox Church*, and Fr. Congar's *Divided Christendom*, Messrs. Geoffrey Bles; Sir Edwyn Hoskyns's *Fourth Gospel* and Mr. Chavasse's *Bride of Christ*, Messrs. Faber and Faber; M. Gilson's *Mystical Theology of St. Bernard*, Messrs. Sheed and Ward; Professor Arseniev's *Mysticism and the Eastern Church*, the Student Christian Movement Press; Abbot Vonier's *Key to the Doctrine of the Holy Eucharist*, Professor E. Allison Peers's edition of *The Works of St. John of the Cross*, and the Dominican Fathers' translation of St. Thomas Aquinas, Messrs. Burns, Oates and Washbourne; Professor Dodd's *History and the Gospel*, Messrs. James Nisbet and Co.; Mr. E. I. Watkin's *Philosophy of Mysticism*, Messrs. Thomas Baker.

I am also grateful to the Dacre Press for allowing me to make use of several passages from books by myself previously published by them. The Appendix to Chapter XII, the whole of Chapter XIII and part of Chapter IX are based upon material previously published in *Theology*, which has been made use of with the approval of the Society for Promoting Christian Knowledge.

CONTENTS

xi

CHAPTER I

THE INCARNATION OF THE WORD OF GOD

I

THE doctrine of the Incarnation involves two mutually inter-related truths, either of which raises great problems for the human intellect, but both of which are in essence so simple that they can be stated in two English sentences of words of one syllable taken from the Gospel itself. The first is "The Word was God"; the second, "The Word was made flesh." The maintenance of the former was the primary concern of the first of the four great ecumenical councils, that of Nicaea; the maintenance of the second was the primary concern of the other three, those of Constantinople, Ephesus and Chalcedon. The first of these texts assures us that Christ is truly God, the second that he is truly man. They provide the data for all Christological discussion, and, while the subtlety of such discussion may be judged by the degree to which it can explain and reconcile them, its orthodoxy is to be determined by its faithfulness to them.

In the two great Catholic confessions which the controversies of the early Christian centuries bequeathed to the Church these two truths are proclaimed with incandescent clarity in phrases whose elaborateness, while it is in striking contrast to the simplicity of the Biblical words, neither adds to nor subtracts from their content.

Thus the Niceno-Constantinopolitan Creed first of all asserts the Church's belief

"in one Lord Jesus Christ, the only-begotten Son of God, begotten of the Father before all the ages, Light from Light, Very God from Very God, begotten not made, consubstantial with the Father, through whom all things were made."

Then it goes on to declare that this same Lord

"for us men and for our salvation came down from heaven, and was made flesh of the Holy Ghost and Mary the Virgin, and was made man."

Similarly, the *Quicunque vult* insists that

"the right faith is that we believe and confess that our Lord Jesus Christ, the Son of God, is God and Man:

"He is God of the substance of the Father, begotten before the worlds; and Man of the substance of his Mother, born in the world:

"Complete God; and complete Man, subsisting by a rational soul and human flesh:

"Equal to the Father as regards the Godhead; less than the Father as regards the manhood.

"And, although he be God and Man, nevertheless he is not two, but is one Christ: one, however, not by the conversion of Godhead into flesh, but by taking up of manhood into God.

"He is altogether one, not by conversion of substance but by unity of person; for, as rational soul and flesh is one man, so God and Man is one Christ."

The Incarnation thus means that the divine Word or Son of God united to himself in the womb of Mary a complete human nature, complete in both body and soul. His body was made of the substance of Mary by the overshadowing of the Holy Ghost; his soul, like other human souls, was created by God and infused into his body.[1]

The Person[2] of this human nature was not created, as in the case of all other human beings; it was the pre-existent Word or Logos. Hence the doctrine of the virginal conception of Christ is entirely congruous with the idea of the Incarnation; for we are not concerned with the production of a new person, but with the assumption of a new nature by a Person who already exists. The divinity of the Person is derived from his eternal generation by God the Father, in virtue of which he is, as it were, the Father's

[1] This statement must not be taken as implying the cruder type of creationist doctrine, which would suggest that the human soul has no organic relation with the body and so is free from all effects of heredity. Some form of creationism seems indeed to be necessary if the human soul is, as a Christian is bound to hold, a transcendent spiritual entity; traducianism involves either that the human soul is compounded out of factors derived from the parents (in which case it must be of a quasi-material nature, and its unity, instead of being the internal unity of a spiritual being rooted in an order transcendent to the body, will be purely external and accidental) or else that the human soul, like that of the lower creation, is nothing more than a property of the body which gradually becomes more clearly marked as the body develops. The truth which traducianism is intended to safeguard is amply provided for by creationism, if it is remembered that God, in creating a new soul, does not design it without regard to the body which it is to animate, but creates precisely that soul and no other which, in union with the body that human procreation and heredity have provided, can enter into the unique and unrepeatable unity of a particular human being.

[2] I.e., the subject of all the human experiences and activities. See p. 4 f. *infra*.

alter ego, the perfect image in which the Father expresses and to which he communicates everything that he himself is. The humanity of the new nature, on the other hand, is derived from the miraculous conception by Mary, in which the divine over-shadowing and the human fiat are most wonderfully blended. We need not deny that it would have been within the scope of divine omnipotence for the Word of God to become incarnate through the process of an ordinary human conception and birth from two parents, but we can, I think, at least say that if the Incarnation is what Catholic dogma teaches it to be, namely the assumption of human nature by a previously existing divine Person, the doctrine of the virginal conception most precisely corresponds to the requirements of the case.

There is thus in Christ a new creation of manhood out of the material of the fallen human race. There is continuity with the fallen race through the manhood taken from Mary; there is dis-continuity through the fact that the Person of Christ is the pre-existent Logos. In Christ human nature has been re-created by the very God who was its first creator; and the new creation is effected, not like the first creation by the mere decree of omni-potent will—"Let us make man in our image"—but by the Creator himself becoming man and moulding human nature to the lineaments of his own Person. Christ is thus quite literally the Second Adam, the Man in whom the human race begins anew; but while the first Adam was, for all his innocence, only God's creature, the Second Adam is the Creator himself. In him human nature is made afresh, and in him the mysterious distortion which succeeding generations have inherited from man's first disobedi-ence, and which theology knows as original sin, has no place.

Christ's manhood is thus impersonal, not in the sense that Christ is not a person, but in the sense that the function in relation to his nature which would ordinarily be performed by a created human person is performed by the uncreated and pre-existent Person of the divine Word. The difficulties that this raises are obvious, for, it will be asked, if Christ has no human person, how can he be completely man? It is well known how in the early Church both Apollinarians and Nestorians came to grief over this question. Apollinarius, in his conviction that the subject of the human life of Christ must be none other than the Eternal Word, taught that the place which in any other man would be occupied by the rational soul or *nous* was in this case taken by the Word

B

himself. As a consequence Christ was left without a rational soul, and, since the rational soul is one of the components of human nature, this meant that his human nature was incomplete; Christ was not perfectly and fully man. And the notion on which in recent years Dr. Relton has laid so much stress,[1] that the Word includes in himself all that is properly involved in the human rational soul, does not really meet the objection, for it would still be true that in becoming man the Word had not *taken* to himself a full human nature and, as the orthodox fathers were never tired of insisting, what he did not take he did not redeem.[2] The Nestorians, on the other hand, with their emphasis upon the completeness of Christ's humanity, were unable to find a place where the divine Word could be dovetailed into it; all that they could provide for was a very close external association or conjunction between the Man Jesus and the Word who is God. For them, in the incarnate Christ there were two subjects, not one. (The later monothelite assertion that in Christ there was no human will is open to the same fundamental objection as the Apollinarian view, though it maims the manhood to a lesser degree.) It was therefore a real step forward when orthodox Christology, in order to describe the element which is present in other men but absent in Christ, was led to adopt the terms *prosopon* and *persona*, which were not the names of any of the constituents of human nature. Every part of human nature could thus without qualification be attributed to Christ, while it could still be affirmed that the subject of all the human activity was not human but divine. Nevertheless, like most formulations of orthodox belief, while providing an accurate statement of the fact which any orthodox Christology must accept, the assertion that in Christ there is a divine but no human *persona* does not in itself explain anything. For, we naturally want to know, what does *persona* mean? What is this factor in a human being which is not a constituent of the human nature but is nevertheless the subject of all the human experiences and activities? To answer this question—so far as it can be answered—we must make some digression.

[1] See ch. ii *infra*. It is not of course implied that Dr. Relton is himself an Apollinarian. It should be added that recent research seems to have shown that Appollinarius did not in fact teach that the Word brought human nature with him from heaven. (Raven, *Apollinarianism*, p. 185 f.; Prestige, *Fathers and Heretics*, p. 222 f.)
[2] Cf. Greg. Naz., *Ep.* ci: Τὸ γὰρ ἀπρόσληπτον, ἀθεράπευτον.

II

The Greek-speaking writers of the early Church, who took the leading part in the Christological discussions, had two words of which the Latin word *persona* became the recognized equivalent. These were *prosopon* (πρόσωπον) and *hypostasis* (ὑπόστασις). *Prosopon* was originally not a philosophical term at all; it was an ordinary word for "face." It was thus conveniently taken to signify, in Dr. Prestige's phrase, "the external being or individual self as presented to an onlooker,"[1] or, as Dr. Sellers puts it, "a person as seen from the outside."[2] The word *hypostasis*, the literal English rendering of which would be "under-standing," had two senses, the active sense of "that which gives support" and the passive sense of "that which lies beneath." Thus, in its philosophical application, it could signify either a concrete object or the stuff out of which the concrete object was made. These two nuances closely correspond to the two meanings which Aristotelian philosophy gave to the word *ousia* (οὐσία), which is in derivation the abstract noun corresponding to the verb "to be." In Aristotle, the *prote ousia* (or "first being") is the concrete essence realized in an individual, while the *deutera ousia* ("second being") is the nature which it may share with others of its kind. In Trinitarian theology the former of these usages came to prevail in the case of *hypostasis* and the latter in the case of *ousia*. Thus the definitive formulation of the doctrine of the Trinity comes to be given in the words, "three *hypostases* in one *ousia*," and the Council of Nicaea declared that the Son of God was of the same *ousia* (*homoousios*)[3] with the Father.

How then does the Latin term *persona* come in? Tertullian, at the end of the second century, describes the Word and the Spirit as *personae* of the Father, and here, says Dr. Prestige, *persona* "is much more the concrete presentation of an individual than, as is commonly alleged, the holder of the legal title to a hereditament."[4] The other Latin term which Tertullian introduces is

---

[1] *God in Patristic Thought*, p. 157. Prestige denies (ad loc.) that in Patristic usage *prosopon* ever meant a mask and gives a quotation from Clement in which this sense is definitely excluded (cf. p. xxviii). He also denies emphatically that the Sabellians spoke of three *prosopa* in the Godhead and that the word *prosopon* became discredited through its association with Sabellianism (p. 160 f.).

[2] *Two Ancient Christologies*, p. 46.

[3] For the way in which even in the term *homoousios* the different shades of meaning of *ousia* remained, see Prestige, *God in Patristic Thought*, p. 267 f.

[4] *Ibid.*, p. 159.

substantia; he contrasts it with *natura.* "*Substantia* belongs to the individual object, but its *natura* may be shared between a number of objects."[1] Thus "the expressions, *unius substantiae* or *una substantia*, as applied to the Trinity, involve unity and identity, as well as equality, of substance."[2] The result of this is that the phrase that comes to be the classical Latin expression of orthodox Trinitarian belief is "Three *personae* in one *substantia.*" Here *substantia* corresponds to *hypostasis* only in the general sense which, as we saw above, *hypostasis* relinquished to *ousia.* *Substantia* has thus become the Latin equivalent to *ousia*, and we may note that, in Latin scholasticism, *substantia prima* and *substantia secunda* are the regular renderings of *prote ousia* and *deutera ousia* respectively.

Thus we get the situation that, in theological usage, *substantia* becomes the equivalent, not of its etymological congener, *hypostasis*, but of *ousia*, both *hypostasis* and *prosopon* being translated by the Latin *persona.*

One other pair of words must be recognized. These are the Greek *physis* (φύσις) and the Latin *natura*, both of which signify the kind of being that an individual is. They are thus equivalent to *substantia* in the sense of *substantia secunda*, or, if they do refer to *substantia prima* it is at most in the sense of the nature as it is realized in the individual (*natura individualis*) and not of the individual (*suppositum*) in which the nature is realized.[3]

The upshot of all this in the Christological realm is that when St. Leo the Great wishes to describe the manner of the Incarnation he writes that two *naturae* and *substantiae* (i.e., as regards the human element, *substantia secunda*, for *substantia prima* here would be sheer Nestorianism) meet together in one *persona*;[4] and the Chalce-

---

[1] *God in Patristic Thought*, p. 220.   [2] *Ibid.*, p. 221.
[3] To avoid verbal confusion a note in the form of a summary may be useful here. In the case of an intelligent being, substance (i.e., *substantia prima* in its most restricted sense), *suppositum* and *persona* are identical. We may distinguish as follows, taking Socrates as our example:

   Substantia:
     1. *Substantia prima*, i.e., substance as determined to the individual:
       (a) *Suppositum* (in an intelligent being this is called *persona*): *id quod est*, namely Socrates.
       (b) *Natura individualis: id quo est*, namely human nature as it is in Socrates, "socrateity."
     2. *Substantia secunda*, i.e., substance considered in abstraction from its determination to the individual, *id quo est*, namely manhood in general. This is also called *natura* or *essentia* in the strict sense, and *quidditas.*

[4] *Salva igitur proprietate utriusque naturae et substantiae et in unam coeunte personam.* . . . (*Tome*, 3.)   (However, *et substantiae* is omitted in E. Schwartz's critical Text.)

donian Council acclaims his exposition and defines that two *physes* concur in one *prosopon* and *hypostasis*.[1, 2]

We must now turn to the famous definition of "person" given by Boethius: *Persona est rationalis naturae individua substantia*, "a person is an individual substance of a rational nature." At first sight this would seem to be inconsistent with the usage already laid down. For we have said that in the triune Godhead three Persons cohere in one substance and that in the incarnate Lord two natures or substances cohere in one Person; now Boethius is telling us that a person *is* a substance of a particular kind. Furthermore, we saw that for St. Leo substance and nature were the same, while Boethius talks about a substance *of* (which presumably means *possessing*) a rational nature. Now it is, of course, possible that Boethius, who was a doubtful sort of Christian in any case, is not in entire agreement with St. Leo and the Chalcedonian fathers. On the other hand, both he and they derive their language from the same philosophical tradition, and Boethius's definition of "person" has been generally accepted by Christian theologians and has been defended by St. Thomas himself.[3] I think that the clue is to be found in the adjective *individua*. It is "individual substance" that is in question, that is, *substantia prima* in its most concrete application: not the specific essence which the person shares with other individuals of its kind, nor even that essence taken in conjunction with the individual characteristics shared by no one else, but the individual himself in whom that essence is realized with those characteristics, the *suppositum* in the strictest sense. Thus the person is the concrete individual and all

---

[1] σωζομένης δὲ μᾶλλον τῆς ἰδιότητος ἑκατέρας φύσεως, καὶ εἰς ἓν πρόσωπον καὶ μίαν ὑπόστασιν συντρεχούσης . . .

[2] It should be stressed that neither the Greek nor the Latin statement of the doctrine of the Trinity implies that the three Persons are merely numerically different individuals of the species "God"; that would be sheer tritheism. In their theological application the words receive a new depth of meaning as they are applied to what is *ex hypothesi* a unique case. The complete interpenetration of the persons in the Godhead is altogether different from the mere sharing by individuals of a common specific form; this is what was forgotten in the early twelfth-century controversy that raged round Roscellinus. Nevertheless, the only language that there is in which to discuss it is the language of human thought, which in this instance was largely derived from contemporary philosophy; it is therefore important to inquire into its philosophical nuances, even while we recognize the transformation which it underwent.

An exhaustive discussion of the vicissitudes undergone by the various terms in the course of theological discussion and controversy is given by Prestige, *God in Patristic Thought*, chs. viii–xi. How early the tendency to think of the Trinity in logical rather than in ontological terms appears may be seen from his ch. xiii, "The Triumph of Formalism."

[3] See *S. Theol.*, I, xxix, 1, in relation to the Trinity; III, ii, 2 ad 3, in relation to the Incarnation.

that finds realization in him: he who is, and what he is, in their concrete union. Now, in the case of any ordinary human being we hardly ever find it necessary to distinguish, except in thought, between the *who* and the *what*; the person and the nature go together. There is no person without a unique individual rational nature proper to it, and no individual rational nature without its unique person. The question therefore does not press itself as to whether the nature is to be understood as what the person *has* or as what the person *is*; the nature is the person in its concrete activity and individuality. There are only two exceptions to this, and these are the two I have mentioned above: namely, the Holy Trinity and the incarnate Word. In Christ, the Catholic Faith assures us, there is no human person, while the human nature is complete. Here, then, the *who* and the *what* must of necessity be distinguished, for, while the latter is created, the former is God himself. When, therefore, we speak about the Man Christ Jesus, we must use the word "person" in its most restricted and rigid sense, as meaning the subject of the human life to the exclusion of all that goes to make that life up. Otherwise we shall be confusing God with his creation, the infinite with the finite.

III

So then we come back to the notion from which this digression began, of a human nature, altogether complete in every respect, but having no created subject of its acts and experiences, since its subject is the eternal and only-begotten Son and Word of God. The doctrine of *enhypostasia*, which Dr. Relton has so fully expounded in his *Study in Christology* and which he derives from the sixth-century theologian Leontius of Byzantium, provides a convenient way of expressing this fact, though I am not certain that it gives us anything very much more. According to it, the humanity of Christ is neither *hypostatic* (that is, possessing a human person) nor is it *anhypostatic* (that is, without a person altogether), but it is *enhypostatic* (that is, it is constituted in the person of the divine Word).[1] Later theologians have not on the whole done much to clear up the problem,[2] and we may indeed suspect that in this

---

[1] Relton, *Study in Christology*, p. 71. According to Prestige, the original meaning of *enhypostatos* was simply "having an objective individual existence." (*God in Patristic Thought*, pp. 174, 274.) He has a far less favourable estimate of Leontius than has Relton.

[2] See, e.g., the summary of the views of Scotus, Suarez, Cajetan and Billot given in A. Tanquerey's *Brevior Synopsis Theologiae Dogmaticae*, p. 409, or for a more detailed discussion, E. Hugon, *The Mystery of the Incarnation*, Part III, ch. ii.

matter we are approaching the point where human reason becomes powerless and all things end in mystery. We may observe, however, that there is no insuperable difficulty in the fact of a function which normally requires a separate person to exercise it being in a particular case assumed by one who already holds a higher office; as instances we might take that of the multiplicity of ministries successively appropriated by Mussolini in his heyday or of a Pope becoming Prefect of a Congregation. We may further remark that a very similar problem arises in the example which the *Quicunque vult* takes as the closest parallel which can be found in the natural order to the supernatural fact of the Incarnation. "As rational soul and flesh is one man," it tells us, "so God and man is one Christ." Now in the case of a sub-human animal the soul is, to all appearance, merely an immanent principle concerned solely with the life of the body and having no existence apart from it; the soul is just a quality of the body, by which a living body is distinguished from a lifeless one; when we say that a horse or an eagle has a "sensitive soul" we mean nothing more than that the matter of which it is composed is organized according to a particular pattern of life, equine or aquiline as the case may be. When, however, we come to the case of man, the rational being whose soul, according to Christian belief, is a substantial spiritual entity transcendent to the body and capable of surviving the body's destruction, we are faced with the problem of explaining the fact, given to us in experience, that the soul is the subject not only of man's transcendent rational and spiritual activities but of his sensitive "animal" life as well, of those very functions which are equally the property of the lower creatures in whom the soul has no self-subsistence whatever. Whatever detailed solution we may have to offer to this problem, the plain truth is that the sensitive life of an animate being, which in itself requires no subject other than that which life on the sensitive level itself supplies, can, without the least maiming of this sensitive life (and indeed to its great ennobling and enrichment), receive as its subject a spiritual entity whose own mode of being is of a radically higher order. Man does not possess a sensitive soul and a rational soul, existing side by side like the Logos and *nous* in the Nestorian Christ. But neither, on the other hand, is his sensitive life incomplete because he is rational; we can hardly suppose that when in the course of biological evolution some sub-human creature received from the Creator that spiritual soul which made him into the first man,

some sub-human element had to be removed to make room for it,
as the *nous* had to be absent to make room for the Logos in the
Christ of Apollinarius. The whole range of animal life was caught
up into the higher mode of life proper to a spiritual and rational
being, yet without any destruction in the process; not, we might
perhaps venture to say, by the conversion of spirit into ape, but
by the taking of apehood into spirit. As the schoolboy said, animals
are imperfect beasts, man is a perfect beast. It would, of course,
be highly dangerous to press this parallel to excess, and in comparing the relation of spirit to animal in man with the relation of
Godhead to manhood in Christ it is imperative to take account
not only of the similarities but also of the differences.[1] In particular, we must remember that the one case is on the natural level
and the other on the supernatural, and that the hypostatic union
of Godhead and manhood in Christ is altogether unique. In the
case which we just imagined, of the formation of the first man,
there would be a lifting up into the human order of a being that
already existed on the animal plane. Indeed, the expression which
was used a few sentences back was not altogether accurate; it was
not *apehood* that was taken up into spirit so much as *an ape*. In the
Incarnation, however, as we have seen, we are forbidden to suppose that the Word assumed to himself an already existing man.
What was assumed into God was not a man but manhood. Here,
then, the comparison breaks down; nevertheless, if we remember
where it ceases to apply it is of real value. For the Catholic Creed
itself authorizes us to make use of it, and, the limitations of our
finite minds being what they are, it cannot be wrong to employ it,
not in order to deny or to modify the content of revealed truth but
in order to make it less difficult for us to accept it.[2] Having then
used the illustration for what it is worth, we must simply reaffirm
that, not by confusion of Substance but by unity of Person, God
and Man is one Christ.

[1] St. Thomas remarks, following St. Augustine, that the similarity would be even
greater than it is if there were, as some have falsely maintained, only one intellect in
all men; he has his eye, of course, upon the Averroists. (*S.c.G.*, IV, xli.)

[2] We may remark here, once and for all, that it is no defect in an illustration that it
fails to hold in every respect. The only thing that it can illustrate perfectly is itself:
"everything is what it is and not another thing." What is important, in making use
of illustrations, in order to explain the less-known by the better-known, is to make it
clear in what respects they hold and in what respects they fail. I shall try to do this,
either explicitly or implicitly, throughout this book.

IV

There is one further important respect in which the parallel between the union of soul and body in man and the union of Godhead and manhood in Christ is illuminating. In both cases we are faced with a combination which on antecedent grounds we might well consider to be altogether impossible. If we were not so used to being human beings we should find it hard to credit the possibility of the union of two elements so disparate as matter and spirit in that unity of substance which we call man. The difficulties raised for scholastic philosophy by the doctrine that a man is one substance whose form is the soul and whose matter is the body are well known; it took all the ingenuity of which St. Thomas Aquinas was possessed to rebut the argument of Averroes, based, so it was claimed, upon Aristotle, that, since the multiplication of individuals within a species is due to the various portions of signate matter with which the one specific form is united, the soul when separated from the body must lose its individual identity and be merged into one universal mind which is common to the whole human race.[1] We can therefore hardly be surprised at the popularity which in the post-medieval period was enjoyed by the doctrine of Descartes, who conceived the human being as consisting not of one substance in which two elements, body and soul, were mysteriously united, but as two substances existing in some kind of loose conjunction, so that man became, in the vivid phrase of Maritain, "an angel driving a machine." (The Christological parallel to this is, of course, Nestorianism.) If, however, it is difficult to concede the possibility of a substantial union in man of two elements so disparate as spirit and matter, it is far more difficult to admit the union of Godhead and manhood in the one Christ, since we are now dealing not with two different orders of created being but with the infinitely greater gulf that separates the Creator from the creature. It is therefore not to be wondered at that, in addition to the heresies of Apollinarianism and Nestorianism. which postulate insufficient modes of union between the human and the divine in Christ, we find another set of heresies which distort one or other of the terms which are united. Thus Eutychianism, with its teaching that the human nature of Christ was absorbed into the divine, was an attempt to destroy the gulf by

[1] See the extended discussion in *S.c.G.*, II, lxxiii–lxxviii.

annihilating the created term; a union between Godhead and manhood in which the two elements retained their character as uncreated and created respectively being too difficult to admit, the created element had to lose its identity by being fused with the uncreated. Many of the modern theories which describe themselves as "kenotic" reproduce the same error in an inverted form: that Christ should be, in the full sense of the words, both God and man seems ridiculous; therefore the Godhead must be compressed or amputated to bring it down to the human level. The extreme kenoticists might be surprised to be told that their views were based upon the same fundamental premiss as those of their *bêtes noires*, the Eutychians, but such is nevertheless the case. Neither party can bring itself to admit that the one Christ is, without qualification, both God and man. Kenoticism is thus the counterpart of monophysitism; it is in fact monophysitism of a different kind. Whereas the monophysitism of the Eutychians absorbed the human nature into the divine, that of the kenoticists absorbs the divine nature into the human.

Another method of trying to overcome the gulf is by closing it up before the bridge-building begins; that is to say, by adopting at the start a view that Godhead and manhood, so far from being of essentially different orders of reality, are of the same kind and differ only in degree. There are two ways of doing this. One is by treating man as essentially divine, and this would seem to be the logical outcome of Berdyaev's doctrine of "theandrism"—Godmanhood—even if he himself hesitates to drive it to its extreme conclusion.[1] The other way is by treating God as finite, and this tendency is evident in the writing of many English theologians of recent years. One form in which it appears is in evolutionary Christologies, which look upon Christ as nothing more than the supreme manifestation of the indwelling of God in the human soul; in these, the notion of the Incarnation as the invasion of the created order by a transcendent deity is ignored because there is no serious recognition that God is transcendent at all. It may, however, take other forms in which the departure from traditional Christology is less immediately evident.

Against all these aberrations it is necessary to state the traditional doctrine in all its apparent impossibility and to bear the reproach which orthodoxy always invites. For orthodox Christology, in its developed no less than in its Biblical stage, is to the

---

[1] See, e.g., *Freedom and the Spirit*, ch. vi.

Jews a stumbling-block and to the Greeks foolishness; but to them that are saved, both Jews and Greeks, it is Christ the Power of God and the Wisdom of God. God is infinite, self-existent, and immutable; man is finite, altogether dependent, and enmeshed in the temporal order; Christ is, without qualification, both God and man. Is it possible, without weakening our grasp of these truths to see, even to some slight degree, how they are compatible?

It is, I think, worth while to remark that the fundamental problem is not in the logical but in the ontological order. We are not concerned primarily with proving that a certain set of propositions can be stated without self-contradiction, but with convincing ourselves that a certain act—namely, the union of human nature with the person of God the Word—is possible to the divine omnipotence. These two questions, it is true, cannot be altogether separated, at least by anyone who claims to be in the main stream of Christian tradition; for, God being himself the Truth, if something is inherently impossible not even God can do it. It is, however, important to insist that, so long as something is not inherently ✓ impossible, God can certainly do it if he wills. The Incarnation may be—indeed, we must affirm that it is—altogether beyond the power of any created agent to effect; but that is not the point. The question is not whether it is easy, but whether it is possible.

When we have put the question in this form, the answer to at least part of it is obvious. Considered merely as an exercise of the power of God over his creature, the assumption of human nature by God is certainly possible. It is he who has made that nature; like every other being in the universe, God himself alone excepted, it has been drawn out of non-existence by him; it is altogether under his control, and he is incessantly present to it at the very root of its being, in the creative act by which he preserves it from moment to moment. If he wishes to exalt it to hypostatic union he can.[1] This is obvious, but it is not the whole of the problem. For the Incarnation is, at least at first sight, not only something happening to human nature, but something happening to God. "The Word was made flesh," the Gospel tells us. "He came down from heaven," says the Creed. Is this compatible with the infinity and immutability of God? This is the real question.

---

[1] It may be remembered that the general teaching of the scholastic theologians is that, whether or not it would have been fitting for God to have assumed a sub-human nature, it would, considered absolutely, have certainly been *possible*.

V

It must be said quite plainly that neither the Incarnation nor anything else can involve any change in God himself. God is altogether immutable and impassible. It is true that a number of prominent theologians in recent years have shown themselves ready to dismiss the immutability and impassibility of God as an importation into the Christian religion from Greek philosophy which must now be dismissed if proper emphasis is to be laid upon the tender element in God's relation with his creation, though in this they are quite out of line with the tradition of Anglicanism.[1] Thus Dr. Matthews asserts that the traditional doctrine of the divine impassibility "is surely very near to a rejection of the belief that God loves the world or human persons at all," and is prepared to attribute immutability to God only in the sense of moral steadfastness.[2] Again, Dr. Relton has written that "the revelation of God in Christ was for ever a refutation of his 'impassibility,' " and accuses St. Cyril of Alexandria of an "unethical conception of God." He asserts that "if the Heart of God thus revealed [sc. in Christ] is a heart of mercy and compassion, redemptive love and consequent suffering are not alien to him, and the doctrine of his impassibility, as we have seen, will have to be modified."[3] He maintains, in fact, that the philosophic basis of the doctrine of the impassibility of the divine Logos is the Platonic doctrine of the Absolute rather than the Christian doctrine of God.[4] It would, however, seem to be true that, so far from the doctrine of divine impassibility being an importation into Christianity from Greek philosophy, the denial of that doctrine is an importation into Christianity from the philosophy of the post-Cartesian period, with its reluctance to conceive of God as truly infinite and as essentially of a different order from his creatures. If God is finite, then it is indeed true that compassion must involve passibility; it is only for an infinite being that compassion and impassibility are compatible. I may perhaps be allowed to quote in this connection some words which I have written elsewhere:

[1] Thus Hooker writes: "This admirable union of God with man can enforce in that higher nature no alteration, because unto God there is nothing more natural than not to be subject to any change." (*Eccl. Pol.*, V, liv, 4; ed. of 1888, II, p. 234.)

[2] See *God in Christian Thought and Experience*, pp. 227, 254. How deeply the doctrine of divine impassibility is rooted in the Christian tradition is shown in Dr. J. K. Mozley's book, *The Impassibility of God.*

[3] *A Study in Christology*, pp. 57, 160.   [4] *Ibid.*, p. 55.

"There is no need whatever for us to overlook or minimize the truth which the Bible throughout so plainly teaches: that God enters into the most intimate details of the life of all his creatures, that he rejoices in our happiness and sympathizes with our sorrows, that he is glorified by our good acts and grieved by our sins. We will go further and say that the intensity with which our actions as personal beings affect him is infinitely greater than that with which they affect our fellow human beings, for God, as our Creator and Preserver, is present to us more closely than we are present to ourselves. But when that has been said, it must be added that even this is infinitely surpassed by the beatitude which God enjoys in the interior fullness of his own divine life, which it therefore can neither augment nor diminish. Therefore there is no incompatibility between the compassion and the impassibility of God."[1]

Whatever, then, the Incarnation means, it cannot imply that any change takes place in the divine Word. With St. Thomas we must affirm our belief in "the Word of God, proceeding forth yet leaving not the Father's side."[2] This is indeed most clearly asserted by the *Quicunque vult* in its affirmation that Christ is one "not by the conversion of Godhead into flesh but by taking up of manhood into God." It is, as a matter of fact, rather startling to reflect how many modern English discussions of Christology adopt precisely the standpoint which the *Quicunque vult* here repudiates. They take as their starting-point human nature as it is known to us, and then in effect inquire what must happen to the divine Word if he is to be compressed within its limits; they hardly ever start by considering the mode of existence of the divine Word and then ask what must happen to human nature if it is to be united to him. Their Christology thus becomes a degradation of the divine Person rather than an exaltation of the human nature. It is therefore hardly surprising that so many of them condemn scholastic Christology as monophysite in tendency, and that they are on the whole so sympathetic to Nestorius and so critical of St. Cyril.

In becoming incarnate the divine Word does not cease to exercise his divine functions as the eternally begotten Son of the Father and as the source (with the Father) of the procession of the Spirit, or his cosmic functions as the creator and sustainer of the universe. He adds to these all the functions of a complete human

---

[1] *He Who Is*, p. 111.
[2] *Verbum supernum, prodiens nec linquens Patris dexteram.*—Office-hymn for the Blessed Sacrament.

life which go to make up the complex which is human nature. In this he manifests his divinity in terms of humanity—"the Word was made flesh and dwelt among us *and we beheld his glory*"—but the assumption of human nature, like the creation of the world, while it *manifests* his divinity, does not either augment or diminish it. Both creation and incarnation have their *terminus ad quem* within the finite order; neither the dependence of the world upon the divine Word in creation nor the assumption of human nature by him in hypostatic union "adds up with" his divine mode of existence in the triune life of the eternal Trinity, for this last mode not only begins but terminates as well within the infinite and uncreated order.[1]

VI

Creation and incarnation are thus closely comparable in one important respect, though their differences are not less important than their similarities.[2] Each has its *terminus a quo* in the infinite order and its *terminus ad quem* in the finite. Each is a relation of the divine Word to his creation. The differences must now be noted. In the first place, creation is an activity of the whole Godhead *ad extra* and not of any special one of the three Persons, though each of the Persons is concerned in it in his own proper mode.[3] The subject of the Incarnation, on the other hand, is the Second Person alone; it is *the Word* that was made flesh, though in bringing this about the other two Persons were not without their part: "the Holy Ghost shall come upon thee, and the power of the Most High shall overshadow thee."[4] Secondly, while creation plants out creatures, as it were, in a relative (though only relative) independence of God, the Incarnation unites one particular element in creation (namely the human nature of Christ) to God. Thirdly,

---

[1] *Terminus ad quem* does not, of course, here mean purpose or final cause. I am thinking simply of creation as a relation *of* God (*terminus a quo*) *to* the world (*terminus ad quem*), and of incarnation as a relation *of* the Word (*terminus a quo*) *to* Christ's manhood (*terminus ad quem*).

[2] As Fr. Thornton writes, using the terminology of the "philosophy of organism": "To the question: how can the eternal Word possibly express his absolute mode of being in and through a completely human organism? we must raise the prior question: how can there possibly be a human organism at all, framed as it is by incorporation of eternity into succession? And behind this lies the more ultimate question: how can there be a succession in which patterns are woven by continual entry of the new on to a field of repetitive energy? In so far as we are here face to face with difficulties of the imagination, the Incarnation does not introduce fresh difficulties which are not already implicit in the idea of creation." (*The Incarnate Lord*, p. 229.)

[3] Cf. St. Thomas Aquinas, *S. Theol.*, I, xlv, 6, 7.   [4] Luke i. 35.

while God's presence of immensity at the ontological root of every
creature is indeed unthinkably intimate, since he is the ground of
its very existence and of its continuance from moment to moment
—as the scholastics say, God is present in his creatures "by
essence, presence and power"—nevertheless it is not to be compared in this respect with the hypostatic union in Christ, whereby
the divine Word enters into the very mode of life of a created
being and, we might dare to say, becomes part of his creation.
"The Word *was made flesh—σὰρξ ἐγένετο.*"

> "Behold, the great Creator makes
>   Himself a house of clay,
> A robe of virgin flesh he takes
>   Which he will wear for ay.
>
> "Hark, hark, the wise eternal Word,
>   Like a weak infant cries!
> In form of servant is the Lord,
>   And God in cradle lies."

God, says a much-quoted liturgical prayer, has wonderfully
created the dignity of the substance of man, but he has yet more
wonderfully renewed it: *mirabiliter condidisti, mirabilius reformasti.*

Let us follow this thought a little further. *In relation to God*, we
may say, creation is not in time, for God who creates is not in time.
But *in relation to creatures* it is in time, because creatures are in time,
and time is the mode of existence with which they are created.
Creation is thus a relation spanning the gulf between time and
eternity; it is, in the scholastic phrase, real in the creature but
only logical or "rational" in God. That is to say it involves a
change in them—indeed that total and radical change which
draws them out of non-existence into existence—but it involves
no change in him. So also the act of incarnation *in relation to the
Person of the Word* is not in time, for, as God, the divine Word is not
in time; but *in relation to Christ's human nature and to us* it is in time,
for Christ's human life is lived in time and so is ours. And, like
creation, the relation of incarnation is real in the creature but
logical in God.[1] We may further add that the mere fact of incar-

[1] Cf. *S. Theol.*, III, ii, 7c: "Every relation which we consider between God and the
creature is really in the creature, by whose change the relation is brought into being;
whereas it is not really in God, but only in our way of thinking, since it does not arise
from any change in God. And hence we must say that the union of which we are
speaking [sc. the Incarnation] is not really in God, except only in our way of thinking
(*non est in Deo realiter, sed secundum rationem tantum*); but in the human nature, which is a

nation does not of itself involve that the Word became man at a
particular date, any more than the mere fact of creation of itself
involves that the world began to be at a particular date. So far as
reason can tell us, the world *might* have always existed in complete
dependence upon the creative *fiat* of God; and if it had, the divine
Word *might* have been always incarnate in it. We know that *in
fact* the world had a beginning, whether we date it as 4004 B.C.
with Archbishop Usher or as 10,000,000,000 B.C. with Professor
Eddington, and we know that *in fact* the Incarnation took place
at a particular epoch, which a combination of liturgiology and
historical criticism might lead us to denote as March 25th, 4 B.C.;
but in itself neither the idea of creation nor that of incarnation
necessarily involves a temporal beginning. But, as was remarked
above, in stating the parallel between creation and incarnation we
must not ignore their differences. The relation between God and
the creature set up by creation is a relation between two different
substances or *supposita*; in the case of a rational creature it is a
relation between persons, a personal God and a personal creature,
for, in the phrase of Boethius already quoted, person signifies "an
individual substance of a rational nature." The relation between
the Godhead and the manhood in Christ is, in contrast, a relation
between two natures which are united in one Person. The Person
of Christ is thus in one sense simple, and in another sense composite. As St. Thomas remarks:

> "the Person or hypostasis of Christ may be viewed in two ways.
> First, as it is in itself, and thus it is altogether simple, even as the
> Nature of the Word. Secondly, in the aspect of person or hypostasis
> to which it belongs to subsist in a nature; and thus the Person of
> Christ subsists in two natures. Hence though there is one subsisting
> being in him, yet there are different aspects of subsistence, and
> hence he is said to be a composite Person, inasmuch as one being
> subsists in two."[1]

Thus, as we have already seen, incarnation implies an immeasurably closer relation between the Creator and the creature than is
implied by creation. Also, we must add, there is a particularity,
and indeed a localization, about it which creation does not import.

---

creature, it is really." It is important to notice that really (*realiter*) does not mean
"truly," as in modern English usage; it is simply the adverb corresponding to the
noun *res*. The scholastics constantly draw the distinction between qualities, etc., that
are *real* and those that are *logical* or *rational* (*secundum rationem*), that is between those
that involve a change in the nature of a being and those that merely involve a change
in its relation to others.   [1] *S. Theol.*, III, ii, 4c.

Since every being, God alone excepted, is created, creation is an entirely general relation which holds in regard of every finite being. Incarnation, in contrast, holds only with regard to one particular type of created being, namely manhood, and indeed one particular individualized instance of manhood, namely the manhood of Christ. It is indeed true that the manhood of Christ is universal in the sense that, considered apart from the divine Person to whom it is united, it is *anhypostatic*; the Word did not unite to himself the nature of any previously existing man, of John the Baptist or Herod or Tiberius Caesar. But, considered in its union with its divine Person, it is *enhypostatic* in him and is altogether concrete. There is one and only one historical individual in whom the Word was made flesh, Jesus of Nazareth, the Son of Mary, born in a particular stable in the town of Bethlehem on a particular night in a particular year. It is his human nature that is the manhood taken by the divine Word, not that of Socrates or Peter or John, not that of the Virgin Mary herself. The manhood of Christ is thus from one point of view entirely universal; it belongs to no *human* person in the whole of creation, but only to the Person of God the Word. But in its union with him it is entirely concrete and particular.

Considered from the side of God, both creation and incarnation are, as we have already seen, timeless, because God himself is timeless. But considered from our side, from the standpoint of the created temporal order, either relation may be considered under two aspects. Creation can either signify the divine act by which a creature began to be—"In the beginning," says Genesis, "God created the heaven and the earth"—or it can signify the incessant act of preservation by which God from moment to moment prevents it from falling back into that non-existence to which its own insufficiency would otherwise doom it: "As the production of a thing into existence depends on the will of God," writes St. Thomas, "so likewise it depends on his will that things should be preserved; hence if he took away his action from them all things would be reduced to nothing."[1] Similarly, incarnation can either mean the act by which, at a particular moment on the first Lady Day, the divine Word united human nature to himself in the womb of Mary, or it can mean the continuous act by which from that moment until the end of time his human nature is bound to his divine Person, so that he is man for evermore. And in either case it is of the utmost importance that the second aspect should

[1] *S. Theol.*, I, ix, 2c.

C

not be forgotten. In the case of creation, its neglect led to the deism of the eighteenth century, with its idea of God as the absentee owner who brought the world into existence a long time ago but has had no intimate concern with it since; in the case of incarnation it was, as we shall see, badly under-emphasized in one of the most influential of modern Christological discussions, that of Charles Gore.

VII

In the incarnate Lord, then, two natures, a divine and a human, are inseparably and unconfusedly united in one divine Person. We must now recognize that the two natures are not both related to the Person in precisely the same way. The Person of the Word and his divine nature are, in the scholastic phrase, really identical and only logically distinct; he is God, and God *is* everything that he *has*. Christ's Person is the Person of God the Son; his divine nature is the nature of God; and the whole Godhead is eternally and necessarily possessed by each of the three Persons of the Trinity. Any separation of the divine nature, even in the least detail or degree, from the Person is inconceivable; wherever the Person is, there is, necessarily and unchangeably, his divine nature also.[1] The divine Person and the human nature, on the other hand, although they are united to each other in the most intimate way—by the assumption of manhood into God, as *Quicunque vult* puts it; by a union which is not accidental but substantial, as St. Thomas says[2]—are not absolutely identical. The divine nature belongs to the Word from all eternity, in virtue of the very fact that he is the Word—"before all ages, πρὸ πάντων τῶν αἰώνων," in the words of the Nicene Creed—while his human nature was taken by him at a particular moment in the world's history. He is "God of the substance of the Father, begotten before the worlds," but he is "Man of the substance of his Mother, born in the world." He *became man*; he never "became God."

Thus, when we think of the incarnate Lord, we must recognize in him the two natures, divine and human, coinhering in the unity of the divine Person with whom the divine nature is really

---

[1] Thus St. Thomas argues that "the divine act of intelligence [the act which is the eternal generation of the Son] is the very substance itself of the one who understands." (*S. Theol.*, I, xxvii, 2 ad 2; cf. xiv, 4.)   [2] *Ibid.*, III, ii. 6.

identical. The Definition of the Council of Chalcedon is quite clear about this. It does not merely assert that the divine Word is the subject of two natures, but that "*our Lord Jesus Christ,*" that is to say, the historic individual who suffered under Pontius Pilate, is "acknowledged in two natures, unconfusedly, unchangeably, indivisibly, inseparably, the difference of the natures being in no way removed because of the union, but rather the property of each nature being preserved and (both) concurring into one Person and one hypostasis."[1] This point is even more strongly emphasized in the famous *Tome* of Pope Leo, which the Chalcedonian Council so enthusiastically acclaimed.

> "Accordingly," Leo writes, "while the distinctness of both natures and substances was preserved, and both met in one Person, lowliness was assumed by majesty, weakness by power, mortality by eternity; and, in order to pay the debt of our condition, the inviolable nature was united to the passible, so that, as the appropriate remedy for our ills, one and the same 'Mediator between God and men, the Man Christ Jesus,' might from one element be capable of dying, and also from the other be incapable. Therefore in the entire and perfect nature of very man was born very God, whole in what was his, whole in what was ours."[2]

It is thus not merely of the divine Word but of the historic Christ, "the Man Christ Jesus," that Leo asserts the duality of natures, and in the last sentence he affirms that *within the sphere of the Incarnation* God is whole not only in what is "ours" but also in what is "his": *In integra ergo veri hominis perfectaque natura verus natus est Deus, totus in suis, totus in nostris.* Further on he writes:

> "The selfsame who is very God, is also very man: and there is no illusion in this union, while the lowliness of man and the loftiness of Godhead meet together (*invicem sunt*). For as 'God' is not changed by the compassion (exhibited), so 'Man' is not consumed by the dignity (bestowed). For each 'form' does the acts which belong to it, in communion with the other; the Word, that is, performing what belongs to the Word, and the flesh carrying out what belongs to the flesh; the one of these shines out in miracles, the other succumbs to injuries. And as the Word does not withdraw from equality with the Father in glory, so the flesh does not abandon the nature of our kind. For, as we must often

[1] Trans. from Bindley, *Oecumenical Documents of the Faith*, p. 297.
[2] Trans. from W. Bright, *St. Leo on the Incarnation*, p. 113.

be saying, he is one and the same, truly Son of God and truly
Son of Man."[1]

Shortly after this there comes the famous passage:

"He who, as man, is tempted by the devil's subtlety, is the
same to whom, as God, angels pay duteous service. To hunger, to
thirst, to be weary, and to sleep, is evidently human. But to satisfy
five thousand men with five loaves, and give to the Samaritan
woman that living water, to draw which can secure him that
drinks of it from ever thirsting again; to walk on the surface of the
sea with feet that sink not, and by rebuking the storm to bring
down the 'uplifted waves,' is unquestionably divine. As then—to
pass by many points—it does not belong to the same nature to
weep with feelings of pity over a dead friend, and, after the mass
of stone had been removed from the grave where he had lain four
days, by a voice of command to raise him up to life again; or to
hang on the wood, and to make all the elements tremble after day-
light had been turned into night; or to be transfixed with nails,
and to open the gates of paradise to the faith of the robber; so it
does not belong to the same nature to say, 'I and the Father are
one,' and to say, 'The Father is greater than I.' For although
in the Lord Jesus Christ there is one Person of God and man, yet
that whereby contumely attaches to both is one thing, and that
whereby glory attaches to both is another: for from what belongs
to us he has that manhood which is inferior to the Father; while
from the Father he has equal Godhead with the Father."[2, 3]

[1] Trans. from W. Bright, *St. Leo on the Incarnation*, p. 115. Bindley very misleadingly
translates *invicem sunt* by "have their separate spheres." Dr. Jalland observes that
"'invicem' in Leo's usage never means 'alternate' but rather 'reciprocal' or
'mutual'." (*St. Leo the Great*, p. 494; cf. p. 458.) Cf. Sellers, *Council of Chalcedon*, p. 237.
[2] Bright, op. cit., p. 116. Dr. Jalland gives the reading, for the concluding words:
"nevertheless it is not the same thing to say that an insult is common to both (natures),
as to say that the glory is common, etc.," and adds: "This appears to mean that while
the sufferings attributable to the one Person are attributable to the Godhead only by
divine permission, the honour attributable to the Manhood is only to be regarded as
a consequence of the unity of Person" (op. cit., p. 457). He has, however, informed
me in a letter that he now thinks this rendering cannot be justified and agrees with
Bright's. The Latin is *Aliud tamen est unde in utroque communis est contumelia, aliud unde
communis est gloria*, and the obvious meaning (which fits in well with the context) is
that there is one thing (*sc.* the humanity) from which common contumely attaches to
both humanity and divinity, and another (*sc.* the divinity) from which both enjoy a
common glory.
[3] It is perhaps unnecessary to say that the remarks about patristic Christology in
this chapter are not intended as a complete exposition. If such is needed it may be
found most readably and authoritatively stated in Dr. G. L. Prestige's *Fathers and
Heretics*.

CHAPTER II

SOME MODERN DISCUSSIONS OF CHRISTOLOGY

I

THE passage from the *Tome* of Leo with which the last chapter ended has proved a real stumbling-block to most modern English Christologists. Thus Dr. Charles Gore, while recognizing that it can be paralleled in others of the fathers, says (the italics are his own) : " *This is a point on which—it must be emphatically said— accurate exegesis renders impossible to us the phraseology of the Fathers exactly as it stands,*" and asserts that "Beyond the rare words of our Lord about his own essential being, such as [St. John x. 30, "I and my Father are one thing"] or St. Matthew xi. 27, 'No one knoweth the Father save the Son'—beyond such words and the accompanying divine claim on men which such words are necessary to interpret and justify, there is very little recorded in our Lord's life— may I say nothing?—which belongs to the divine nature *per se* and not rather to the divine nature acting under conditions of manhood."[1] Even Dr. Frank Weston remarks rather regretfully that St. Leo "does show a leaning to the Cyrilline school of thought."[2] Dr. H. M. Relton, while speaking on the whole with great approval of Leo, asserts, with reference to the teaching of the last sentence of the quotation from the *Tome* just given, that "Leo's doctrine of the 'Communicatio Idiomatum' is the most questionable part of his theology as found in this letter, because by it he preserves so rigid a distinction between the two natures as seriously to imperil the reality of their true union," and further maintains that "Cyril and Leo by this usage introduce a doctrine of Communicatio Idiomatum which is subversive of the unity of Christ's Person."[3]

In reply to such criticisms as these it must, I think, be said that, so far from the doctrine of *communicatio idiomatum* overstressing the distinction between the two natures, its whole intention is to maintain the union and interplay between them. This can be seen from the actual words in which St. Leo states it :

---

[1] *Dissertations on Subjects connected with the Incarnation*, pp. 166, 165.
[2] *The One Christ*, p. 334.   [3] *A Study in Christology*, pp. 49, 64.

"Accordingly, on account of this unity of Person which is to be understood as existing in both the natures, we read, on the one hand, that 'the Son of Man came down from heaven,' inasmuch as the Son of God took flesh from that Virgin of whom he was born; and on the other hand, the Son of God is said to have been crucified and buried, inasmuch as he underwent this, not in his actual Godhead, wherein the Only-begotten is coeternal and consubstantial with the Father, but in the weakness of human nature."[1]

In other words, although we cannot attribute the properties of the human nature to the divine nature or those of the divine nature to the human nature, we can attribute the properties of the human nature to God the Son and those of the divine nature to the Man Jesus, since "God the Son" and "Jesus" are both personal names and there is only one Person, who may be named from his union with either nature indifferently.[2] As a matter of fact, the real source of the objection would seem to be an assumption that the divine nature, considered as distinct from the divine Person, can be excluded from the sphere of the Incarnation altogether, as if in the Incarnate Lord there were simply a divine Person united to a human nature. Thus there seems to be an implicit denial of the truth that the divine Person and the divine nature are really identical and only logically distinct; it is assumed that, just as the human nature has no part in the cosmic activity by which the eternal Word preserves the universe by his creative *fiat*, so also the divine nature has no part in the incarnate life of the Man Jesus. But the fact is that, because the divine nature cannot be separated from the divine Person when human nature is assumed by him from Mary, the two natures are to be seen in the incarnate Lord united without confusion. In the words of Leo already quoted "although in the Lord Jesus Christ there is one Person of God and man, yet contumely attaches *to both* by one thing and glory attaches *to both* by the other."[3] The only modern work on Christology in which full weight has been given to this consideration outside the Roman Communion is, so far as I know, Dr. F. J.

---

[1] Bright, *St. Leo on the Incarnation*, p. 117.

[2] If it is true, as many modern Biblical scholars hold, that the words "Son of Man" do not mean, as St. Leo thought, simply "human being" but a pre-existent heavenly figure as in the Book of Enoch, the argument is not affected in its essence, although certain Biblical texts can no longer be used to illustrate it. In any case, it is doubtful whether the phrase "Son of Man" can be entirely divested of the connotation of "human being," as is shown by its use in the Book of Ezekiel.

[3] See p. 22 *supra*. The point is not only that the contumely and the glory arise from the two different natures (*aliud . . . aliud*) but also that each of them inheres in the one Christ who is God and man (*in utroque communis*).

Hall's book, *The Kenotic Theory*, which deserves far more attention than it has in fact received. The point was, however, perfectly plain to Hooker, who writes:

> "Forasmuch as the Word and Deity are one subject, we must beware we exclude not the nature of God from incarnation, and so make the Son of God incarnate not to be very God. For undoubtedly *even the nature of God itself in the only person of the Son is incarnate*, and hath taken to itself flesh. Wherefore incarnation may neither be granted to any person but only one, *nor yet denied to that nature which is common unto all three*."[1]

At this point it will be well to touch upon the question of the *kenosis*, the "self-emptying" which St. Paul attributes to Christ in a famous verse in the Epistle to the Philippians, though I shall discuss the matter more fully in the next chapter. "Have this mind in you," writes St. Paul, "which was also in Christ Jesus, who, being in the form of God, counted it not a prize to be on an equality with God, but emptied himself, taking the form of a servant, being made in the likeness of men."[2] In recent years this passage has often been taken as implying that, in becoming incarnate, the divine Word divested himself of certain of his attributes, or at least of the power to exercise them; in some extreme forms of kenotic theory it has even been maintained that during the period of his humiliation the divine Word ceased to be, in any genuine sense of the word, God at all. This is not the place for a long exegetical discussion, but a few remarks may be permitted. (1) In the first place, the assumption, made by Gore among others,[3] that "emptied" (ἐκένωσεν) implies that the Word stripped himself of some element or elements proper to his divinity, is very doubtful; sound exegetical authorities can be quoted against this view. Thus Dr. Marvin Vincent says, in the International Critical Commentary, that the verb is "not used or intended here in a metaphysical sense to define the limitation of Christ's incarnate state, but as a strong and graphic expression of the completeness of his self-renunciation. It includes all the details of humiliation which follow, and is defined by these."[4] Dr. Maurice Jones endorses the view that "the verb 'emptied' . . . does not require a genitive of the secondary object, and Christ did not empty himself of anything but *poured himself*, emptying his

[1] *Eccl. Pol.*, V, li, 2: ed. of 1888, II, p. 221. Italics mine.
[2] Phil. ii. 5–7 (R.V.).   [3] *Dissertations*, p. 89.   [4] *I.C.C.*, Philippians, p. 59.

fullness into us."[1] Professor J. H. Michael tends to the view that there is a reference to the suffering servant in Isaiah who "poured out his soul unto death."[2] None of these writers interprets the verb *ekenosen* as signifying any kind of evacuation of the Godhead. (2) There are, as Dr. E. H. Gifford argued,[3] strong reasons for understanding "being (ὑπάρχων) in the form of God" as meaning not "having been God" but "continuing to be God in very essence." (3) The words "counted it not a prize to be on an equality with God" can mean either "counted his equality with God not as a usurpation (but as something belonging to him by right)" or "counted his equality with God not as something to hold on to (but as something which he might willingly let go)." In either case, there is a marked contrast between the "form of God" (μορφὴ θεοῦ), or God's essential nature, and "equality with God" (τὸ εἶναι ἴσα θεῷ), which may denote merely a dignity of honour which can be laid aside without any essential change.[4] The passage is thus susceptible of a great variety of interpretations. An extreme kenoticist may render it: "When he was in the form of God, he did not look upon this equality with God as something to be clung to, but emptied himself of it and took instead the form of a servant." But it might equally well be read thus: "Continuing to be essentially God and counting his equality with God as belonging to him by right, he poured himself out upon us by taking in addition the form of a servant." And there are a number of possible renderings intermediate to these two. It is thus, to say the least, hazardous to attempt to derive from the text in Philippians the doctrine that the Incarnation involves a change in the divine nature of the Word.

II

Gore, whose work I have already described as having provided one of the most influential of modern Christological discussions, was concerned to rebut the doctrines of the extreme kenoticists by stating the kenotic theory in a mild form. He summarizes his teaching as follows:

"The divine Son in becoming man must, we conclude, have accepted, voluntarily and deliberately, the limitations involved

---

[1] Westminster Comm., *Philippians*, p. 31. Cf. Prestige, *Fathers and Heretics*, p. 341.
[2] Moffatt Comm., *Philippians*, p. 90.   [3] *The Incarnation*, p. 11 f.   [4] *Ibid.*, p. 22 f.

in really living as man—even as sinless and perfect man—in feeling as a man, thinking as a man, striving as a man, being anxious and tried as a man. Jesus does not indeed appear in the Gospels as unconscious of his divine nature. He knows he is Son of the Father. He 'remembers' how he came from God and would go back to God. But he appears none the less as accepting the limitations of manhood. And St. Paul, I say, gives us the hint which directs our vision. This was no failure of power. God is love, and love is sympathy and self-sacrifice. The Incarnation is the supreme act of self-sacrificing sympathy, by which one whose nature is divine was enabled to enter into human experience. He emptied himself of divine prerogatives so far as was involved in really becoming man, and growing, feeling, thinking and suffering as man."[1]

Elsewhere Gore writes:

"The Incarnation of the Son of God was no mere addition of a manhood to his Godhead: it was no mere wrapping around the divine glory of a human nature to veil it and make it tolerable to mortal eyes. It was more than this. The Son of God, without ceasing to be God, the Son of the Father, and without ceasing to be conscious of his divine relation as Son to the Father, yet in assuming human nature, so truly entered into it as really to grow and live as Son of Man under properly human conditions, that is to say also under properly human limitations. Thus, if we are to express this in human language, we are forced to assert that within the *sphere* and *period* of his incarnate and mortal life, he did, and as it would appear did habitually—doubtless by the voluntary action of his own self-limiting and self-restraining love—cease from the exercise of those divine functions and powers, including the divine omniscience, which would have been incompatible with a truly human experience."[2]

It will not, he says,

"suffice to say that the Son was limited in knowledge, etc., *in respect of his manhood*, so long as we so juxta-posit the omniscient Godhead with the limited manhood as to destroy the impression that he, the Christ, the Son of God, was *personally* living, praying, thinking, speaking, and acting—even working miracles—under the limitations of manhood. . . . Within the period and sphere of his incarnate and mortal life, he the eternal Son was, doubtless by his own act and will, submitting himself to the limitations proper to manhood. The real Incarnation involves a real self-

[1] *Belief in Christ* (edition of 1922), p. 225. [2] *Dissertations*, p. 94.

impoverishment, a real self-emptying, a real self-limitation on the part of the eternal Word of God."[1]

Gore agrees with the general consensus of the fathers that the divine Word continues to exercise outside the sphere of the human life his divine and cosmic functions, but he insists that we must not bring the absolute divine state of the Son side by side with the picture of his humiliation.[2] And he has to admit that "the great bulk of the language of ecclesiastical writers" is against him.[3] Indeed he even goes so far as to disapprove of "the general teaching of the Catholic Church for many centuries about our Lord"[4] —a damaging admission in a writer whose general theological position was as orthodox as Gore's. And, as Dr. Knox and Dr. Vidler have remarked, there is the great difficulty on Gore's view of knowing what was the relation of the consciousness of the eternal Word to that of the incarnate Lord.[5] And Gore, even towards the end of his life, was obliged to admit the justice of such a charge.

"No doubt," he wrote, "such a conception raises questions to which we can find no full answer. Thus—Is the self-emptying to be conceived of as a continual refusal to exercise the free divine consciousness which he possessed, or as something once for all involved in the original act by which he entered into the limiting conditions of manhood? And I think if we are wise we shall not attempt to answer the question. We have not the knowledge of the inner life of Jesus which would make an answer possible. Or again, we are asked how we relate this 'limited' condition of the Son as incarnate with his exercise of all the cosmic functions of the eternal Word—what the New Testament calls 'the sustaining' or 'bearing along of all things' or the holding all the universe of things together—and again I think we had better give no answer."[6]

III

It was this question to which Frank Weston, who had heard Gore deliver the Bampton Lectures on the subject of the Incarnation in 1891, addressed himself in his book, *The One Christ*. Weston is absolutely clear that the Incarnation cannot involve any modifi-

---

[1] *Dissertations*, p. 203.   [2] *Ibid.*, p. 206.   [3] *Ibid.*, p. 202.
[4] *Ibid.*, p. 205. How repugnant to the whole tradition of Christendom is the "kenotic" view is shown by Friedrich Loofs in his learned article in *E.R.E.*, VII, p. 680 f.
[5] *The Development of Modern Catholicism*, p. 145.   [6] *Belief in Christ*, p. 226.

cation of the activity of the divine Word in either the divine or the
cosmic sphere; he is altogether convinced of the immutability of
God. And he is also clear that the subject of the human life of
Christ is the Person of the divine Word. But he sees the Word
adding to himself a new mode of existence by imposing upon
himself a law of restraint affecting that mode of existence alone,
and under that mode living a fully human life in which his
freedom and knowledge are altogether circumscribed by the
limitations proper to human nature as such. For Weston, the
Word has not, as Gore sometimes seems to suggest, rendered
himself helpless by one act of self-abandonment in the past; rather
he incessantly restrains himself by a continuous act of self-limitation, in virtue of which he refrains, within the sphere of the
incarnate life, from enjoying his divine privileges. Here is Weston's
own summary of his theory:

> "We postulated the distinction between the eternal, universal
> relationships of the Son of God, and the new, particular relation-
> ships that make up the world of the Incarnate and his redeemed
> people. In the former sphere we found all the unlimited activities
> of the eternal Son for all time, activities from which he has never
> ceased; and among them we found the promulgation of the law of
> self-emptying which he imposed upon himself: the law of self-
> restraint that was to make possible the second set of relationships,
> the sphere of the Incarnation.
>
> "Within the sphere of the Incarnation we found the eternal
> Son living under that law of self-restraint, by which the limits of
> his manhood at every moment are constituted as the limits of his
> consciousness and freedom as Incarnate Son of God. We saw him
> unconscious of any self that is too great to be mediated by the
> human soul that he had joined to himself; he who is God, possessing
> all the attributes of God, lives entirely and utterly under conditions
> of manhood. Apart from his manhood he has no existence as
> incarnate, although all the while he lives and reigns in the eternal
> sphere as the unlimited Word of the Father."[1]

Again:

> "The Incarnate lives under the conditions of manhood, in the
> particular relations that he assumed, thereby limiting his divine
> powers; but there is no wall of partition. Behind all the special
> relationships that make up the sphere of the Incarnation lies the
> divine will, unlimited, powerful, and free, of the eternal Son,
> dwelling in the bosom of the Father. But within the sphere so

[1] *The One Christ*, p. 320.

constituted, within those special relationships, we find no signs of
the presence of divinity unconditioned by manhood.

"Thus in fact there is a link between the two spheres, and no
gulf at all; and the link is the divine Will of the eternal Son,
willing to manifest himself only in the measure in which manhood
can reveal him."[1]

Weston's theory has many strong points. It makes it quite clear
that there is no alteration in the divine and cosmic activities of the
Word as a result of the Incarnation. And, by maintaining that the
self-limitation involved in the human sphere was not just the result
of one heroic act, performed at some moment in the past and
depriving its agent of even the abstract possibility of withdrawal,
but is a continuous and incessant activity by which the divine
Word *remains incarnate*—a point on which, as we saw, Gore was
undecided—Weston provides a conception of the highest value.
For, when we consider the incarnate Lord moving towards his
Passion, with all the anguish both of body and of soul that it brings
with it, we see him not just undergoing the consequences of an
irrevocable past decision but accepting stage by stage a whole
series of sufferings of increasing intensity, which culminate in the
unimaginable desolation of the Fourth Word from the Cross and
from which he is perfectly free physically to escape. This is, I must
point out, in full accordance with the Biblical evidence. "Thinkest
thou that I cannot beseech my Father, and he shall even now send
me more than twelve legions of angels?"[2] "I lay down my life
that I may take it again. No one taketh it away from me, but I lay
it down of myself. I have power to lay it down, and I have power
to take it again."[3] And, by postulating a limitation of divine
power which does not involve its actual abandonment, Weston's
view allows for the glorification of Christ at his ascension, a fact
which the extreme kenotic theories find it extremely difficult to
assimilate.

"It seems clear," he writes, "that if the Logos had once laid
aside, completely and entirely, his divine powers in order to enter
upon a certain new sphere, he could never have resumed them
without going outside that limited sphere. The power necessary to
the resumption of the divine attributes could only be his again after
he had ceased to live in the limited sphere. In which case the
Incarnation has no permanency, and the mediatorial work of
Christ is not everlasting. And it is also fairly clear that even if the

[1] *The One Christ*, p. 130.   [2] Matt. xxvi. 53.   [3] John x. 17-18.

abandonment is conceived as taking place within the sphere of the Incarnation, so that the power of resuming the divine attributes is always present to the Incarnate; yet at the time of the glorification of the manhood the process of self-abandonment has to be changed to a process of self-limitation.

"It is surely a much richer thought that the self-limitation is continuous from the moment of the conception onwards; that at every moment he willed to live in conditions of manhood, and that in his acceptance of the law that governs this life lies the value of the Incarnation as an act of divine self-sacrifice. In time and through eternity the Christ is God the Son, self-limited in manhood."[1]

Weston further remarks that the life of Christ

"begins in the womb of Mary: it does not end on Mount Olivet. It is the endless life into which the sons and daughters of God are taken by Christ and in which they live in him and with him—his mystical body, his Church. Whatever then we postulate of the manner of the incarnate life on earth must bear some relation to the manner of it in Heaven all down the ages. . . . We can be saved only by the life of the Son of God made man; by the life of God made over to us through manhood; and it is from the divine Saviour in Heaven that we look for aid. But if the fulness of deity cannot exist with manhood, in spite of limitation; if nothing short of abandonment of the divine powers will make possible the union; then we must confess that we have no certainty that in Heaven the divine fulness can be brought to us in and through the glorified manhood."[2]

Weston's criticisms of theories of self-abandonment are of the highest value, and we may freely admit that his Christology marks an immense advance on that of Gore. Nevertheless, his positive doctrine has its defects. As Knox and Vidler remark, Weston is "weak as a philosopher; he does not realize that in speaking of the Incarnation and the risen and ascended Lord we are dealing not with changes in the eternal nature of God, but with the relation of the timeless Being of God to his manifestation in history."[3] Weston in fact also overlooks the point that was stressed earlier on, that the relation of incarnation, being a relation of the infinite to the finite, while it is real in the human nature is logical in the Person of the divine Word. Hence, as Knox

[1] *The One Christ*, p. 124.   [2] *Ibid.*, p. 126.
[3] *The Development of Modern Catholicism*, p. 219. The assertion of these authors that Weston is also weak on the critical side is of perhaps less importance in view of the movement of Biblical study since the date of their work.

and Vidler observe, he involves himself in unnecessary difficulties in his discussion of the coexistence in Christ of two modes of existence, a human and a divine. These details can however be easily put right.[1] A more serious criticism is made by Dr. Relton, who points out that, according to Weston,

"all the activities of the unlimited Logos are confined to the sphere of his eternal, universal relations, and when he acts in the sphere of the incarnate state, his divine powers are always conditioned by, and mediated through, his manhood. . . . The question that presents itself to our mind," he continues, "is whether the evidence derived from the self-revelation of Jesus Christ does not contain data which make it hard to believe that, in his incarnate state, his self-consciousness of his deity was *wholly* conditioned by, and mediated through, the manhood he had assumed; and, further, whether his divine powers were circumscribed within this same limit. . . . We contemplate his filial consciousness, which marks his relationship to God as unique; differing not in degree but in kind from ours, and which was, moreover, the medium and channel through which has been conveyed to the world that insight into the very heart of God, which constitutes the claim of Christianity to be a complete and final revelation. . . . If it be urged that we can set no limit to manhood's capacity for mediating such a divine revelation, because we have no knowledge of the powers of a sinless manhood as a vehicle for the self-manifestation of God to men, we admit the point, but prefer to take refuge in the thought that, after all, sinless perfection is something differing not only in degree but in kind from anything human, and to this extent is as unique in the Person of Christ as was his filial consciousness. The uniqueness of his relationship to God as 'of one substance with the Father' is the foundation for the finality and completeness of his revelation. The uniqueness of his sinless perfection is the foundation of his atoning work in redemption. Are we to believe that his work both as Revealer and as Redeemer was conditioned by, and mediated through, the limitations of the man-

---

[1] Thus Weston writes: "I have based the self-restraint of the incarnate Son upon an act of will which he made as the unlimited Word of the Father: an act once made and never to be altered; whereas the usual view is that his self-restraint is due to a series of acts within the sphere of his Incarnation." (*The One Christ*, p. 323.) Such an act of self-restraint, however, since it is a relation of the infinite to the finite, will be *ex parte Dei* not "once made" at a moment of time but timeless, while *ex parte humanitatis* it will be, if not a "series of acts," at any rate one continuous act enduring from the moment of the Incarnation for ever; the antithesis is only apparent. The criticism of this point made by Relton (*Study in Christology*, p. 218) can therefore be evaded. I should add that by "the usual view" Weston means the usual view of the fathers, not that of modern Christologists.

hood he assumed? We hesitate to answer this question in the affirmative, in view of the above considerations."[1]

Relton then asks whether the Gospel portrait of the earthly life of Jesus Christ is conceivable upon any other hypothesis than that at every moment of his earthly life he was transcendent above, and yet immanent in, the manhood he had assumed.

"The Alexandrian and Cyrilline Christology," he says, "leave us with the eternal, unlimited Logos as the subject of the manhood. Both, however, recognize some form of self-limitation on the part of the Logos in his incarnate state, whereby the divine nature is restrained, and the manhood thus allowed to act humanly. This leaves the door open, so to speak, for the Logos to exercise his divine powers and prerogatives *to the full*, if and when he wills to do so. Dr. Weston invites us to close this door, and in this way not only to escape many difficulties, but to secure a much more consistent and comprehensible Christology. We should like to do so, but the risk seems too great. If we turn away from this most enticing form of kenotic Christology, what is the alternative?

"Let us see what can be said for the doctrine of the Enhypostasia."[2]

Dr. Relton is thus one of the very few modern writers who take altogether seriously the fact which is expressed by saying that the Person of the divine Word and his divine nature are really identical and only logically distinct. If this is so, then the divine nature cannot be excluded from the sphere of the Incarnation. How Dr. Relton actually develops his statement of the doctrine of Enhypostasia in modern terms I shall now go on to consider.

IV

Dr. Relton starts, with Leontius of Byzantium, from the Cyrilline position that the ego of the God-Man was the divine unlimited Logos. The manhood of Christ

"had no existence prior to the Incarnation, but became hypostatic, and received its subsistence, and consequently its completeness, when the divine Logos became its Ego. The manhood of Christ in the Christology of Leontius was thus more than a mere accident of the Godhead, and yet less than an independent individual person."[3]

[1] *Study in Christology*, p. 218.   [2] *Ibid.*, p. 222.   [3] *Ibid.*, p. 225.

In reinterpreting this doctrine in modern terms, Relton takes as his fundamental concept that of consciousness or self-consciousness, and he claims that the Enhypostasia enables him to avoid the pitfalls into which other modern Christologists who have built upon this same concept have fallen.

> "If we are to think in terms of 'personality' instead of 'sub-stance,' then the whole trend of modern thought in the field of Christology is to secure that the self-consciousness of Jesus be a single consciousness moving always as a spiritual unity. This, and this alone, it is felt, will safeguard the reality of the Gospel portrait, which from first to last presents us with the *One* Christ. We have," he says, "examined theories which are attempts to secure this single consciousness, and have given reasons for our inability to regard them as fully satisfying all the conditions of the problem. Now the doctrine of the Enhypostasia, as we interpret it, secures that the self-consciousness of the God-Man is a single-consciousness which is not purely human, nor merely human, but truly human, and this because, and only because, it is at the same time truly divine. Therefore it, and it alone, could be the subject of both natures, and be the basis of their union within the Person of Christ."[1]

Relton goes on to say that

> "the basis of the doctrine is the fact that the divine Logos, prior to the Incarnation, already possessed everything needful to enable him to live a truly human life. . . . The human and the divine," he maintains, "are not two contradictory, but two complementary terms, and the less is contained in the greater. His divine self-consciousness was, in virtue of its divinity, a truly human self-consciousness."[2]

Indeed, he goes so far as to assert that

> "the manhood of Christ, if it had possessed a human Ego only, would have been incomplete. Hence the Logos as its Ego was the sole condition which could secure its completeness. We may not speak of Christ's manhood as being real and complete except on one supposition, namely, that its personality was divine."[3]

In Christ there is thus one self-consciousness which is both divine and human, indeed which is fully human only because it is divine.

> "Is it inconceivable," Relton asks, "that he who is perfect Personality could become personal in the flesh and live a truly

---

[1] *Study in Christology*, p. 226.   [2] *Ibid.*, pp. 226, 227.   [3] *Ibid.*, p. 228.

human life? If he possesses in a perfect degree that which is most distinctive of manhood, i.e., personality, is it inconceivable that his Ego, infinite in its divinity, could nevertheless be the Ego also of the manhood he assumed? Is it inconceivable that his self-consciousness should be a single divine unique consciousness, giving him a knowledge of himself as the divine unlimited Logos in virtue of its unlimited extension, eternal character, and all-embracing fullness, and yet at the same time giving him a know-ledge of himself as the human Son of man circumscribed by the limitations inherent in a finite existence?"[1]

Relton insists that such a consciousness would be in its divine character unlimited and would therefore mediate to Christ the knowledge of his relationship to the eternal Father and be the source of his work as the revealer of God to men, while at the same time it would be truly human and would be subject to all the laws that govern the growth of our personality as finite limited beings in a finite world (the limitations that in us are the effects of sin being alone excepted).

"The divine Ego contains the human, and yet is not exhausted by that fact. The single unique divine self-consciousness of the incarnate Christ is the universal, revealed in and through the particular, embracing the latter and yet not limited by its range. Of the incarnate Christ we may say that the form of his consciousness was human, but its content was divine. Its range, viewed from one standpoint was unlimited—viewed from another standpoint, was limited and yet none the less *self*-limited. It was the subject of both natures. . . . The doctrine of the Enhypostasia secures for the Christ in his incarnate state a range of consciousness passing out beyond the limits of a finite mind. The same self-consciousness could mediate two sets of knowledge—all that he knew as God, all that he came to know as the result of his earthly experiences in the days of his flesh."[2]

Relton rightly remarks that the outstanding difficulty in his view is the question as to how the particular can perfectly embody its own universal.

"How," he asks, "could the particular man, Christ Jesus, be nevertheless the Universal Man, the Second Adam, the archetype and representative man, belonging not to any one age, but claimed as the ideal of every age? The same difficulty, viewed from another standpoint, is this: How a single, unique, divine self-consciousness could be at once unlimited and yet limited?"[3]

[1] *Study in Christology*, p. 229.   [2] *Ibid.*, p. 233.   [3] *Ibid.*, p. 234.

D

He argues, however, that paradoxical as it may sound, the Gospels show us a Christ who, without any alternation of personality, manifests with complete naturalness and self-coherence, this double character.

"However incredible or logically impossible such a phenomenon may appear, the fact remains that in the Person of Jesus Christ is revealed One who was a particular man, and yet the Universal Man; One, moreover, whose consciousness was at once limited and unlimited, finite and circumscribed yet infinite and uncircumscribed in its range, human and yet divine, divine and yet human. If we say that it is intellectually inconceivable and historically impossible, the facts reprove us. Faith can grasp it. The Gospels record it. Is there any hypothesis which will cover it? The doctrine of the Enhypostasia is the one which we venture to suggest. It is based upon grounds which make it at least conceivable to the human mind. It does not solve the problem, because the problem is ultimately insolvable by any finite mind. It postulates a logical impossibility—the particular cannot embody its own universal. But the Person of Christ is the bankruptcy of human logic."[1]

For much that Dr. Relton says we may indeed be grateful. There were all too few theologians who were prepared in 1917, to insist, in the face of the prevailing liberal reconstructions of the historic Christ, upon the radically supernatural and transcendent character of the Jesus of the Gospels; it required more courage then than it does to-day, when the labours of Hoskyns and others have shown how impossible it is to eliminate the supernatural element from the sacred text. And it is refreshing to see an Anglican writer, in the full noon of liberalism, starting from a professedly Cyrilline and Alexandrian standpoint. There are, however, I would suggest, certain respects in which he seems to have made unnecessary concessions to the *Zeitgeist*, in particular by his transference of the whole Christological problem from the ontological to the psychological plane. I have urged already that the classical Christian formula, "Two natures, a divine and a human, united in one divine Person," does not render the humanity of Christ incomplete, even while it implies that he has no human person, simply because "person" is a purely ontological term and does not denote a psychological constituent of human nature. When, however, Relton translates "one divine Person" by

[1] *Study in Christology*, p. 265.

"one divine consciousness," with the corollary that this divine consciousness takes the place which a human consciousness would otherwise occupy, he leaves the human nature incomplete, just as Apollinarius did when he put the divine Word in the place of a human *nous*. Nor is it, I think, satisfactory to rejoin, as Relton does, that the divine consciousness includes in itself all the essential requirements of a human consciousness—that, as he says, "there exists in God himself a human element,"[1] that only God could be perfectly man[2]—the same point could be urged in favour of Apollinarius, with whose teaching Relton shows a rather alarming sympathy.[3] And if it be asked why such a view will not do, seeing that it provides what may reasonably be held to be a full human existence, the answer is that it does not allow for a full human nature as *taken* by Christ; there is not a complete "taking up of manhood into God," since one of the elements of human nature, namely the consciousness, is not taken by the divine Word but rather supplied by him. And "what he did not take he did not redeem." The fact is that the formula "one consciousness" involves either that the human nature is left incomplete, in which case we have a view closely similar to Apollinarianism and mono-thelitism, or else that the human nature is absorbed into the divine, and this is virtual Eutychianism. Furthermore, we can preserve the orthodoxy of "one consciousness" only by equating "consciousness" with "person," and this seems frankly impossible. For the person is the ultimate subject of the whole human life, in which consciousness is only one element; there is the whole sub-conscious and unconscious realm in addition and there is the realm of sensitive and vegetative life. Person and consciousness thus differ not only in their status as subject and operation respectively, but also in the width of their scope. Finally, it must be observed that it is one thing for logic to be rendered "bankrupt," as Relton says,[4] and another for it to be murdered. There is bound to be at the heart of the Incarnation a mystery which the human mind cannot pierce—it is indeed both ridiculous and irreverent to ask what it "feels like" to be God incarnate—but when one has been led to admit that one's theory actually "postulates a logical impossibility" it may be suspected that the theory is defective. I

---

[1] *Study in Christology*, p. 269.   [2] *Ibid.*, pp. 227–8.
[3] *Ibid.*, Part I, ch. i. It is, however, very doubtful whether Apollinarius actually taught the doctrine of an archetypal manhood in the Logos; see C. E. Raven, *Apollinarianism*, p. 185.
[4] "The Person of Christ is the bankruptcy of logic" (*Study in Christology*, p. 234).

am not trying to pass judgment *de haut en bas* or accusing of mere conventionality a discussion which in many respects ran clean counter to the prevailing theological trend of the time, when I suggest, as one looks back upon Dr. Relton's work from a standpoint which is a quarter of a century later, that his really false step was made when he translated the classical Christology from ontological into psychological terms. The person-nature terminology was, in effect, devised precisely in order to free Christology from the complications of contemporary psychology; it is a pity if we in the twentieth century fall into the very snare which our fifth-century forefathers so skilfully eluded.[1]

V

The three distinguished theologians whose Christology I have just discussed illustrate a continuous line of development of thought in the attempt to work out a theory which would be in its essence identical with the classical Christian doctrine as it was formulated by the Council of Chalcedon, while none the less meeting what were felt to be the legitimate demands of contemporary thought, with its strong emphasis upon psychology. They were all committed to explicit acceptance of Catholic doctrine, and made every attempt to adhere to it and defend it. In this they were in marked contrast with such professed kenotic extremists as Dr. H. R. Mackintosh. In the case of Weston, at any rate, it is impossible for anyone who is acquainted with the part which he played in the controversies of his day or with his pastoral letter on *The Christ and His Critics* to have the least doubt of his determination to defend in all its fullness the Catholic doctrine of the Word-made-flesh. We have, however, seen reason to suppose that both Gore and Relton made unnecessary concessions to the climate of their times. It may perhaps be suggested that their real weakness lay in the assumption that contemporary categories of psychology were capable of providing an adequate medium for the expression of Christological doctrine. One result of this was that their attention was diverted from what might have been a far more fruitful and constructive task, namely the exposition and explanation, to a world to which the Chalcedonian doctrine was altogether

[1] Need it be said that, in writing as I have of consciousness in this paragraph, I am not implying that consciousness is a separable "part" of the human mind and forgetting that it is a mode of operation? The point is that consciousness is something that the individual *has* (*quod habet sed non est*), in contrast with the person which is who the individual *is* (*quod est et non habet*).

unfamiliar, of the precise content and implications of that doctrine itself and of the terms in which it has been historically embodied. Nevertheless, their work is worthy of the highest gratitude for its uncompromising repudiation of those systems, all too common at the time, which viewed the Incarnation under a purely evolutionary aspect and for their insistence that the Christ differs not merely in degree but in kind from every other being who has ever lived or will ever live on this planet. None of them could have made so unguarded a statement as that to which one of Dr. Relton's critics committed himself, that "what is *ex hypothesi* potential in all men—that is, the complete union of the human with the divine—was actualized in" Christ,[1] with its suggestion that the actualization of this potentiality in any one of us would—and presumably, if we attain the end for which God has made us, one day will—leave no difference between us and the incarnate Lord; Relton is quite clear about the difference between the hypostatic union of the two natures in one Person in Christ and the adoptive union of Christians into him.[2]

The conclusion to which all this points is, I suggest, that the really important thing for Christology is that it should quite fearlessly move within the orbit of those conceptions which are proper to it and resist the temptation to transfer itself into the modes of thought of other sciences. (This is, I will add, entirely compatible with the performance of the always imperative task of explaining the Faith to the contemporary world in language that it can understand.) The harm that can come to a science when it deserts its own proper categories of explanation for those of another science which has more contemporary appeal is very evident to-day. The last century witnessed the attempt to reduce both psychology and biology to departments of mechanical science, with deleterious results from which those studies are only now beginning to shake themselves free. At the same time, the attempt was being made to reduce physics to mathematics, though at the present day it might seem to be à moot point whether physics is to be brought under the sway of logic or of psychology.[3]

---

[1] *J.T.S.*, vol. xx (1919), p. 187.   [2] *Study in Christology*, p. 190.

[3] I must make it quite plain that I am not intending in the least to deny the legitimacy of mathematical physics or of any other science, but only to affirm that, whatever use physics may make of mathematics, it is concerned with sensible being as its object, while mathematics has as its objects certain abstractions of quantity and number. Cf. Maritain, *The Degrees of Knowledge*, chs. i and iii. One might also refer to the attempts to reduce mathematics to logic, and logic to symbol-shuffling, both of which seem fairly clearly to have failed. See Russell, *Principles of Mathematics*; Gonseth, *Fondements des Mathématiques*, ch. x; Ushenko, *Problems of Logic*.

One invariable consequence follows the attempt to discuss the problems of one science in the categories of another, namely, that the subject-matter proves to be recalcitrant to the treatment; this intransigence is then interpreted as the sign of an ir ner contradiction. M. Étienne Gilson has remarked upon this in the course of some very penetrating observations on the philosophical discussions of such scientific authorities as Professor Eddington and Sir James Jeans.

"In 1930," he writes, "Sir James Jeans decided to deal with philosophical problems in the light of contemporary science. The upshot was his most popular book: *The Mysterious Universe*. Now, if the universe of science is mysterious, what is not? We do not need science to tell us that the universe is indeed mysterious. Men have known that since the very beginning of the human race. The true and proper function of science is, on the contrary, to make as much of the universe as possible grow less and less mysterious to us. Science does it, and she does it magnificently. . . . The true reason why the universe appears to some scientists as mysterious is that, mistaking existential, that is, metaphysical, questions for scientific ones, they ask science to answer them. Then they are puzzled, and they say that the universe is mysterious."[1]

Similarly, when Dr. Relton writes that "the Person of Christ is the bankruptcy of logic,"[2] and that the doctrine which he himself has expounded "postulates a logical impossibility,"[3] or when Dr. William Temple asserts that the Chalcedonian formula is "a confession of the bankruptcy of Greek Patristic Theology" and "represented the breakdown of theology,"[4] may it not be replied that there is, as a matter of fact, not the least inadequacy in the Chalcedonian formula itself, which states the truth concerning Christ in its own proper terms as a question of ontology to which the concepts of person and nature are entirely suitable, and that the contradiction appears only when the attempt is made to state it in terms of the quite different science of psychology, and, we

---

[1] *God and Philosophy*, pp. 122–3. Cf., on the method of modern physics, Max Born, *Experiment and Theory in Physics*.
[2] *Study in Christology*, p. 234.   [3] *Ibid.*, p. 265.
[4] "The Divinity of Christ" in *Foundations*, pp. 230–1; cf. *Christus Veritas*, p. 134. I have not discussed the Christology of Dr. Temple in detail, but it may be noted that he too conducts his discussion in psychological terms. "Until Christianity itself had led to the formation of a tolerably adequate conception of personality," he writes, "it was inevitable that the problem should be set in terms of Substance or Nature." (*Christus Veritas*, p. 131.) I agree; but I am not sure that this was altogether a misfortune. Dr. Temple's own bias towards psychology is seen in his equation of "personality" with "will." (*Ibid.*, p. 150.)

might add, in terms of a modern version of psychology which has been erected on purely naturalistic bases without any reference to the Christian doctrine of man? That the doctrine of the Incarnation may have consequences in the psychological sphere we need not deny—I shall refer to some of them later—but the doctrine is not itself a matter of psychology, and thus any attempt to identify, for example, "person" with "consciousness" or with "personality" (in the commonly accepted modern sense of that term) can lead to nothing but confusion. I shall therefore conclude this section by quoting the central passage of the great formula of the Council of Chalcedon, a statement which, while its explanation to the world of the present day may need much patient effort of exposition, does not, I would most emphatically urge, require either apology or modification.

"Wherefore," declares the Council, "after the example of the holy fathers, we all with one voice confess our Lord Jesus Christ one and the same Son, the same perfect in Godhead, the same perfect in manhood, very God and very Man, the same consisting of a reasonable soul and a body, of one substance with the Father as touching the Godhead, the same of one substance with us as touching the manhood, like us in all things, sin except; begotten of the Father before the worlds as touching the Godhead, the same in these last days, for us and for our salvation, born of the Virgin Mary, the Mother of God, as touching the manhood, one and the same Christ, Son, Lord, Only-begotten, to be acknowledged in two natures (ἐν δύο φύσεσιν); without confusion, without conversion, without division, never to be separated (ἀσυγχύτως, ἀτρέπτως, ἀδιαιρέτως, ἀχωρίστως); the distinction of natures being in no wise done away because of the union, but rather the characteristic property of each nature being preserved, and concurring into one Person and one subsistence (εἰς ἓν πρόσωπον καὶ μίαν ὑπόστασιν), not as if Christ were parted or divided into two Persons, but one and the same Son and Only-begotten God, Word, Lord, Jesus Christ; even as the Prophets from the beginning spake concerning him, and our Lord Jesus Christ hath instructed us, and the Symbol of the Fathers hath handed down to us."[1]

[1] It should be noted that the only psychological terms occur in the words ("of a reasonable soul and a body") which insist on the completeness of the manhood of Christ; the statement of the relation of the Godhead and the manhood to each other is entirely in terms of person (*prosopon*), subsistence (*hypostasis*) and nature (*physis*). It is not, of course, that these terms were simply taken over in their current applications by Christian theology. The precise theological meanings which they ultimately came to bear were arrived at only after long discussion and controversy. See, e.g., Prestige, *God in Patristic Thought, passim*; Sellers, *Two Ancient Christologies*, p. 46 f.

VI

We might summarize this discussion by saying that the modern Christological writing which we have examined has tended, in spite of much in it that is illuminating and stimulating, to suffer from two grave defects. One, to which I have just been referring, is a reluctance to discuss Christology in its proper terms, which are ontological, and an anxiety to transpose it into the realm of the more fashionable science of psychology; this can, I think, best be described as a failure of theological nerve.[1] The other, which I touched upon earlier, equally manifests a concession to the prejudices of the contemporary mind; it is the assumption that the Incarnation is to be viewed primarily as a compression of the divine into the framework of the human, rather than as an exaltation of the human to the level of the divine. It is true that such an attitude may seem superficially to receive some sanction from the language of the two most widely used of the great Catholic creeds. The Apostles' Creed lays almost all its emphasis upon the human nature of the Son of God: "who was conceived by the Holy Ghost, born of the Virgin Mary, suffered under Pontius Pilate, was crucified, dead and buried." Nothing is said about his pre-existence. The Nicene Creed adds the statement, which may well scandalize the philosophers, that he "came down from heaven and was made flesh," though it also asserts in uncompromising terms his coeternity and coequality with the Father. But, on any showing, this is precisely what we should expect in formularies which are, or are based upon, the confessions required of candidates for baptism; the ordinary Christian is not to be expected to entangle himself in philosophical discussions but to accept the plain facts of the Gospel and to express them in the same concrete and straightforward language that he uses in describing the experiences of his daily life. A baby has been born from a human mother and is lying in a stable at Bethlehem; he is, so the Church assures us, the very God who made the universe and whose dwelling is in heaven; how else can we express this than by saying, simply and uncompromisingly, that he has "come down from heaven," that he has been "made flesh," that he has been "made man"? When, however, we pass beyond the mere recogni-

---

[1] Dr. Prestige significantly remarks that "psychology, in ancient times at least, was ever the parent of heresy." (*Fathers and Heretics*, p. 228.)

tion of historical fact and ask how this miracle is possible—when, for instance, we inquire how the incarnation of the divine Word is compatible with his immutability as God—we are led to those more subtle and philosophical statements which we find in the Chalcedonian definition and the *Quicunque vult*. He came down from heaven—yes; but heaven is not a "place," whereas the earth is; or, if heaven is a place, it is one of a very different kind from the earth. Therefore, the "descent" which we observe is relative not to heaven but to us. How, then, did this descent, this coming down, occur? Not, replies *Quicunque vult*, by the conversion of Godhead into flesh, but by taking up of manhood into God. There is no contradiction between the two statements, but the second tells us how the first is to be understood. It is right for the ordinary Christian—and for the philosopher too, for when he stands at the font or kneels at the altar he is as "ordinary" as anyone else—to state his faith in the most commonplace and straightforward way that he can; but it is also necessary to remember that because we are enmeshed in the created order—because we are, so to speak, at the thin end of the Creator-creature relation—we habitually see everything upside down. Therefore, what, when expressed in the language of our experience is a making of God into flesh, is, when expressed from the divine standpoint, an exaltation of manhood into God. And it is God's standpoint, not ours, that expresses the ultimate truth.

This does not imply, I must repeat, that there is in the Church an intellectual *élite* who know the real facts, while any loose form of words will do for the *hoi polloi*. Each form of words is a true expression of the Faith, and it is even more necessary for the philosopher than for anyone else to confess that the Son of God "came down from heaven," for, just because he is more conscious of the divine impassibility, he needs all the more safeguarding from the danger of turning the Incarnation into a mere theophany. And it may be suggested that the Church of England has shown real wisdom in making the *Quicunque vult*, as well as the Apostles' and the Nicene Creed, the property of the laity, for in so doing it removes all suggestion that the true faith is the possession of an esoteric body distinct from the main mass of the Church.

If we may compare natural things with supernatural ones, we might find a parallel to this in such a form of words as "The sun sets in the west each evening," which might be found on the lips of astronomers and plain men alike, in spite of the fact that the

scientific description of the phenomenon has to be given in terms
not of the "setting of the sun" but of the "rotation of the earth on
its axis." The use of the former phrase does not imply that the
speaker rejects the Copernican astronomy or believes that the
earth is flat; but neither can the phrase be conveniently super-
seded by a more "scientific" statement, as we shall see if we try to
formulate in accurate astronomical language the regulations about
the lighting of bicycle-lamps or the blacking-out of windows in
war-time. As soon, however, as anyone inquires "why" or "how"
the phenomena of sunrise and sunset are to be understood, the
reference to the earth's rotation becomes quite indispensable.[1]

VII

I shall conclude this chapter with a few brief remarks on the
long and elaborate work of Fr. Lionel Thornton, C.R., entitled
The Incarnate Lord, which Professor Hodgson has described as the
greatest theological work that has appeared in his lifetime.[2] The
reason why I have not discussed it earlier in this chapter is that it
stands for the most part outside the general idiom of modern
Christological discussion, being based upon a "philosophy of
organism" which has considerable affinities with the thought of
Dr. A. N. Whitehead. Fr. Thornton's adoption of this system as
a medium for Christology would seem to be due to an admirable
desire to preserve that conception of the universe as a hier-
archically graded and organic whole which was so prominent a
feature of medieval thought, while meeting at the same time the
demands of modern evolutionary theories and avoiding the difficulties that are commonly felt to be inherent in the medieval
doctrine of determinate species. For an exposition and criticism
of Whitehead's own system I may perhaps refer the reader to what
I have written elsewhere;[3] in the present connection I would only
say that I cannot help feeling doubtful whether Fr. Thornton's
work really owes as much to that of Whitehead as he himself, with
the humility of the true scholar, is inclined to think. I certainly
agree with Dr. Hodgson that Fr. Thornton "never fell into the

---

[1] This illustration must not, of course, be pressed beyond the limits of its immediate
application. In the case of sunrise and sunset the "appearances" might be "saved"
by some other form of astronomical theory than the Copernican, and in any case the
question lies entirely within the sphere of human reason, unlike the question of the
Catholic creeds, in which the supernatural indwelling of the Holy Spirit in the Church
has its part.   [2] *The Doctrine of the Trinity*, p. 228.   [3] *He Who Is*, ch. xi.

temptation to assimilate the historic revelation to the demands of the philosophical system," but that, "on the contrary, he brought into the philosophy from the Christian revelation what it needed to make that system work, to save it from the necessity of postulating pan-psychism in order to account for the movement in the universe."[1] Thus, while Whitehead writes that "it is as true to say that God creates the World, as that the World creates God,"[2] Thornton insists that "the essence of religion consists in the concrete dependence of incomplete created individuality upon absolute individuality as it exists in God."[3] Again, whereas Whitehead tells us that "neither God, nor the World, reaches static completion. Both are in the grip of the ultimate metaphysical ground, the creative advance into novelty. Either of them, God and the World, is the instrument of novelty for the other,"[4] Thornton points out that "if God is dependent upon creation for his self-expression in the sense that creation is the necessary object of divine activity, then there is no identity between God and the eternal order."[5] And, in dealing with Christology, Thornton is altogether determined to be orthodox. "The intention behind all the language employed," he says, referring to his own exposition, "was the intention to reaffirm, in terminology relevant to modern ways of thought, precisely that doctrine which was slowly formulated in a succession of ecumenical councils," and he adds that "how far that intention has been adequately embodied in the statement must be left to the judgment of the Church."[6] His actual statement of the union between the Godhead and the manhood in Christ is perhaps sufficiently exemplified in the following extract:

"The humanity of the Incarnate Lord is not a static metaphysical entity, but a spiritual organism. We have not to search, as some have supposed, for a central core which must be abstracted to make room for the eternal Logos. All the principles of unity which exist in any other human organism exist also in him. But whereas in created human beings the highest law of being is that transcending principle of unity which is proper to a human organism on the level of spirit and which flows down from the creative activity of the eternal order, *this is not the highest law of being in the Incarnate Lord.* The highest law of being in his case is the law of being proper to deity. There is no abrogation of other laws

---

[1] Loc. cit.   [2] *Process and Reality*, p. 492.   [3] *The Incarnate Lord*, p. 362.
[4] *Process and Reality*, p. 493.   [5] *The Incarnate Lord*, p. 397.   [6] *Ibid.*, p. 253.

of being. In his organism are all the laws of being which exist in each of us. But even the highest of these, that which constitutes him 'the man Christ Jesus,' is not the highest law of his Being. *It is not, therefore, that principle of unity which determines his status.* His human organism has the creaturely status which is proper to humanity, just as the constituent parts and elements in our complex organisms each have their proper status in the cosmic series, notwithstanding their being built into a spiritual organism. The human body is not less physical because it is taken up into a spiritual organism and has become an organ of spirit. Neither is the human organism less human because it is taken up into union with the eternal Logos and has become the organ of his deity. Just the reverse."[1]

The language of the above passage is indeed different from that of the fathers and the councils; nevertheless it is, I think, abundantly plain that Fr. Thornton's meaning is identical with theirs. By making his statement in terms of metaphysics and not of psychology he is able to maintain that the subject of Christ's human nature is the person of the Logos without finding it necessary to remove from the human nature any of its own constituents. In St. Leo's phrase, Christ is "whole in what is his, whole in what is ours." In saying that the highest law of being on the human level, namely that which constitutes him as the particular man Jesus that he is, is present in Christ, but that it is not the highest law of his being and so is not the principle of unity which determines his status, Thornton is in effect saying that in Christ there is a complete and concrete human nature, but that this human nature is personalized not by itself or in itself but by and in the pre-existent Person of the divine Word. As he says elsewhere, "*the principle of individuality in the Incarnate Lord is Absolute Individuality as it exists in the Person of the Eternal Word*,"[2] and while insisting with the fullest possible emphasis that there is a fundamental difference of kind between humanity and deity,[3] he is able also to write:

"The perfect human organism of Jesus Christ is not less but more truly and profoundly human than ours can ever be. It is not less but more individual. For it conforms to that absolute principle of individuality which is the creative ground of our human

[1] *The Incarnate Lord*, p. 237 (italics in original). With the last three sentences of this passage, cf. pp. 4–7 *supra*.
[2] *Ibid.*, p. 282 (italics in original); cf. p. 232.   [3] *Ibid.*, ch. v.

organisms and the very fountain from which flows our created and incomplete individuality."[1]

The conclusion would seem to be that Fr. Thornton succeeds as well as anyone can hope, in producing a restatement of Christian dogma which is not also a distortion of it. How far such a restatement is of lasting value will presumably depend upon the permanence or impermanence of the philosophical system which is its framework; I suspect that the philosophy of organism has somewhat declined in popularity since 1928. One might perhaps also doubt whether the philosophy of organism does in fact offer the best medium for the expression of theological truths; Fr. Thornton's exposition has frequently been accused of obscurity and turgidity, but perhaps the fault lies not so much with him as with Whitehead, whose writings offer almost or quite as much difficulty to the reader. Be that as it may, it is, I think, extremely significant that the most thorough attempt that has been made to discuss Christology in terms of modern thought is altogether orthodox, even though we may rightly lament with Dr. Hodgson[2] that it has received from the theological and philosophical world nothing like the attention that is its due.

---

[1] *The Incarnate Lord*, p. 283.   [2] Loc. cit., *supra*.

CHAPTER III

GODHEAD AND MANHOOD IN CHRIST

I

I INTEND in this chapter to devote some further discussion to the problem with which the kenotic Christologists were occupied, for whether or not we interpret the word *ekenosen* in the famous passage in Philippians as implying a real modification in the attributes of the divine Word, the fact remains that all that men experienced of the incarnate Lord in the days of his earthly life was manifested to them through the medium of his human nature. It will be well to repeat that all that faith necessitates in this matter is the acknowledgment that in the incarnate Christ the two natures, divine and human, are united in the one divine Person of the Word without either nature being thereby rendered incomplete or confused with the other, although a wonderful and unique union exists between the two; in the Chalcedonian phrase, they are neither confused, nor altered, nor divided, nor ever to be separated. The Christian must believe this; he is not obliged to explain it. But if he does venture on the task of explanation, what is above all necessary is that he should not subtly deform the dogma in order to get a problem that is more amenable to his powers of explanation; that way all the heresies lie. In theology, as in other intellectual pursuits, cooking the working is disreputable; but cooking the question is unforgivable.

I have already remarked that the Incarnation is not to be thought of as the compression of the divine Word within the limits of human nature but as the exaltation of human nature to the level of Godhead by its union with the Person of the divine Word. I have also pointed out that both Godhead and manhood are to be found in the incarnate Christ, and that the divine nature is not to be excluded from the sphere of the Incarnation. We have none the less to face the fact that in the incarnate Christ the divine nature is not to be seen in its naked splendour; it is seen only as mediated through the instrumentality of the manhood. Some of his acts are such as any human being could perform, such as

48

eating and sleeping, rejoicing and sorrowing; in others, the manhood, while in no way constrained or suppressed, is clearly
functioning as the instrument of the divine Word acting in his
capacity as God, as when, in his own right, Christ pronounces the
forgiveness of sins or raises Lazarus from the dead; but in no case
is the divine nature seen acting in separation from the human.
The two natures are distinct and their union is unimaginably
intimate; they are never separated and never confused.

Now the question which troubled the kenoticists was how it was
possible for the divine Word to be united to human nature in this
way without his own freedom, omnipotence and omniscience
being curtailed. The human nature was felt to be a kind of fetter
by which, to a very marked degree, the Word was restricted from
his normal and proper activity. But there is in fact no reason to
suppose that this is so. Is it not far more reasonable to suppose
that the human nature of Christ is to be viewed not as a fetter but
as an instrument? If the Word is to be active in the world, not
merely in the external mode of creator and sustainer but by
entering himself into its own life, what more adequate instrument
than a human nature could he assume? For he is, as Scripture
tells us, "the image of the invisible God (εἰκὼν τοῦ θεοῦ τοῦ
ἀοράτου),"[1] "the impress of his substance (χαρακτὴρ τῆς ὑποστάσεως
αὐτοῦ),"[2] and man is made in God's image.[3] Furthermore,
man is God's vice-gerent in this world and the creature in whom
the world is able to offer freely and voluntarily to God the full
obedience which created being owes to him who made it; God has
made man but little lower than the angels and has crowned him
with glory and honour.[4] Is not manhood then the very instrument
that the divine Word needs if, as the Son of the Father, he is to
enter into the Father's house as its Lord? The very writings that
assure us that Christ is the Father's image tell us that he is the firstborn or heir of all creation and the One in whom the declaration
of the Psalm about the dignity of man is fulfilled.[5] The New-
Testament writers certainly never seem to find the human nature
of Christ an embarrassment to the exercise of his divine prerogatives. In the union of the Word with human flesh, the Prologue

---

[1] Col. i. 15.   [2] Heb. i. 3.

[3] Gen. i. 26, 27. Gore seems to overlook this when, after, as I should say legitimately,
disagreeing with Relton's view of a pre-existent manhood in the Word, he goes to the
extreme of denying that humanity has its eternal counterpart in the Word in any other
sense than that in which all other created things have theirs. (*Belief in Christ*, p. 230.)

[4] Psalm viii. 5. Or should it even be "little lower than God" as in the R.V.?

[5] Heb. iii. 6.

to St. John tells us, the glory of the Word was made visible to us, not that it was impaired or obscured: "we *beheld* his glory, glory as of the only-begotten of the Father."[1] "In him," St. Paul tells the Colossians, "dwelleth all the fulness of the Godhead in bodily form (σωματικῶς)."[2] We may hesitate to say with Dr. Relton that no one but the divine Word could be perfectly human,[3] but we can most emphatically agree that the assumption of human nature is in the highest degree congruous with the Person of God the Son.

Accepting, therefore, the obvious statement that the divinity of the eternal Word can be manifested by the human nature of Christ only to the extent and in the way that human nature is constitutionally and intrinsically capable of manifesting it, we can unreservedly add that human nature is an adequate medium for this purpose. It is not, indeed, that by the exercise of its own powers human nature can aspire to this union; human nature is essentially finite and cannot itself bridge the gulf that separates the creature from the Creator. But what it cannot do for itself God can do for it; it is, by the sort of thing that it is, apt for this union, though it cannot by its own energies achieve it. In the scholastic term, human nature has a *potentia obedientialis*, a purely passive capacity, for hypostatic union; but there is all the difference in the world between a passive capacity and a positive repugnance.

We must, furthermore, beware of assuming that the limitations proper to human nature as such are the same as the limitations that we experience in ourselves. There is every reason for believing that human nature as it exists in us, who are members of a fallen race and have added to our misery by the commission of numberless sins of our own, is a terribly frustrated and mutilated version of what human nature is meant by God to be. Whether or not we agree with the traditional catalogue of the supernatural endowments given by God to Adam in Paradise and lost through the Fall (immunity from concupiscence, suffering and death; dominion over the lower creation; and so on), we can hardly deny that human nature when free from the effects of sin, both original and actual, must vastly exceed, both in its active powers and its passive

---

[1] John i. 14. [2] Col. ii. 9.

[3] *Study in Christology*, p. 227. It is, of course, metaphysical, not moral, perfection that is in question; if man had not sinned he would have certainly been *morally* perfect. But as regards metaphysical perfection, may we not distinguish? In his own created order man is capable of metaphysical perfection. But by the hypostatic union manhood is exalted to an order of perfection higher than its own, it is "taken up into God"; and this is a greater perfection for it still.

capacities, anything known to us in ourselves. Furthermore, we must expect that human nature when united to the Person of God the Son may, without any destruction of its genuinely human character, surpass even that excellence which it would manifest in an unfallen but merely created being. "If it be asked," writes Robert Wilberforce,

"what effects were produced by personal union with Deity upon man's nature, we are assured that gifts greater than tongue can utter or heart conceive were bestowed upon it. For this is the very meeting-place of heaven and earth, the union of glory and humiliation; herein the two worlds of the infinite and the finite touch upon one another; by this we see what God can bestow, and of what man is susceptible."[1]

The kenoticists would therefore seem to have gone astray at the start by their assumption that human nature must of necessity be recalcitrant to the divine Word. Nor can they validly plead in their support the Gospel narrative. Both Weston and Relton have shown in their consideration of the evangelical material that we are presented with the picture of one who was completely human and yet whose human nature was altogether subject to the action of its divine Person as being the perfect instrument of the latter.[2] There is indeed an element of constraint in the Gospels: "The Son of Man must suffer many things";[3] "I have a baptism to be baptized with, and how am I straitened till it be accomplished."[4]

---

[1] *The Incarnation of our Lord Jesus Christ*, p. 134. Cf. this passage from Hooker:
"As therefore we have showed how the Son of God by his incarnation hath changed the manner of that personal subsistence which before was solitary, and is now in the association of flesh, no alteration thereby accruing to the nature of God; so neither are the *properties of man's nature* in the person of Christ by force and virtue of the same conjunction so much altered, as not to stay within those limits which our substance is bordered withal; nor the *state and quality* of our substance so unaltered, but that there are in it many glorious effects proceeding from so near copulation with Deity. God from us can receive nothing, we by him have obtained much. For albeit the natural properties of Deity be not communicable to man's nature, the supernatural gifts, graces and effects thereof are." (*Eccl. Pol.*, V, liv, 5: ed. of 1888, II, p. 234; italics in original.)
And again:
"There is no doubt but the Deity of Christ hath enabled that nature which it took of man to do more than man in this world hath power to comprehend; forasmuch as (the bare essential properties of Deity excepted) he hath imparted unto it all things, he hath replenished it with all such perfections as the same is any way apt to receive, at the least according to the exigence of that economy or service for which it pleased him in love and mercy to be made man. For as the parts, degrees, and offices of that mystical administration did require which he voluntarily undertook, the beams of Deity did in operation always accordingly either restrain or enlarge themselves." (*Ibid.*, 6, p. 236.)
[2] *The One Christ*, ch. ii; *Study in Christology*, Part III, ch. 3.
[3] Luke ix. 22.　　　　[4] Luke xii. 50.

F

But this is not a constraint laid upon his divinity by his manhood; it is rather a constraint laid upon his actions by the perfect obedience of his human will to the will of the Father and to the purpose for which he has come into the World: "As the Father gave me commandment, even so I do."[1] And in the execution of this obedience his divine dignity is not diminished but manifested; when he stands before Pilate, it is he, not Pilate, that is the judge; when he is nailed to the Cross, he is reigning from the tree. That the Incarnation does not involve any emptying away of his divinity is nowhere more clearly shown than in the fact, to which the Gospel plainly bears record, that the very experiences and incidents which in any other case than his would be utterly shameful become, when he assumes them, the manifestation of the power and the glory of God. We must therefore not confuse together the act by which the divine Word holds his human nature in union with his Person, and the acts of his human will by which, in the human nature, in complete concurrence with the divine will which as God he shares with the Father, he submits, in whatever way is appropriate to the actualities of the particular situation, to the limitations of our fallen state, in order to identify himself with us, to share our lot and to work our redemption.

Again, while, as has been said, we must, in considering those acts of the incarnate Lord which exceed the forces of human nature as we know it in ourselves, recognize the distinction between the powers that are proper to unfallen humanity and those that are the property of the Creator alone, we must also note that the line of demarcation between these two is in practice difficult for us to draw precisely. For instance, when Christ stills the storm, are we to see this miracle as an exercise of divine omnipotence or as an exercise of that lordship over the lower creation with which man was endowed in his state of innocence but has lost through sin? It is extremely difficult to venture a confident opinion upon this. Some of Christ's miracles and utterances are clearly possible to him only because he is God; and there are a whole host of words and acts which any one of us could say and do; but in between these there is a mass of material concerning which we are unable, owing to our ignorance of the precise limits of unfallen human nature as such, to say with assurance whether we are witnessing the action of God making use of human nature as the pure instrument of his omnipotence or are witnessing the exercise of the

[1] John xiv. 31.

powers of perfect human nature. It is none the less important for a correct understanding of the Incarnation to understand the difference in principle that there is between the two. For, among other consequences, the former of these must be for ever beyond our attainment, whereas we may expect the latter to be restored to mankind when the incorporation of the human race into Christ is complete.

II

The problem of kenosis is usually posed with particular reference to Christ's human knowledge; Dr. Hodgson has indeed gone so far as to suggest that the question of the knowledge of the incarnate Lord is the major Christological issue of recent times, as the question of the relation between his two natures was at the time of Chalcedon.[1] And it is widely held that both the demands of contemporary thought and the deliverances of Biblical criticism make it necessary for us to admit that our Lord was ignorant of certain facts which we know to-day and even that on some points he was positively in error. Some would go so far as to urge that he was, at any rate at the beginning of his ministry and possibly even to its end, unconscious of his divine sonship, a view which involves the remarkable consequence that we know more about him than he knew about himself. Others would insist that he was infallible in all matters relating to his Person and his redeeming work, while ignorant or even sometimes definitely mistaken about certain questions in the natural order. This last view seems to be particularly vulnerable to the sting of the question which the Lord himself put to Nicodemus: "If I told you earthly things and ye believe not, how shall ye believe if I tell you heavenly things?"[2] On the other hand, there are obvious difficulties in supposing that, in the plain and obvious sense of the words, the human mind of the Babe of Bethlehem was thinking, as he lay in the manger, of the Procession of the Holy Ghost, the theorems of hydrodynamics, the novels of Jane Austen and the Battle of Hastings.

Now it is, I think, well to realize that the difficulties which have been raised concerning our Lord's human knowledge rest not nearly so much upon established results of critical study as upon a prevailing mood of thought. The assertion that Christ was mistaken, for example, in believing in the existence of evil spirits and in diabolic possession is obviously based upon a philosophical

[1] *And Was Made Man*, ch. i.   [2] John iii. 12.

prejudice rather than upon critical grounds, a prejudice which is, moreover, by no means universally shared by those who have to do with extreme cases of mental derangement. And the rejection of our Lord's eschatological teaching as the product of a mistaken expectation of an imminent end of the world has been dangerously undermined by the work of such scholars as Professor C. H. Dodd, who have shown that, in the Gospel teaching, the "end of the world" means something far more profound than any merely historical catastrophe.[1] Again, the points on which Christ's knowledge of the Old Testament has been alleged to be at variance with the certain findings of Biblical study[2] are purely incidental to arguments *ad hominem*, in which our Lord is making clear the implications of his opponents' beliefs and unfolding the content of the Old-Testament conceptions; there does not seem to be any direct advertence to the points on which he is alleged to have been in error at all; he is merely conforming to the conventions of contemporary speech. There is indeed the famous passage in which he declares his ignorance of the day and hour of the end of the world,[3] but no new problem is raised by this. It is discussed at length by the fathers with a variety of interpretations; we shall return to it later. Nevertheless, the question of Christ's human consciousness having been raised, we cannot avoid discussing it; I must, however, repeat that Christological doctrine is not primarily psychological but ontological. No amount of discussion of our Lord's psychology can have any *direct* bearing on the Catholic creeds and the Chalcedonian definition. We must first assert without qualification that in the incarnate Lord two natures, a divine and a human, are inseparably and unconfusedly united in the divine Person of the eternal Word; any psychological discussion is subsequent and subsidiary.

I have said already that, in virtue of the real identity between the divine Person and the divine nature, we must acknowledge in the incarnate Christ not one nature but two, and that we must not relegate the divine nature to the divine and cosmic spheres and exclude it from the sphere of the Incarnation.[4] Dr. F. J. Hall has laid great emphasis upon this point in particular relation to the

---

[1] The point is not that the end of the world and the Second Advent have no historical character as chronologically future, but that in his union with Christ the Christian receives already a participation in those events for whose temporal fulfilment he must wait until the end of history. See ch. vi. *infra*.

[2] E.g., Mark xii. 36 and parallels; Mark ii. 26.

[3] Mark xiii. 32.   [4] See p. 20 f., *supra*.

question of Christ's human knowledge in the book to which I have already referred.[1] He insists that, whatever limitations we may feel bound to admit in the human nature of Christ, those limitations cannot be asserted of the Incarnate Lord as such, for in him there is also to be recognized the divine nature in which omniscience is perfect and complete. Christ is, in St. Leo's phrase, "whole in what is his, whole in what is ours." We cannot indeed admit that, in his human nature, he is either morally peccable or intellectually mistaken, for his human nature is not fallen like ours but is perfect. Nevertheless, we can readily agree that human nature, just because it is finite, has certain inherent and essential limits; hence, Hall concludes, we need not assert omniscience of it, while we must assert omniscience of the divine nature which is, equally with the human, involved in the Incarnation. We must however suppose, he holds, that Christ's human mind is able to turn to the divine mind and draw from it whatever knowledge is appropriate to the human nature at its actual stage of development and to the needs of the particular situation.

Such a view is, of course, not altogether devoid of difficulties, but this is inherent in the nature of the problem; as I have already suggested, it is futile to try to answer the question as to what it "feels like" to be Christ. In the last resort the Incarnation must involve a mystery, even if it cannot involve a contradiction. In Gore's Christology the ultimate problem was how the incarnate mode of existence of the Word was to be related to his divine and cosmic activities; in Relton's it was how a universal could be its own particular; in Weston's how the Word could be simultaneously the subject of two modes of existence. And the strong point of Hall's theory is that it accepts without reserve or embarrassment the Chalcedonian formula, and distinguishes clearly between the ontological and the psychological sphere. If I feel it necessary to amplify the line which he follows, it is not because I believe it to be based upon false suppositions but because I do not think he has sufficiently developed the consequences for the human nature of its union with the divine, that is to say, in theological terms, that he has not adequately considered the implications of the *communicatio idiomatum*. The only difference between his view and that which I shall expound will lie in the fact that, while he conceives the infusion of supranormal knowledge into Christ's human soul as being directly communicated from the divine knowledge on

[1] *The Kenotic Theory.* See p. 25 *supra.* Cf. Sellers, *The Council of Chalcedon,* p. 347

each occasion in whatever way is proper to the particular situation, I shall argue that there is a permanent infusion into the human soul of all knowledge that it is intrinsically capable of receiving.

III

There is a sound principle of scholastic psychology which teaches that human knowledge, in contrast with that which we may suppose to be proper to pure spirits, is based upon the deliverances of the senses; this is a consequence of the fact that we are composite beings consisting of body and soul in a mysterious and intimate union. *Nihil in intellectu quod non prius in sensu*: there is nothing in the intellect that was not first in the senses; and this principle need not be substantially modified if we are ready to admit, with some modern mystical theologians, that it is possible, at least under the influence of grace, for human beings to achieve a direct, though obscure, knowledge of spiritual realities, including God himself, by pure species and not through the intermediation of sensible things.[1] It remains true that sensible experience is the normal, and all but invariable, medium of our knowledge of external beings. Human nature is in essence psycho-physical, and in the human soul sensitive and intellectual activity are compresent and interrelated. And since in a finite human being person and nature are really identical and only logically distinguishable—for, as Boethius says, a person *is* an individual substance of a rational nature—our knowledge is necessarily of this composite type. In Christ, however, the Person is really distinct from the human nature; the nature with which the Person is really identical is not the human but the divine, and in this it shares in the omniscience which is the inalienable possession of the Godhead. Is it therefore unreasonable to suppose that the content of Christ's human mind will include not only that experimental knowledge which is acquired by him in the course of his development from infancy to manhood in a way substantially the same as, though immeasurably more consistent and unimpeded than, the way in which we acquire ours, but also an infused knowledge which is directly communicated to his human nature from

---

[1] Cf. the paper by Abbot Chapman on "What is Mysticism?" in his *Spiritual Letters*. He adds that, when knowledge is received by pure species, the mind will perforce "translate" it into the terms of its normal experience, *convertit se ad phantasmata*, and in this there is room for much error. (Op. cit., p. 304; cf. Chapman's article on Mysticism" in *E.R.E.*, IX, p. 95.)

the divine Person who is its subject, and which is a participation in the divine omniscience and is limited only by the receptive capacity of human nature as such? It does not seem to be always recognized that there is a definite distinction between the knowledge that a human nature can acquire by its own efforts and that which it is capable of receiving; what I can know if I am told it is not coextensive with what I can myself find out. Let us take the extreme case of the question whether Jesus knew in his human soul that he was God. It is sometimes urged that the knowledge that one is God is, so to speak, too much for a human soul to contain. But there is surely a confusion here. It is, of course, true that no human soul, not even that of the incarnate Word, can concentrate into itself the fullness of the divine activity; there must always be operations of deity which lie beyond its limits. Furthermore, while it is reasonable to suppose that the Lord Jesus, by his life of obedience to the Father's will, his study of the sacred Scriptures and his perfect performance of the religion of the ancient people of God, may have come by a purely human process of "experimental" knowledge to the realization that he was the Messiah, it is hardly likely that any such process can have led to the knowledge that he was, simply and without qualification, God. Nevertheless, the acceptance of the proposition, "I am God," is not in itself impossible to the human mind; there are alive to-day a fairly large number of people who have achieved it, though they are mostly confined to madhouses. It is notable that one of the charges made against Jesus was that he "made himself equal to God,"[1] and that his adversaries, who could not bring themselves to accept his claims, were forced to consider that he "had a devil and was mad."[2] The mere belief that one is God is not therefore impossible to a human mind; the only question is whether it is true and whence it is derived. It is not, I think, unreasonable to suggest, with all the diffidence and reverence that a question of such transcendent mystery demands, that the knowledge of his deity, while beyond the limits of his experimental knowledge, is present in Christ's human mind by infusion from the Person of the divine Word to which it is united.

The consequences of such a suggestion may indeed seem to be alarming. If the content of Christ's human knowledge is limited, not by the power of his mind to discover but only by its capacity to receive, if there is communicated to it from the Person of the

[1] John v. 18. [2] John x. 20.

Word everything that it is possible for a human mind to know, are we not bound to view the human growth and development which the Gospels depict, and which seems to be a necessary consequence of his human birth and upbringing, as a mere illusion? Are not the accusations of the kenoticists, that a strict adherence to the Chalcedonian and patristic Christology inevitably leads one into a virtual or implicit docetism,[1] justified? Are we not after all being asked to believe that the Babe of Bethlehem, as he lay in the manger and even as he lay before birth in his mother's womb, was thinking about the theorems of hydrodynamics and the Battle of Hastings? I would suggest that the answer to this objection lies in the recognition that human knowledge is a far more elaborate and complicated faculty than Christologists have always realized.

It is, for example, only too often assumed that if something is "known" at all it must be in the forefront of one's conscious attention, that the question, "Does the individual N know the proposition p?" is as simple and admits of as immediate an answer as the question, "Is the proposition p written on the blackboard in the lecture-room?" How superficial such an assumption is may be seen if I put to myself the question whether ten minutes ago I knew my own name. It is hardly possible to deny that I did; nevertheless it is quite certain that I was not thinking about it at that instant. And the inadequacy of the "blackboard" view of knowledge becomes even clearer if we reflect upon the complicated and mysterious character of human memory or upon the vast regions of the soul which lie beneath the level of conscious attention. Frequently, for example, we are unable for a long period to recall some fact which we desire to make use of; then it suddenly, as we say, "occurs" to us. Are we or are we not to say that it was "there" in the intervening time?

I must make it quite plain that I am not just asserting that the non-experimental knowledge of Christ is merely "not being thought about" or that it is "buried in the unconscious." That would involve treating his psychology as if it was in every respect identical with ours and would be so gross a simplification as to border upon irreverence. But I urge most strongly that the human mind, even as we know it in ourselves, is a very mysterious

---

[1] That is, the heresy, present in the first days of Christianity and apparently the object of refutation in 1 John i. 1, which considered the human nature of Christ as unreal and illusory.

thing, and that if the "blackboard" theory is inadequate when applied to us, it is *a fortiori* inadequate when applied to the incarnate Lord. Is it impossible to suppose that there is in his human mind what we might perhaps call a "stratification" of knowledge in such a way that, quite apart from the experimental knowledge which he acquires by the normal human use of intellect in conjunction with the senses, the Christ includes in himself, by infusion from the omniscience which his divine Person possesses through its real identity with the divine nature, the possession of everything that is in principle knowable by man, while the exercise of this knowledge is adjusted, with the most exact and exquisite accuracy, to the precise needs of every situation with which he is confronted?[1] Once again, with all necessary reservations, we may compare natural things with supernatural. Consider a "perfect" mathematical lecturer, who, we will suppose, knows "all about" his subject and also has complete understanding of the mental equipment and development of his class. He knows precisely how much they can take in at any particular stage; he always keeps within the bounds that are set for him by the limitations of his hearers, and thus, without any undue forcing of the pace, leads them on gradually to a fuller knowledge of the subject; he has many things to tell them but they cannot bear them now. He may be able to see the solution of a particular problem in a flash of intuition, or he may be able to solve it in two or three lines of working. But his insight into the minds of his class is such that he will always adopt a method of expression and calculation which it

---

[1] Cf. again the second quotation from Hooker quoted in note 1 to p. 51 and the following passage which immediately follows it:

"From hence we may somewhat conjecture how the powers of that soul are illuminated, which being so inward unto God cannot choose but be privy unto all things which God worketh, and must therefore of necessity be endued with knowledge so far forth universal, though not with infinite knowledge peculiar to Deity itself. The soul of Christ that saw in this life the face of God was here through so visible presence of Deity filled with all manner graces and virtues in that unmatchable degree of perfection, for which of him we read it written, 'That God with the oil of gladness anointed him above his fellows.' " (*Eccl. Pol.*, V, liv, 7; ed. of 1888, II, p. 236.)

And again:

"The principal powers of the soul in man are the will and understanding, the one of which two in Christ assenteth unto all things, and from the other nothing which Deity doth work is hid; so that by knowledge and assent the soul of Christ is present with all things which the Deity of Christ worketh." (*Ibid.*, lv, 8; p. 245.)

It is perhaps well to remark here that there is an essential difference between the knowledge which God has as God and that possessed by any human soul, even the human soul of Christ. For example, any knowledge of future events that a human soul has, however complete it may be, must be a knowledge of them *as future*, whereas the divine knowledge of them is not strictly speaking *fore*knowledge at all. God, in his eternal being, simply *knows*.

is within their capacity to understand; he will choose a long
elementary method which they can follow rather than a brief but
advanced one that will be beyond them. If his insight into their
minds and his self-adjustment to the concrete reality of the
situation are really "perfect"—and here, of course, we make an
assumption to which the most successful teacher can only approxi-
mately conform—he will be so sensitive to their limitations as to
be unable to make use of any method which it would be beyond
their power to assimilate; furthermore, this adjustment will not be
forced but entirely spontaneous. Thus to a particular question he
may reply, "I can't tell you the answer to that," because he has
so fully and naturally adjusted himself to the mentality of the
questioner that the answer is not in the realm of their common
ratiocination. Yet the knowledge is none the less included in the
content of his own equipment, and if the same question is put to
him by a more advanced student the answer may be immediately
forthcoming.

This is, it need hardly be said, only a very rough and remote
illustration, but it may help to indicate that a complete inter-
communication between the divine and human in our Lord is
compatible with the fullest reality of his human nature. In some
such way, I suggest, we may understand the crucial passage in
which the incarnate Lord expresses ignorance of the date of the
Last Day. At least the illustration points to the possibility of
reconciling the three essential points in any doctrine which avoids
the extremes of docetism on the one hand and kenoticism on the
other. These are: (1) Knowledge that is employable at any given
moment may be limited not by an abrupt refusal of the will to
allow the intellect to advert to it, but by a steady spontaneous
activity by which, with perfect insight, both will and intellect
adjust themselves to the concrete exigency of each successive
situation. (2) The admission of ignorance in a particular case is
neither, on the one hand, a mere affectation such as it would be
difficult to reconcile with truthfulness nor, on the other, the sign
of absence of knowledge in the mind itself considered in its totality.
(3) The conformity of the mind to the situation being perfect,
positive error is altogether excluded from the utterances that
Christ makes.

IV

The chief defect in the illustration just made use of lies in the fact that Christ's supranormal knowledge is infused from his divine Person, while the mathematician's knowledge, however comprehensive it may be, is altogether "acquired" and "experimental." A closer parallel, though one from a less familiar realm, is provided by the supernatural knowledge of God which is characteristic of the higher levels of mystical experience (though it may be present inchoatively and rudimentarily in the earlier and lower grades of prayer) and which is described by scholastic theology as knowledge of God and of divine things by the infusion of pure intellectual species. In this we have a communication of knowledge to the soul, not through the normal human medium of the senses but by the direct information of the soul by God. This knowledge is of necessity obscure and perplexing, for the divine Being who is its object infinitely exceeds the capacities of understanding possessed by a finite intellect; indeed the mind can receive it at all only because God acts not simply as the mind's object of knowledge but also as the medium through which it knows and as the energizing force by which the mind is brought into operation. God is, of course, in himself supremely knowable, and he is closer to us than is any other being. Nevertheless, we cannot see him by our own powers, because he infinitely exceeds our finite capacity; in his presence, says St. Thomas, we are like the owl or the bat in the presence of the sun. They are unable to see the sun, not because it is invisible but because their sight is so weak.[1] In mystical knowledge, then, the soul knows God because God lifts it up into his own being and gives it a participation in the knowledge by which he knows himself. This knowledge is unfamiliar and perplexing; it is altogether different from the soul's normal knowledge of other beings, which is obtained in a piecemeal way through the intermediation of the senses, *per compositionem et divisionem*, by comparing things with one another and distinguishing between them. Considered *ex parte objecti*, with reference to the divine being who has made himself its object, this knowledge is infallible; he who is known is the Truth itself and he cannot deceive. But when the soul tries to describe this object to itself, when it tries to relate this knowledge to knowledge obtained by

[1] Cf. *S. Theol.*, I, i, 5 ad 1; xii, 1c.

the normal means, and above all when it tries to tell other people about it, it is faced with an enormous problem of interpretation and translation. It has to make comparisons and form images, although the divine object of its experience is such as no image can adequately represent; in returning to its normal realm of thought it must perforce make use of sensible representations (*convertit se ad phantasmata*); hence *ex parte subjecti*, as the mind actually formulates to itself and to others the content of what it has experienced, this knowledge and its expression are liable to all the confusion and fallibility to which the mind of a corporeal and fallen being is subject. The fact that, in the accounts which even many of the great saints have given of their "revelations," delusions and even absurdities are frequent is frankly recognized by mystical theologians.[1] And, even when error is avoided, this knowledge remains intractable to the task of translating it into the terms of normal knowledge.[2] The soul undoubtedly retains the knowledge as its most precious possession, and it overflows into the discursive levels of the mind. In so far as is relevant to the handling of any particular situation, to that extent and in the necessary manner it may become available; nevertheless, in any situation what is accessible in the empirical realm is only a partial and, we might say, "lowered" expression of it. In the last resort the mystic must say, "My secret is my own."[3, 4]

Now when we compare this with the infused human knowledge of Christ there are both similarities and differences to be noted. In this latter case the infusion takes place, not by an elevation of the soul in which the subject remains still a separate person from God and retains his own individuality, but by the union of an impersonal human nature to the person of God the Word himself. Thus there is no difference between the Person who communicates the knowledge and the Person who receives it, though there is a difference between either and the nature in which the knowledge is received. And this nature is a perfect and sinless one. There is no possibility of positive error in the reception of the knowledge or

---

[1] See, e.g., Poulain, *Graces of Interior Prayer*, p. 321 n.

[2] Every mystic stresses the essential impossibility of adequately conceptualizing or describing the experience. See, e.g., St. John of the Cross, *Living Flame*, II, 21; III, 48. (Peers's trans., Vol. III, pp. 150, 186.)

[3] Isa. xxiv. 16 (Vulg.): *Secretum meum mihi.*

[4] A remarkably readable and full exposition of the scholastic doctrine of mystical experience will be found in the article by Abbot Chapman to which reference has already been made, in the *Encyclopaedia of Religion and Ethics*, Vol. IX, pp. 94–7, *s.v.* "Mysticism, Christian, Roman Catholic." See also p. 211 f. *infra.*

even in its translation into the discursive mode of thought and expression. Nevertheless the translation is conditioned by the inherent characteristics of discursive and corporeal knowledge as such. Thus, however complete and adequate is the response, both of word and of act, which the incarnate Lord makes to every situation which confronts him, there is bound to be a core of knowledge which is altogether present by infusion in his human mind and yet, by its very nature, defies translation on to the normal discursive human level, not, we must repeat, because *he* is in any way unwilling or impotent, but because *it* is inherently untranslatable.

It is, as I have already said more than once, irreverent and futile to try to pry too deeply into the psychology of God incarnate, but the comparison just made may have its uses. For it takes its stand upon the nature of infused knowledge as such; and its argument is simply that Christ possesses an infused as well as an experimental human knowledge, that the former can never be translated in its totality on to the plane of the latter, but that the latter is the plane on which Christ makes the utterances recorded in the Gospel narrative. The work of translation is always precisely adjusted to the concrete situation, but there is a secret core which is simply untranslatable, while it is none the less included in the content of Christ's human mind. Any infused knowledge, whatever its type, is bound to be in one respect or another, "ineffable."

There is, I would suggest, an unfortunate misunderstanding to which the phrase "incommunicable knowledge," which is often used in this context, is exposed. It is often taken as meaning that there are certain truths of which Christ is conscious but which he conceals or dissembles either because he is not willing to reveal them or because he does not feel morally at liberty to do so. In the latter case there would be a close parallel with the example which Weston used, of the obligation of a priest to respect the seal of the confessional. But, in fact, "incommunicable" does not mean "that which ought not to be revealed" but "that which cannot be revealed." The obstacle to communication lies not primarily in the will of the speaker but in the character of the knowledge. Having regard to the conditions of the Incarnation, there is a simple impossibility of fully translating the infused knowledge on to the discursive and experimental plane. We may see a parallel here to the famous remark of St. Thomas about the things which do not come within the scope of divine omnipotence, because they "cannot have the aspect of possibility," and of which "it is better to say that they cannot be done than that God cannot do them."[1] The only relevant difference is that, whereas in the case just cited the impossibility is constituted by the necessities of logical consistency, in the case of our Lord's knowledge it is constituted by the inherent character and structure of the human nature which he has assumed and of the mind which is an element in it.

It may be added that, in spite of the objections of many modern writers, there does not seem to be anything repugnant to sound doctrine in the common teaching of Roman theologians, following St. Thomas, that our Lord possessed in his human soul, from the first moment of his life, the Beatific Vision of the divine Essence.[2] The difficulties seem to rest upon two false assumptions: the first, that such a beatific knowledge would, like the experimental knowledge, be discursive and would involve the consequence that, from the moment of the infusion of his soul into his embryonic body, Christ was ratiocinating about every being in the universe and every truth of logic and mathematics; the second, that the Beatific Vision admits of no degrees and that therefore its enjoyment is incompatible with real human growth and development. But the scholastics assert quite firmly that beatific knowledge is not discursive but intuitive; it therefore partakes of that same character of untranslatability and incommunicability that is the property of the infused knowledge which we have just been considering, and it will partake of it to an even greater degree. They further agree that, while the Beatific Vision is a seeing of the whole essence of God, it is not a whole seeing of it (it is seen *totam, sed non totaliter*). In St. Thomas's words, "Since the created light of glory received into any created intellect cannot be infinite, it is clearly impossible for any created intellect to know God in an infinite degree,"[3] and this argument is explicitly extended to the human nature of Christ: "the soul of Christ sees the whole Essence of God, yet does not comprehend it; since it does not see it totally."[4]

[1] *S. Theol.*, I, xxv, 3c. St. John of the Cross writes, no doubt on the basis of his own experience, that in the transforming union the soul at times "is wont, . . . without knowing how this comes to pass, to see itself so far withdrawn and separated according to this higher and spiritual part, from the sensual and lower portion, that it recognizes in itself two parts so distinct from each other that it believes that the one has nought to do with the other. . . . The operation is now wholly spiritual, and the soul receives no communication in its sensual part." (*Dark Night*, II, xxiii, 14; Peers, I, p. 482.)
[2] *S. Theol.*, III, x. Cf. Hooker, "The soul of Christ . . . saw in this life the face of God." (*Eccl. Pol.*, V, liv, 7: ed. of 1888, II, p. 236.)
[3] *S. Theol.*, I, xii, 7c.   [4] *Ibid.*, III, x, 1 ad 2m.

Now if we recognize that in Christ as man there is a real development from the embryonic stage through infancy to manhood, a development in which soul as well as body takes part (since at every moment the soul must be precisely adapted to the body with which it is united), we should expect to find a real development in Christ's possession of the Beatific Vision, for it will not be enjoyed by the soul of a baby in the same manner as by the soul of a man. If we hold, therefore, that Christ always enjoyed the Beatific Vision, we are not committed to the view that it had precisely the same character when he lay in the womb of Mary as when he hung on the Cross; if its mode was conditioned by the manhood which he had assumed, it was presumably also conditioned by the character of that manhood at each moment. There is therefore room for a real development to take place; and this consideration will apply not only to the beatific but to the infused knowledge as well.[1]

V

We need not claim to have removed every element of mystery from the doctrine of the Incarnation; indeed any theory that professed to do so would stand self-condemned. But we may claim, if not to have demonstrated, at least to have shown the possibility of the reconciliation of a real omniscience in our Lord's human nature with an equally real growth and development. We have, I venture to hope, preserved the truth on which Dr. Relton lays such stress, that the Gospel narratives "reveal to us One who was not only a truly human personality, but One whose deeds and words at times marked him as a transcendent Personality, unlimited in the range of his consciousness, revealing things which not even a perfectly human but finite mind could embrace, doing things beyond the capacities of a finite man however perfect."[2] We have been able to agree that the subject of the manhood of the incarnate Lord is the *unlimited* Word. For, although a human mind, even when it is the mind of Christ, is inherently finite when considered in abstraction from its person, it is, when considered in

---

[1] It must be admitted that St. Thomas seems reluctant to draw this last conclusion. He says that in neither the infused nor the beatific knowledge did Christ advance, since from the beginning he had them perfectly. (*S. Theol.*, III, xii, 2 ad 1m.) But he is obviously mainly concerned with the acquisition of new facts, which he restricts to the experimental knowledge, rather than with the question which we are here concerned with. I suspect that in any case St. Thomas was handicapped by the imperfect embryological knowledge of his time. (Cf. *S.c.G.*, IV, xliv.)

[2] *Study in Christology*, p. 253.

relation to its inherence in the divine Word from whom it receives its concrete subsistence, elevated to the level of his infinite Godhead. We have not, however, found it necessary, with Relton, to reject the doctrine of the divine impassibility,[1] or to assert that only God can be perfectly human,[2] to speak of a single consciousness at once human and divine,[3] or to express the union of the two natures in psychological terms. We have tried to keep psychology in its proper place, namely in the discussion of the content of Christ's consciousness, though even here I should hesitate to affirm that psychology is adequate to explain the facts. We have avoided the opinion of Gore, to which even Weston made concessions, that the subject of the incarnate life is not the unlimited but the limited Word. And we have, I think, been able to accord to the Chalcedonian definition and to the *Tome* of Leo a more enthusiastic and unqualified approval than they have on the whole received from the writers whom I have just named. In making this claim we need not profess to be wiser than our fathers. The possibility of this change of emphasis is mainly due to the fact that theology has begun to recover in recent years its consciousness of being a science in its own right, dealing with its own proper problems by means of its own proper concepts. And in all that I have said, beyond the affirmation of the defined dogmas of the Catholic Church, I should wish to be understood as speaking with that tentativeness and reserve which is fitting for the human mind when it ventures to investigate the deep things of God. It may be added that the view of Christ's human knowledge which has been expounded seems fully consistent with the general scholastic doctrine that this knowledge includes three different elements, namely the perfect human participation in the Beatific Vision, an infused knowledge of all things that are humanly knowable, and an acquired knowledge derived by the ordinary process of human experience.[4] But any such statement must be safeguarded by pointing out that these three different kinds of knowledge are on different levels or in different spheres, and are not merely three different methods by which knowledge is acquired in the same sphere.[5] Only so can we avoid docetism in one of its many forms.

---

[1] *Study in Christology*, p. 160.   [2] *Ibid*, pp. 227–8.   [3] *Ibid*., p. 230.
[4] Cf. *S. Theol.*, III, ix–xii.
[5] The best modern Roman-Catholic writers are anxious to assert this. Cf. the following passage from Dr. J. P. Arendzen:
"We are always tempted to think that the different spheres of knowledge are only different in the category of the objects known, whereas they differ also in the very mode of knowing. These things are difficult for us to follow, because they are beyond

I need only reaffirm, in bringing this chapter to a close, that its purpose has been simply to expound the traditional Catholic doctrine of the Incarnation as, under the guidance of the Holy Spirit, the Church was led to formulate it against the Christological heresies of the first centuries, in order that we may have a sure foundation on which to base our subsequent discussions of the nature and implications of the Christian life. It has seemed desirable, in doing this, to devote some space to several of the more important of recent Anglican Christological writings, but it is obviously impossible to attempt a systematic exposition of the whole of Christology in the space of a few pages. I have been concerned merely to affirm the doctrine of the two natures, a human and a divine, united without confusion, without conversion, without division and inseparably, in the one divine Person of the eternal Word, the only-begotten and consubstantial Son of God the Father, and to maintain that this union consists not in the conversion of the Godhead into flesh, but in the taking up of manhood into God.

---

the sphere of our own experience. But given the possibility of different modes of knowledge, our reason can see that a thing may be unknown in a lower sphere though known in the higher, and that even while Christ's soul and conscience remained an absolute unity, Christ could truly know and yet also in another sense not know the Day of Judgment.

"It is remarkable," he adds, "that after the Resurrection, in answer to the query of the Apostles regarding the future, Christ only answers: 'It is not *yours* to know.' All knowledge was then completely his, even in his normal, natural consciousness and in a human way." (*Whom Do You Say——?*, p. 178.)

F

CHAPTER IV

INCARNATION AND ATONEMENT

I

IN the preceding chapters I have attempted to expound the doctrine of the Incarnation as being the re-creation of human nature by its elevation into union with the pre-existent Son and Word of God, who is the Second Person of the Ever-blessed Trinity. I have urged that, while it is highly necessary to give full emphasis to the truth that in the incarnate Lord the eternal Word is living a fully human life and really undergoing the whole range of experiences which a concrete human nature unavoidably entails—a truth upon which both Bible and Creeds insist when they tell us that "the Word was made flesh" and that the Son of God "came down from heaven"—it is also of the greatest importance to maintain that, in the words of *Quicunque vult*, this Incarnation, this "enfleshment," of the Word took place "not by the conversion of Godhead into flesh, but by taking up of manhood into God." In subsequent chapters I shall endeavour to show that this doctrine is the essential foundation of the life of the Christian and to draw out some of its implications. Before doing this, however, it will be well to round off the first part of our task by attending to one or two points which, while they have fallen outside the line of thought which has been pursued, are important for a full understanding of the theme and for the avoiding of misconceptions.

It will almost certainly have been felt by some readers that the stress which I have placed upon the Incarnation as effecting the re-creation of human nature has led to a virtual ignoring of the central position which, both in the New Testament and in the experience of Christians, belongs to Calvary and the Cross. Some may see in this the insurgence of hellenism and humanism against the transcendental Hebraism of the Gospel message; others may recognize it as typical of "Catholicism" in contrast to "Protestantism" and accuse me of the capital sin of "evacuating the Cross of Christ." But whatever precise form the objection may

take, it is sufficiently typical of a large body of Christian sentiment—and, I readily admit, sufficiently important in itself—to
call for careful consideration. Briefly, the question is whether the
re-creation of human nature, which is the *leitmotiv* of the Gospel,
is to be located in the union of human nature with the Person of
the Word in the womb of Mary the Virgin or in the death of the
Lord Jesus upon the Cross. Is it, in short, Lady Day or Good
Friday that is the supreme commemoration of our redemption?

I would suggest that here, as in the case of so many other
questions that have divided Christians, the real truth is to be
attained by recognizing that the statements of both sides are, if
properly understood, expressions of parts of the truth, or of the
whole truth as seen under certain partial aspects, but that neither
is complete in itself. (This does not imply, I must add, that there
is *never* in Christian theology a clear issue of truth *versus* error; on
the contrary, there are many.) If we limit our attention simply
to human nature as it exists in the concrete individuality of the
incarnate Lord himself—that is, if we think simply of the manhood
of Jesus of Nazareth—we are bound to assert that, from the
moment of its union with the Person of the Word, it is altogether
pure and sinless; in him, considered in abstraction from his
relation to the men and women whom he came to redeem, the
re-creation of human nature is altogether complete, and if
redemption consisted only in the appearance upon the earth of a
perfect human being there would be no need for either crucifixion
or resurrection. The Transfiguration is the demonstration of the
perfection and exaltation of human nature as it is in its hypostatic
union with God the Word; but the descent from the mount and
the treading of the Way of the Cross are the proof that the work
of Christ is not limited to the re-creation of human nature in one
historical individual, even if that individual be God incarnate.

For, as we shall be considering in detail in the latter part of
this book, the ultimate purpose of the Incarnation is not just the
re-creation of human nature in Jesus, but the re-creation of the
whole human race into him; and this involves that, as its representative, he shall in his human nature himself undergo the pains
that both the physical and the moral constitution of the universe
involve for the fallen human race as a consequence of its defection
from the condition in which, and for which, it was first created.

The scholastic distinction between first and second act, or first
and second perfection, may perhaps help to bring out this point.

The "first act" of a being is simply the act by which it *exists*, as a concrete thing with a determinate nature; and it must exist before it can do anything else. Nevertheless, every being exists *for* some end; its very existence implies that it has not only an efficient cause whereby it is thrust out of nonentity into being, but also a final cause *for the sake of which* it exists, some operation or activity which is its justification for existence. It is, of course, being and not operation that is primary; before anything can operate it must exist. Nevertheless, *operari sequitur esse*, and the full perfection of a being is reached only in the "second act" wherein its purpose is expressed. So, reverting to the case of our Lord's human nature, whether with the Scotists we hold that the Incarnation would have taken place even if man had not fallen or whether with the Thomist tradition we tend to the view that its very *raison d'être* is to be the means whereby the Fall is undone, we can in either case agree that, things being as they are and man having fallen, the Incarnation is for the redemption of man. Thus, while the metaphysical integrity and the moral perfection of Jesus are necessarily involved in the Incarnation considered from the aspect of first act, it must be added that the restoration and reintegration of the whole human race is the final end of the Incarnation, and its progressive actualization is the second act of the perfect human nature of Christ. And the link between the two, the bridge that unites the perfect re-creation of manhood in the individual human nature of Jesus with the re-creation of manhood in those who are restored in him, is the historical assumption by him, in the free and perfect obedience of his human will, of both the pain and the punishment that their fallen condition demands.

That we are here in the presence of a profound mystery is abundantly evident. How, we naturally ask, can the restoration of our manhood be brought about by something that happens to the manhood of Jesus? What is the bond between us and him? Even when we are reminded that Christ's manhood is impersonal, so that it inheres not in any human subject but in the Person of the divine Word, does that get us any nearer to an explanation? It tells us that the Incarnation and Passion of Jesus do not mean that *he* is being redeemed, but that does not imply that *we* are. If what requires re-creation is the manhood of *all* human persons, it will hardly help us to be told that the one manhood that has been re-created does not belong to any human person at all. So indeed we might be tempted to argue; and yet both the Gospel and Christian experience unite to assure us that Christ's victory is ours, that God has laid upon him the iniquity of us all and that by his stripes we are healed.

II

Can anything be said that may help to illuminate the obscurity, that may convince us that the doctrine of the Atonement is not nonsense? I think that at least some tentative suggestions may be made. First, we may remark that if the first stage in the re-creation of the human race is the assumption of human nature by God the Word, then *in some sense* what he assumed must be not an entirely abstract set of human characteristics having no relation with our manhood except that of purely external and schematic similarity, but the actual concrete human nature which we possess. There must be more than accidental significance in the concreteness with which the *Te Deum* asserts that what the Son of God assumed in order to deliver it was not merely manhood but man. *Tu ad liberandum suscepturus hominem . . .*[1] On a purely nominalistic view of human nature—that is, on the view that the name "man" when applied to different individuals does not signify any kind of sharing in a common essence but only a purely external and disconnected similarity of appearance and behaviour —there can be no real connection between what happens in Christ's human nature and what happens in mine. On the other hand, we must not be tempted to rush to the opposite extreme of an exaggerated realism[2] which would make the individuality of the multiplicity of human beings a mere illusion and would attribute reality only to a universal manhood laid up in some sort of Platonic heaven; which would see individuals as related to this universal in much the same way as the images of an object in a number of mirrors are related to the object itself, being entirely dependent upon it for their semblance of existence and having no basis of being apart from it. Such a view would be both inconsistent with Christian dogma and ludicrously false to the facts of experience. For it would involve the Averroistic doctrine that our individual souls have no permanent identity, being merely local and temporary embodiments of one subsisting human intellect.

---

[1] "When thou wast about to take upon thee man to deliver him . . ." The Prayer-book translation loses the concreteness of the Latin.

[2] That is, realism in the medieval sense, not in the modern sense which usually involves what the medievals would have called nominalism. Medieval realism taught the reality of the universal; modern realism teaches the reality of the particular.

And it would also involve the plainly untrue consequence that, in everyone who was alive at the moment of the Incarnation the re-creation of manhood and its restoration to full perfection and integrity would have happened instantaneously and, as it were, magically when the Word united manhood to himself, while those who were born subsequently would presumably come into existence with their manhood in this completely restored state. (We may recall here that some of the fathers have been in fact accused, however unjustly, of teaching a "collective" rather than an "individual" incarnation.[1]) Now it is perhaps significant that the philosophical system which became central in the Christian tradition of the West is one that steers a middle course between these two extremes, a moderate realism which holds that the universal exists neither *ante rem* nor *post rem*, but *in re*: a view, that is, in which the universal is concretely embodied in the particular manifestations and in which the only existence that it has antecedently to them is its existence as an idea in the mind of God. Like all *viae mediae* this is a far more subtle and precarious notion to sustain than either of the extreme views which plump for simplicity at the expense of adequacy; and it is, again like all *viae mediae*, susceptible of a number of grades. It is in this, however, that its power mainly resides, for it may well be that the relation of universal to particular is essentially analogical, like so many other philosophical notions, and is by no means realized in the same mode in every instance. It is, in this connection, instructive to compare the problem of the relation between the universal and the particular—which is, of course, for the *philosophia perennis*, closely allied to the problem of the relation between form and matter—as it occurs in the different cases of inanimate beings, angels and men. In inanimate beings the form is entirely at the mercy of the matter and its spatial dimensions; we can cut a lump of paraffin wax in two and get two lumps of wax, we can squeeze two lumps together and get one. The universal appears to reside altogether in its particulars and to have no status apart from them. Also, it is embodied in all of them in the same way; the differences between them are purely minor and secondary. In the case of the angels, if we may for the moment adopt the Thomist doctrine concerning them, the universal is so independent and self-energizing that it individualizes itself; it is entirely indepen-

[1] Thus, for example, Mersch defends Methodius, Hilary and Gregory of Nyssa against this charge: see *The Whole Christ*, pp. 245, 305, 321.

dent of matter, there is thus only one particular for each universal, and every angel is a pure subsistent form and the one and only individual in its species.[1] In the case of man, however, we have an intermediate position which is highly mysterious. We can hardly deny that manhood is a common generic essence in which all men share—the fact that humans procreate humans is enough to indicate this—and this generic essence is far more significant, it is far less a mere association of properties and far more the manifestation of an indivisible principle, than is waxhood or even doghood. Yet, while in the sense just described the universal has in man a primacy over the particular that is found in none of the sub-human creation, there is another sense in which the particular is of supreme importance. For so far is it from being the case that the universal can exist in isolation from its particular manifestation, that Christian teaching tells us that every individual human soul is inherently unique and immortal. If we are to say with the Aristotelians that the form of a man is his soul and the matter of the man is his body, we must add that the supreme dignity of the form of manhood is shown, not, as we might suppose, by its being able to exist apart from all reference to matter and thus as altogether unmultiplied within its species, but by its various exemplifications preserving their own particular individualities even when, as after death, they are for the time being separated from the matter in union with which they were individualized.

III

Now I am far from wishing to maintain that the Christian religion stands or falls with the metaphysics of either Aristotle or St. Thomas, or that the Christian must give equal allegiance to the *philosophia perennis* and the Apostles' Creed. All that I have been trying to do is to show, by discussing the question in the classical language of Western Christianity, that the relation between the universal and the particular is even more mysterious and perplexing in the case of man than it is in the case of other creatures. We cannot say with the nominalists that the assertion of our

[1] If it be held that the Thomist doctrine of angels is unacceptable, one may prefer to adopt the Bonaventuran view, which Mr. E. I. Watkin has expounded in recent years, according to which angels, like men, are composed of form and matter and are individually multiplied within their species. It should hardly need to be added that the "matter" which we are concerned with here is matter in the philosophical sense, not in the sense of modern physical science.

common manhood is a mere linguistic convenience; nor can we say with the extreme realists that the only concrete manhood is a universal one laid up in heaven, so that if that is re-created our own re-creation must be *ipso facto* complete, since we have no reality except as numerically multiplied shadows or reflections of it. How any intermediate position is possible is indeed a mystery; the only hint we have of a solution is provided by the doctrine that the "ideas" of creatures exist, not, as the Platonists would hold, in an eternal realm wherein they are absolutely self-subsistent but in the mind of God, in which "manhood" must mean less than a concrete existent but more than a mere name. (It may thus perhaps be the case that the Thomist doctrine of the divine ideas is due not so much to an importation of Plato into Aristotle as to the baptism of Aristotle into Christ; this is, however, another question.) In any case, the purpose of this discussion has been to show that, if the doctrine of the re-creation of man in Christ is mysterious, it is no more so than is the nature of man himself. Christ's manhood is impersonal, we are told; he is the "universal" man. Hence the re-creation of manhood in him does not *ipso facto* bring about my own re-creation; yet, so I am assured, I can only be re-created "in him." This is a great mystery, and I have not claimed to solve it. I have merely tried to show, by discussing the matter in traditional terms, that man is himself a very strange being, in whom the problem of the relation of the universal and the particular, which is in all beings sufficiently obscure, reaches its climax of difficulty. It is at least remarkable that, both in anthropology and in Christology, the crux of the matter is reached over the question of individuation. It is perhaps not fantastic to suggest that in this correspondence there lies, if we only knew sufficient about human nature, the answer to the question as to how the impersonal manhood of Christ can be the medium of the redemption of all men.

Be this as it may, the essence of the Christian Gospel is the declaration that Christ has in his own self borne both the physical and the moral consequences of human sin. If the human race needed only to be restored in one concrete instance, then there would be no need of the crucifixion; Christ is perfect man from the moment of his conception, and at every moment of his life he makes a perfect offering of obedience and love to the Father, an offering which in a world of sin leads him to the death of the Cross. But since the re-creation of manhood is to be communicated from his human nature to that of the sinners among whom he came to dwell, he has, in his own person but in their place, as the representative man, to reverse their sin. He has to meet the enemy which defeated them and to defeat him. I shall not attempt here to discuss in detail the various elements that are involved in the doctrine of the Atonement; it will, I think, be enough to remark that it is impossible to dispense with either of the two great strands that go to form the Catholic tradition. Christ met the demands of the violated order of the universe, the demands which St. Anselm discussed, in metaphors which some of his followers have perhaps interpreted more literally than he intended, in terms of forensic thought; Christ also, by his perfect obedience and love, challenged and overcame the very forces to which man had succumbed. In the language of traditional theology, he both paid man's debt to God and destroyed the power of the devil. And we must notice that for the fulfilment of both these aspects of redemption it is necessary that he shall be both the consubstantial Son of God the Father and also, in his impersonal and universal human nature, the representative of all mankind. For only God can pay the debt which man owes, and yet it must be paid in the person of man. And only God can overcome man's ancient enemy, while the battle must none the less be fought in human nature, since its fruits are to be communicated to men. The Atonement has of course sometimes been depicted in crude and barbarous terms, yet it is most striking how both the crudity and the barbarity vanish once it is remembered that the Christ who died is both God and man. There is then no opposition between priest and victim, for priest and victim are one. There is no question of an angry Father demanding the blood of a helpless offender, for the Son who meets the demand is himself of the very same substance as the Father, "consubstantial with the Father as touching the Godhead"; Father and Son are together in the transaction, for "God was in Christ reconciling the world unto himself."[1] There is equally no question of the wrong person being punished for the offence, for Christ is one with us in his function as the representative and universal man, "consubstantial with us as touching the manhood."

I shall consider later on what is involved in the communication of the benefits of Christ's Passion to us. Here all we need recognize is that while, considered simply from the point of view of the

[1] 2 Cor. v. 19.

nature assumed, the re-creation of manhood is complete from the moment when the hypostatic union was first set up, yet, considered from the point of view of its applicability to us, the re-creation of manhood is initiated only at the moment when, in his death upon the Cross, Christ has overcome the powers which enthrall us though they never enthralled him. There is thus more than a pious fancy in the remark that the six days of Holy Week are the six days of the New Creation, which culminate in the re-creation of man in Christ on Good Friday as the six days of the old creation culminated in the creation of Adam. For the Crucifixion is not merely a necessary preliminary to our conversion, a *conditio sine qua non*; it is the actual payment of our debt. He "made there, by his one oblation of himself once offered, a full, perfect and sufficient sacrifice, oblation and satisfaction for the sins of the whole world." The death of Christ on the Cross was the re-creation of man, and not merely its antecedent condition. Since Christ is the universal man, his payment of our debt and his victory over our foes were in actual fact our re-creation, even though the fruits of that re-creation can be produced only as, by grace, we live in him. By his Incarnation he took a perfect human nature to himself, by his Passion he identified it with ours, not by a mere metaphysical union but by the personal sacrificial offering of it in obedience and love. There is therefore no question of the Incarnation and the Passion being competitors in the re-creation of man. If it was necessary for manhood to be assumed, it was no less necessary for it to be sacrificed. And because the human nature of Christ was both assumed by him and sacrificed for us, the fruits of the sacrifice can be ours through incorporation into him. But this will be the subject of the next chapter.

CHAPTER V

INCORPORATION INTO CHRIST

I

IT is almost universally assumed to-day that becoming a Christian means in essence the adoption of a new set of beliefs or the initiation of a new mode of behaviour. A Christian would be defined as one who "believes in Christ" or "worships Christ" or "tries to follow Christ's teaching." Now it is far from my purpose to belittle either Christian dogma or Christian ethics. Nevertheless, it must be pointed out that to define the essence of Christianity in terms either of belief or of practice involves the neglect of two principles that are fundamental to all sound theology. The former of these is that the act of God precedes and is presupposed by the acts of man: "Herein is love, not that we loved God, but that he loved us";[1] "Ye have come to know God, *or rather to be known of God*."[2] The second is that what a being *is* precedes what it *does*; our actions are a consequence of what we are, *operari sequitur esse*. It will follow from this that the Christian should be defined not in terms of what he himself does, but of what God has made him to be. Being a Christian is an ontological fact, resulting from an act of God.

What, then, is this act by which God makes a man into a Christian? It is, the New Testament assures us, incorporation into the human nature of Christ, an incorporation by which the very life of the Man Christ Jesus is communicated to us and we are re-created in him. "I am the vine; ye are the branches"; "If any man is in Christ, he is a new creature," or "there is a new creation"; we have been "grafted into" Christ like shoots into a tree.[3] The Christian is a man to whom something has *happened*, something moreover which is irreversible and which penetrates to the very roots of his being; he is a man who has been re-created in, and into, Christ.

---

[1] 1 John iv. 10.   [2] Gal. iv. 9.
[3] John xv; 2 Cor. v. 17; Rom. xi. 13–24. See the detailed working out of this whole theme in Mersch, *The Whole Christ*, Part I, chs. v, ix, x; Ramsey, *The Gospel and the Catholic Church*; Thornton, *The Common Life in the Body of Christ*, ch. ii.

Now the basis of this ontological change by which a man becomes a Christian is the permanence of the human nature of Christ. We have already seen, in our discussion of Christology, how necessary it is to hold that the divine Word really became flesh, that he united to himself, unconfusedly and inseparably, a concrete human nature, and that that human nature, though glorified by his Resurrection and Ascension and no longer subject to the limitations which governed it during the period of his humiliation, is nevertheless still in existence and still fully human.[1] As the Epistle to the Hebrews teaches, it is with his manhood still intact and forever united to his divine Person that Christ has entered into the realm of the "heavenlies," there to make perpetual intercession for us. The re-creation of manhood in Christ was not finished when, in the womb of Mary, he had united a perfect and unblemished human nature to himself, or even when in that human nature, by his death on Calvary, he had, as our representative, offered to the Father the oblation of love and obedience that we were powerless to offer ourselves. The truth is not merely that in Christ the new creation was effected on our behalf, but that through our union with him it is to be brought about in each one of us. Becoming a Christian means being re-created by being incorporated into the glorified manhood of the ascended Christ, so that, in the words of the Epistle to the Ephesians, we are raised up with him and made to sit with him in the heavenly places, in Christ Jesus.[2]

Now the normal and divinely appointed means by which this re-creation is initiated is clearly the Sacrament of Baptism, the sacrament of new birth, of regeneration. The Anglican formularies leave no doubt about this. Sacraments, we are told in the Articles of Religion, are "effectual signs of grace (*efficacia signa gratiae*) . . . by the which [God] doth work invisibly in us," and baptism is "a sign of regeneration or new birth, whereby, *as by an instrument*, they that receive baptism rightly (*recte*, i.e., in due form) are grafted into the Church."[3] "This child," says the Prayer Book, "is by baptism regenerate."[4] The inward spiritual grace of baptism, it tells us in the Catechism, is "a death unto sin and a new birth unto righteousness; for being by nature born in sin, and the children of wrath, we are hereby made the children of grace." God is not, of course, bound to the sacraments, and when sacra-

---

[1] See p. 30 *supra*.   [2] Eph. ii. 6.   [3] Artt. xxv, xxvii.
[4] "Private Baptism of Infants."

ments cannot be had he has no doubt other ways of supplying the grace that is normally mediated through their instrumentality. From very early times the Church has been led to recognize, in the case of the martyrs, that baptism by blood can be a substitute for baptism by water, and, as the actual historical and empirical facts of missionary and evangelistic work have forced upon the attention of theologians the existence of multitudes of souls in good faith who, either because they have never heard the preaching of the Gospel or because they are the victims of invincible prejudice, have not received the Sacrament of Baptism, there has been a progressive widening of the limits that may be assigned to "baptism of desire."[1] None the less, it must be asserted that the normal and divinely instituted means of incorporation into Christ is the Sacrament of Baptism, and we shall see later on that this is not the result of a purely arbitrary and unnecessary decree on the part of God, but is due to the fact that man is in his essence a social being and that, in consequence, his restoration must be not merely an individual putting of himself "right with God" but his insertion into a redeemed community. It is not just a matter of re-created men, but of a re-created human race.

II

It is, I think, necessary here to say something about the much-disputed question whether the restoration of man in Christ is to be thought of in terms of imputation or impartation. That is, does God, in view of the redeeming work of Christ, merely treat men as if they were what they are not, or does he make them in reality different from what they were? Protestant theologians have, in recent years, laid great stress upon the contention that in the New Testament, the Greek word δικαιόω, which has universally been rendered by the Latin word *justificare* and by the English word "justify," does not mean, as the Latin would suggest, to "make righteous" (*justum facere*), or, as the English word commonly means, to "prove in the right,"[2] but rather to "declare

[1] See, for example, Dr. K. E. Kirk's discussion in *Ignorance, Faith and Conformity* and the chapter on "Salvation outside the Visible Church" in the Roman-Catholic scholar Karrer's *Religions of Mankind*. Cf. also the discussion of Islamic and other non-Christian mysticism in Maréchal, *Studies in the Psychology of the Mystics*, chs. v, vi.
[2] " 'Esther,' Richard resumed, 'you are not to suppose that I have come here to make under-handed charges against John Jarndyce. I have only come to justify myself.' " (Dickens, *Bleak House*, ch. xxxvii.) For another "non-theological" use of the word see p. 162 *infra*.

or pronounce acquitted," without any reference to the actual guilt or innocence of the accused person. That is to say, it is maintained that justification, in the New-Testament exposition of the idea, does not assert or imply that any change is brought about in the sinner himself, still less that he is proved innocent of the charges brought against him, but simply that, in spite of his guilt and worthlessness, he is, if he has faith in Christ, treated as if he were innocent, by the imputation to him of the merits of Christ, who has paid the penalty in his stead. It is clear that such a doctrine might well lead to the crudest form of Anselmian doctrine and indeed, as it did in the case of certain of the Reformation sects, to the most disgusting types of antinomianism. It might be argued that the imputation of Christ's merits to me is a purely external act whereby I am let off my punishment in the same kind of way in which a man upon whom a fine has been imposed in a police-court will be released if someone else pays his fine for him, even though he himself may be entirely impenitent and fully deter-mined to commit the crime again at the first opportunity. It might also be argued that, while the imputed merits of Christ absolve me from all guilt, they can do nothing to bring about any real moral change in me, and that I can—and indeed must—go back to the old life with the added comfort that I shall no longer be held accountable for my actions. It is needless to add that the best Protestant theology and spirituality has consistently refused to be led into such extreme and absurd paths. Dr. Gustav Aulén, for instance, in his well-known book, *Christus Victor*, has argued that the true Lutheran doctrine of the Atonement is by no means the Anselmian one, but is what he describes as the "classical view," that the Atonement is in its essence an actual victory over the powers of evil, that "God was in Christ reconciling the world to himself." And, in spite of the many exaggerations of language which have given Luther's opponents the chance to accuse him of holding that so long as a man is justified it does not matter how he behaves, it does not seem to be true that Lutherans have had a low standard of morality; the reverse would seem to be the case. What is, however, true, I think, is that Protestantism, with its reluctance to admit that grace can produce a real supernaturaliza-tion of the soul in its ontological depths, has tended to discount the possibility and legitimacy of the systematic pursuit of super-natural sanctity. While exhibiting in the lives of many the most striking examples of heroic effort for the glory of God and the salvation of souls, and while insisting all the time that human righteousness is "filthy rags," it has, on the whole, been content in the ethical realm with the practice of the natural virtues, relegating the supernatural to the realm not of action but of piety and faith. It has been frequently pointed out that the commercial efficiency of Anglo-Saxondom has largely been due to the fact that the outlook of Protestantism released the restraints that medieval Catholicism (as, for example, in the matter of usury) had maintained upon the ever-present tendency in fallen man to concentrate upon worldly prosperity, and that, paradoxical as it may appear, the insistence of the Reformers that man could do nothing to achieve his own salvation resulted directly in a concentration upon this-worldly ends by banishing moral effort from the supernatural to the natural sphere.[1] Be this as it may, it is impossible to deny that Protestantism has been markedly suspicious of the supernatural virtues. It is not indeed that it has denied the existence of the supernatural as such; nothing could be more plainly supernatural than justification in traditional Protestant theology. But justification has been envisaged as simply an act of God by which man is accounted righteous without any ontological change being made in him.

This does not mean that the Reformers do not expect to see acts of supernatural virtue in the justified man; quite the contrary. But because they do not believe in a real communication of the life of God to the human soul, they are unable to see the man himself as being the subject of these acts. The sole subject, in any real sense, is God, although the merits of the acts are attributed to man by imputation. The supernatural and the natural in the justified man are thus like two parallel streams with no real connection: the former, which is wholly good, is God's operation; the latter, which is wholly bad, is man's. There is thus a sharp contrast with the Catholic doctrine, for in this latter a man's good acts, while they are to be attributed in their entirety to God as primary cause, are none the less to be attributed to man as their secondary and freely acting voluntary cause, whose real efficacy is not destroyed, but is mysteriously and subtly released and confirmed, by the overarching influence of supernatural grace.[2] The

---

[1] Reference may be made to R. H. Tawney's well-known book, *Religion and the Rise of Capitalism*, or to Fanfani's *Catholicism, Protestantism and Capitalism* in illustration of this development.

[2] Cf. the discussion of Luther and Calvin by Mersch in *Le Corps Mystique du Christ*, Vol. II, App. V (not in E.T.), and Maritain's *True Humanism*, ch. i.

Protestant tendency appears with great clarity in Dr. Nygren's compendious work, *Agape and Eros*, in which love (ἀγάπη) in the New-Testament sense is viewed as entirely an activity of God and in which practically the whole of Christian spirituality between St. Paul and Luther comes under more or less violent condemnation for holding that this love is, in a real sense, communicated to man as something which operates in and with him. And it is possible to find Protestant discussions of mysticism whose logical outcome would seem to be that the Catholic mystics simply cannot exist, while even by the more moderate and sympathetic writers of the orthodox Protestant school the mystics have to be condemned as having radically misunderstood their own experience.[1]

Now it is quite easy for the question as to whether justification involves impartation or imputation to be turned into a merely verbal quibble; it depends very largely on what it is that is alleged to be imputed or imparted, as the case may be. To impute a real quality is presumably the same as to impart a fictitious one; and the imputation of an impartation would seem to be the same as the impartation of an imputation. The question can, however, hardly be entirely a verbal one; the difference between the Protestant and Catholic conceptions of mysticism would seem to be sufficient to show that. Nor is the matter to be settled merely by determining the precise meaning of the verb *dikaioō* in the New Testament. The real question is whether or not the justification and regeneration of the sinner bring about a real change in him. Does his nature remain in all essentials what it was, although he no longer vaunts his own independence of God but acknowledges himself to be a sinner, or is he, on the other hand, brought into a new and living union with Christ, through which his whole nature can become supernaturalized, first in its essence and then, as man co-operates with grace, in its operations as well? It is, I would urge, manifest, not only that the lives of the saints themselves clearly indicate that the second alternative gives the true answer, but also that this is what a sound doctrine of God would lead us to expect. For, since God is the Creator, he cannot impute without imparting. What he says "goes." "God said, Let there be light, and there was light."[2] The imputation of the merits of Christ to man is thus a real impartation of them to him, not, of course, as something which he can then possess for his own independent use, but in virtue of his life in and with Christ, as the fruit of Christ's

---

[1] See p. 222 f. *infra.*   [2] Gen. i. 3.

life operating in him.[1] That this view is thoroughly in line with the tradition of Anglicanism may be seen from the following passage from Hooker, which will be a fitting summary for this discussion:

"Thus we participate Christ partly by imputation, as when those things which he did and suffered for us are imputed unto us for righteousness; partly by habitual and real infusion, as when grace is inwardly bestowed while we are on earth, and afterwards more fully both our souls and bodies made like unto his in glory. The first thing of his so infused into our hearts in this life is the Spirit of Christ, whereupon because the rest of what kind soever do all both necessarily depend and infallibly also ensue, therefore the Apostles term it sometime the seed of God, sometime the pledge of our heavenly inheritance, sometime the handsel or earnest of that which is to come."[2]

III

We need not here go into any detailed discussion of the questions, important as they are in themselves, of the relation of justification to faith and works and of the precise connection between justification and baptism.[3] I need only assert that, like every other work of grace, justification has as its primary efficient cause God himself, and that its meritorious cause is the death of Christ, whose merits are not bestowed upon us as a reward for any works of ours but are accepted by us through faith (*propter meritum Domini* and *per fidem*, as Article xi says). The point is this: that the work by which God accepts us in Christ is not a merely external, legal or "logical" fiction, but a supernatural rebirth which brings about an ontological change in us; that in baptism we are brought into a real relation with the glorified manhood of the Redeemer, that in baptism there is a real supernaturalization of our human nature in its essence, which can result, if we co-operate with the grace of God, in a progressive supernaturalization of its operations and in the manifestation of supernatural virtues.

This last remark gives me the opportunity of emphasizing that there is nothing "magical" about our baptismal incorporation into Christ, as if it absolved us of the necessity of moral and spiritual effort. Baptism is the foundation of the Christian life; it is not

[1] See the discussion of merit in Symonds, *The Council of Trent and Anglican Formularies*, ch. iii. [2] *Eccl. Pol.*, V, lvi, 11: ed. of 1888, II, p. 254.
[3] Reference may be made to Symonds, *The Council of Trent and Anglican Formularies*, ad loc., and to A. H. Rees, *The Doctrine of Justification in the Anglican Reformers*.

G

a substitute for it. To whomsoever much is given, of him shall much be required; the reception of baptism is in itself no guarantee of final perseverance and ultimate salvation. Baptism is what the Prayer Book calls it, a new birth; and birth is only the beginning of life in the world, not the attainment of full manhood. Nevertheless, nobody considers ordinary human birth to be unimportant, in spite of the fact that what is born is not a fully grown adult but only a weak and undeveloped child. Similarly, we may lay full stress upon the importance of the new birth by water and the Spirit, for we cannot do anything to speak of until we have been born. Baptism is the entry upon the supernatural life in Christ; it opens up a whole universe of subsequent graces, whose enjoyment is conditional upon the response of the soul itself, but which is of an unbelievable richness and fullness and whose consummation is the Beatific Vision.

Both the necessity of baptism and the ceremony by which it is performed rest not upon human invention but upon divine institution. The outward part—the washing in water and the recitation of the appointed trinitarian formula—is not however wholly arbitrary. The ceremony of washing which Christ adopted was one to which men had already been led to attach a religious significance, and its use as the outward sign of Christian initiation was, from the point of view of its human associations, highly appropriate. For the entry upon the supernatural realm which is bestowed by incorporation into Christ and which is fittingly described as a new birth is also a deliverance from the realm of fallen human nature—the sphere in which man lies under the curse of original sin—and an insertion into the realm of the perfect manhood of Christ. The symbolism of washing is therefore a most adequate expression of this passage from the kingdom of defilement to the kingdom of grace. Thus it is that the Anglican Prayer Book, in the opening prayer of the baptismal office, sees baptism prefigured in the great Biblical incidents in which the element of water plays so prominent a part: the preservation of Noah and his family in the ark, the leading of Israel through the Red Sea, and the Baptism of Christ in the Jordan, wherein, as it asserts, he sanctified water to the mystical washing away of sin.[1] Again, in the Nicene Creed, the one statement that is made about baptism is that it is "for the remission of sins." And, because baptism is

[1] Cf. the passage in 1 Peter iii. 20, 21, in which the ark is expounded as a type of baptism.

not the first but the second birth, it is not only a sacrament of life but also of death: in the words of the Catechism, "a death unto sin, and a new birth unto righteousness." So to St. Paul, the immersion of the catechumen beneath the water of baptism is a burial, and his emergence from it is a resurrection; death to the old life is a necessary element in birth into the new.[1] And since, as we have already seen, it is the death of Christ upon the Cross, as our representative who took upon himself the consequences of our sins, that makes it possible for the human nature that was re-created in him to be accessible to us, it follows that the death through which we pass in baptism is not only a death to the old life but is also the death which Christ himself died. It is with Christ that we die to the old life, and it is with Christ that we rise to the new. Into the great baptismal passage in the Epistle to the Romans St. Paul compresses with admirable conciseness the rich complexity of the Sacrament:

"Are ye ignorant that all we who were baptized into Christ Jesus were baptized into his death? We were buried therefore with him through baptism into death : that like as Christ was raised from the dead through the glory of the Father, so we also might walk in newness of life. For if we have become united with him by the likeness of his death, we shall be also by the likeness of his resurrection; knowing this, that our old man was crucified with him, that the body of sin might be done away, that so we should no longer be in bondage to sin; for he that hath died is justified from sin."[2]

It is possible, if we are not careful, so to concentrate upon baptism as the sacrament of incorporation into Christ's glorified humanity as to forget that it is also the sacrament of washing from sin, the sacrament by which the soul is given a real participation in Christ's death. In actual fact, as we have seen, the two aspects are indissolubly connected, for the manhood of Christ is the manhood in which he died, and it still bears the marks of the Passion. In the vision in the Apocalypse, the Lamb that was seen standing in the midst of the throne was "a lamb as though it had been slain."[3]

In discussing the Incarnation, I laid stress upon the fact that the assumption of manhood by the eternal Word, while it undoubtedly has consequences in the realm of psychology, is not in

[1] Rom. vi. 3–11.   [2] Rom. vi. 3–7.   [3] Rev. v. 6.

itself a psychological but an ontological fact. A similar point must be emphasized here. Baptism is equally an ontological fact, and not one that is immediately in the psychological or moral realm. This can be seen if we consider the statement that was made above, that baptism removes its recipient from the curse of original sin. In the empirical order that simply is not true. If the traditional view is correct which sees human mortality as one of the consequences of the Fall, we can hardly avoid recognizing the fact that the baptized are as subject to physical death as the heathen. And even if we reject tradition on this point, we cannot but admit, with the ninth Article of Religion, that, as regards the effects of original sin upon human psychology,

> "this infection of nature doth remain, yea in them that are regenerated: whereby the lust of the flesh, called in Greek, *phronema sarkos*, which some do expound the wisdom, some sensuality, some the affection, some the desire of the flesh, is not subject to the Law of God."

Although, however, the physical and moral effects of original sin are not magically removed by baptism, the introduction of the soul into the supernatural realm does communicate to it the principle by which its ultimate healing can be brought about. Sanctification is the proper fruit and the ultimate end of the baptismal union. Here, as elsewhere, grace does not annihilate or do violence to nature but heals it and strengthens it and brings it to perfection. There is perhaps a danger that the scholastic tag, *Gratia non tollit naturam sed perficit*, may become a parrot-cry; nevertheless, it expresses a fundamental principle of God's dealing with man, a principle, I must add, which applies in different analogical modes in different cases. It is frequently important to know not merely that grace perfects nature, but what is the precise mode in which it perfects it in a specific instance. To work this out in the case with which we are here concerned would involve nothing less than the composition of a complete treatise on ascetic theology. The fact that it cannot be attempted here is not perhaps of great consequence, since the task has been done with great competence by many writers. All that I need stress is the fact that, while the Christian life is a life not on the level of nature but on that of grace, in it man's natural faculties and capacities are not suppressed but stimulated to act more fully and perfectly; free-will, so far from being destroyed, is liberated and energized.

Man is not less but more free in his natural life as a member of the everyday world of human relationships because he is re-made in Christ and has his true citizenship in heaven. As Fr. Gardeil has maintained eloquently, the obediential capacity which nature has for grace does not mean that nature loses its dignity and its reality as the creature of God, but that it is ennobled and stimulated into unexampled and unprecedented vigour and fullness as grace brings it to its perfection by an interior vivification.[1] As Leontius of Byzantium wrote, "The supernatural does not destroy the natural, but educes and stimulates it both to do its own business and to acquire the power for what is above it."[2] and other Christian writers have echoed his thought through the ages. "Grace finds out man's naturall faculties," wrote John Donne, "and exalts them to a capacity."[3] And in our own time Jacques Maritain has summed up the matter with his usual profundity and clarity.

> "In any supernatural operation," he writes, "two activities are united, but not in juxtaposition: nature does not begin from below what grace completes from above; from the beginning nature only acts as grace has raised it up. If nature and grace *shared* in the performance of supernatural acts, in the vision of God in heaven, in an act of theological virtue here on earth, then there would be brought in an element of mechanical addition. No; it is precisely because our natural powers of action are in themselves in a condition of docility and potentiality with regard to God that supernatural acts rise out of the depths of our nature, from the heart of our soul and our faculties, but *only as* they have been raised up by grace, as they have been *drawn on* by infused qualities towards possibilities which are entirely inaccessible to our nature in itself."[4]

To return, then, to the point which was originally under discussion, the grace of incorporation into Christ, the normal channel of which is baptism, is a supernatural fact in the ontological order which does not of itself immediately produce physical and moral effects; but it does produce such effects mediately and progressively when, and to the degree in which, the soul co-operates with this grace and surrenders itself to its influence. There is no "magic,"

---

[1] *La Structure de l'Ame et l'Expérience mystique*, Vol. ii.
[2] Quoted by Gore, *Dissertations*, p. 277.
[3] Quoted by Husain, *Dogmatic and Mystical Theology of John Donne*, p. 125.
[4] *Degrees of Knowledge*, p. 317. To "share" here means, of course, to divide into two mutually exclusive parts.

no violence, no destruction of free-will; none the less, holiness is the fruit of incorporation into Christ.[1]

IV

It must be added that, in recognizing that justification involves a real impartation of Christ's life to us and a real elevation of us into him, we must not allow the truth to be obscured for which the Anselmian theology stood, namely that sin is a violation of the moral order of the universe and places man under a condemnation from which he cannot extricate himself. Between God and man there is the barrier of debt; there is the divine justice which demands to be satisfied. Sentences such as this, of course, jar most sharply upon many twentieth-century minds. They call up the picture of a savage creditor, demanding, like Shylock, his pound of flesh and apparently not minding whose flesh it is, since it is man who owes it but Christ who pays. I have said something about this in the previous chapter, but I would add here that, although the mystery of the Atonement contains depths that are unfathomable by the human mind, the great truths with which we have just been concerned do at least throw some light upon the mystery. For the doctrine of the Incarnation assures us that Christ did not merely take the place of man, but *became man* and mysteriously renewed the very nature of manhood by uniting it to his divine Person.

> "He sent no angel to our race
> Of higher or of lower place,"

precisely because nothing that an angel could have done would have been of the slightest use. Therefore,

> "He wore the robe of human frame
> And he himself to this world came."[2]

And again, because the Father and the Son are of one substance, they cannot be set over against each other as if the Father were

---

[1] I have not attempted to discuss here the relation between baptism and confirmation, which in the early Church were two parts of one ceremony of initiation. It may well be that, with the separation of the two in the West in the Middle Ages, theologians tended to attribute to baptism some of the effects that properly belong to confirmation, and in consequence to be very vague as to whether confirmation has any specific effects at all. It is at least difficult to admit that incorporation into Christ and initiation into the Church are complete without confirmation.

[2] Cf. Heb. ii. 16: "For verily not of angels doth he take hold, but he taketh hold of the seed of Abraham."

all justice and the Son all mercy. "The Son can do nothing of himself but what he seeth the Father doing; for what things soever he doeth, these the Son also doeth in like manner."[1] Two great truths stand out. The first is that man owed the debt, but only God could pay it; therefore God the Son became man. The second is that the Son who paid it and the Father to whom it was paid are of one and the same substance, essence and nature; hence all suggestions of savagery are excluded. It is perhaps well to stress that the forensic metaphors of "debt," "payment" and the like must not be pressed beyond their proper limit. There are indeed important respects in which atonement for sin is like the payment of a debt; there are others in which it is like the punishment of a criminal; there are others, no less important, in which it differs from both these. There is nothing to which it is precisely similar except itself; there is therefore nothing to worry about in the fact ✓ · that it has to be described under various figures, any of which if pushed to an extreme would result in an absurdity and many of which if pushed to an extreme would be mutually contradictory.

Furthermore, the Atonement involves man's deliverance from the powers of darkness. It should hardly be necessary at the present day to defend the Christian belief in the existence of evil spirits; the assumption that all spiritual beings are benevolent would seem to be antecedently improbable and also difficult to reconcile with the facts of human experience.[2] If, with writers such as Tillich,[3] we replace demons by a category of the "demonic" we raise the fresh difficulty that the demonic has to be considered as a self-contradictory element in existence, for which God as the Creator has to bear the direct responsibility. And Mr. C. S. Lewis's studies in demonic psychology in the *Screwtape Letters* have at least shown that belief in evil spirits is relevant to religion. I shall therefore assume that it is still legitimate to speak about man's deliverance by Christ from the power of the devil.

There have, of course, been Christian writers who held that as a result of sin the devil acquired rights over man, and that therefore the debt which Christ paid by his death was paid not to God but to the devil.[4] Such a doctrine is plainly repugnant; and it failed to gain any permanent footing in Christian thought. It is preposterous to suggest that the devil can have any rights over man

---

[1] John v. 19.   [2] Cf. p. 53 *supra*.   [3] *The Interpretation of History.*
[4] See G. Aulén, *Christus Victor*, p. 63 f.

against God; the utmost that might be conceded would be that man had ceased to have any rights over himself against the devil, and even that would be highly debatable.[1] We cannot therefore admit any notion that Christ either compensated the devil for the loss of his rights or that he tricked the devil out of his rights by, as it were, giving him a cheque that the bank afterwards refused to cash. The debt was due not to the devil but to God; but, although the devil has no *rights* in the matter, he has obtained *power* over man, through man's own perversity and stupidity. The devil is indeed cheated of his prey—*Tulitque praedam tartari* the Church sings, and *Multiformis proditoris ars ut artem falleret*[2]—but it is a prey to which he had no right. And the ultimate truth is that he has tricked himself from the beginning by placing himself on the wrong side. We have to recognize that, so far from showing extraordinary insight, the devil must be an intellect of considerable opacity, since he has actually thought it worth while to fight against God. One of the most telling passages in the *Screwtape Letters* is that in which the demon Screwtape is forced to admit that "the Enemy" (that is, God) has a secret which the demons cannot fathom, and the same point is brought out by Mr. Lewis in his novel, *Perelandra*, in the suggestion that the diabolic intellect only functions on the rational level when this is necessary for the temptation of human beings, since, if they allowed themselves habitually to think, the demons would have perforce to see the futility of their enterprise. A further example is provided by the ridiculous rhodomontade which Satan delivers in *Paradise Lost* in the speech in which he claims the allegiance of the fallen angels. The diabolic enterprise is essentially self-frustrating; in one way or other the devils always succeed in spite of themselves in glorifying God. If they inspire a persecution of Christians, they succeed only in raising martyrs to the altars of the Church; if they encompass the death of the Messiah, they co-operate in the redemption of mankind.

But this is a digression from the main theme, which was simply to emphasize that, in giving due stress to the doctrine of incor-

---

[1] Only the most extreme form of doctrine of total depravity could maintain that, as a result of sin, man had ceased to have *any* rights over himself. The whole conception of the natural law involves that, whatever may be his status over against God, man has not ceased through sin to have rights over himself as against other creatures. And the devil is only a creature after all.

[2] "And spoil the spoiler of his prey"; "That the manifold deceiver's art by art might be outweighed." (Hymns of Venantius Fortunatus, *English Hymnal*, Nos. 94 and 95, Latin of the Breviary version.)

poration into Christ, we are not hereby bound to minimize the doctrine of the Atonement. The Incarnation and the Atonement are inextricably bound together. However mysterious to us the redemptive act may be, the fact remains that, in taking manhood and offering it to the Father in perfect obedience, the eternal Son makes the one full, perfect, and sufficient sacrifice, oblation and satisfaction for the sins of the whole world.

CHAPTER VI

THE RESULTS OF INCORPORATION

I

"THE Three Heavenly Unities," wrote Lord Bacon in his Confession of Faith, "exceed all natural unities; that is, the unity of the Three Persons in the Godhead; the unity of God and man in Christ; and the unity of Christ and the Church—the Holy Ghost being the worker of both these latter unities; for by the Holy Ghost was Christ incarnate, and quickened in flesh; and by the Holy Ghost was man regenerated and quickened in the spirit."[1]

I intend in this chapter to trace out in more detail the consequences of the baptismal incorporation into Christ which we have seen to be the essential basis of the Christian religion, and in order to do this I shall start from the consideration of three fundamental modes of union which bridge in three stages the gulf between God the Father, who is the source of all being, and our own finite selves.

1. First, we must recognize the essential union of the Person of God the Father with the Person of God the Son within the life of the triune Godhead, a union through which the Son, who is eternally begotten of the Father, eternally renders to the Father a perfect offering of adoring filial love, a union which is perfected in the procession of the Spirit and in which the three Persons share the fulness of one another's life by their common possession of the totality of Godhead.

2. Then there is the hypostatic union of human nature with the Person of the eternal Son in the Incarnation, a union in which the human nature, because it has no human hypostasis but is enhypostatized in its union with the Son, is raised to the level of Godhead and on that level is caught up into the eternal filial offering of the Son.

3. Lastly, there is the adoptive union of human beings by

[1] *Works*, III, p. 123; quoted by R. I. Wilberforce, *The Incarnation*, p. 218.

incorporation into the manhood of Christ, whereby, through their union with him, they too, without any destruction of their own personal individuality, are caught up into his filial offering.

The first of these is a union of Persons in one substance, the second is a union of natures in one Person, the third is a union of personal beings through union of their natures.

In the first case the terms that are united are both divine. In the second case one is divine and the other is created. In the third case both are created, for while, considered in its union with the Word, the human nature of Christ is divinized, considered in itself it is a creature.

In one sense, the first union is the closest of the three, for the divine Persons entirely possess one another in their complete mutual interpenetration (*perichoresis, circumincessio*). In another sense, the second is the closest, for the two natures, the divine and the human, concur in the concrete existence of one personal being.

The three unions are thus altogether different in their characters; if we forget this we shall fall into the most grotesque heresies. And each of them is enshrouded in mystery. In the first case we are unable to understand how, without being confused with one another, three Persons can each of them possess the same concrete essence in its totality. In the second case the problem is how one Person can be at the same time the subject of two natures, and moreover of two natures which are completely distinct, since one is divine and the other human. In the third case the problem is how, without losing our personal individualities, we can be incorporated into the concrete human nature of another man, namely Jesus Christ. Nevertheless, taken together, the three unities bridge the gulf between the Father and us: essential union of the Person of the Father with the Person of the Son; hypostatic union of the Person of the Son with the human nature of Christ; adoptive union of our human nature into his.[1]

To follow out the implications of this, I do not think we can do better than take as our starting-point the answer in which the Prayer-Book Catechism describes the effects of baptism. "My baptism," it says, "wherein I was made a member of Christ, the child of God, and an inheritor of the kingdom of heaven." Let us take the three parts of this in turn.

[1] It should be noted that "essential union" means union *in* the same essence, "hypostatic union," union *in* the same hypostasis, and "adoptive union," union *by* adoption.

"A member of Christ." I have already said as much about this as we need at the moment. By baptism, without loss of personal identity, we are incorporated into Christ, that is to say, established *in corpore Christi*, given an ontological union with, and participation in, his glorified human nature, so that all that he possesses in it becomes ours. In him we are new creatures; he is the vine, we are the branches; the glory which the Father gave to him, he has given to us.[1]

"The child of God." Christ is the Son of the Father, by nature, in essential union; in his human nature dwells all the fullness of the Godhead bodily, in hypostatic union; we are one with him in his human nature, by adoptive union. Therefore, since all that he has he communicates to us, we are the sons of God by adoption and grace, as he is the Son of God by nature. This is not just theological theorizing; it is the teaching of the New Testament.

"When the fullness of the time came," wrote St. Paul to the Galatians, "God sent forth his son, born of a woman, born under the law, that he might redeem them which were under the law, that we might receive the adoption of sons. And because ye are sons, God sent forth the Spirit of his Son into our hearts, crying, Abba, Father. So that thou art no longer a bondservant, but a son; and if a son, then an heir through God."[2]

Again he writes to the Romans:

"Ye received not the spirit of bondage again unto fear, but ye received the Spirit of adoption, whereby we cry, Abba, Father. The Spirit himself beareth witness with our spirit, that we are children of God: and if children, then heirs."[3]

This Biblical doctrine, we must notice, is not that we are all sons of God by the mere fact of our natural birth; or if we are, we are sons who have fallen away from sonship into servitude, we have left the Father's house and gone into a far country and have been reduced to living with the swine. True sonship is restored to us only in Christ; but in him it is a far more wonderful sonship than that which we had lost.[4] Adam, says the Lucan genealogy of Christ, was the son of God;[5] he was made, Genesis tells us, in God's image, after God's likeness;[6] he was God's son by nature, by

[1] John xvii. 22.   [2] Gal. iv. 4–7.   [3] Rom. viii. 15, 16.
[4] See the eloquent passage on the Prodigal Son in Thornton's *Common Life in the Body of Christ*, p. 131.
[5] Luke iii. 38. The word "son" is not in this verse in the Greek, but is supplied by comparison with verse 23.   [6] Gen. i. 26.

creation. We who are restored in Christ have a far greater privilege, for our sonship is an adoption by grace into the sonship of him who is not _made in_ God's image but _is_ that image itself, "the ✓ image of the invisible God, the heir of all creation,"[1] "the impress of his substance."[2] Wonderfully as God created the dignity of man's substance, he has yet more wonderfully renewed it. In the mystery of his foreknowledge "he chose us in [Christ] before the foundation of the world . . . having foreordained us unto adoption as sons through Jesus Christ unto himself."[3] It is in Christ alone that we can cry, "Abba, Father." The Lord's Prayer, the _Pater noster_, is the Church's prayer, the prayer of those who dare to approach God with the name "Father" upon their lips only because the sonship which they had forfeited has been restored to them in Christ.[4] It is of the highest significance that, in the great Christian liturgies, it is only when the divine Victim has been brought mystically before the Father as the unique mediator between God and man, and in his sacramental presence, that the Church dares to offer the prayer which Christ taught it to say. "Vouchsafe, O Lord, that we may dare with boldness and without condemnation to call on thee, the heavenly God, as Father, and say——"[5]; "Instructed by the Saviour's precepts and taught by divine commandment, we dare to say——"[6]; "As our Saviour Christ hath commanded and taught us, we are bold to say——"[7]: "Our Father . . ." In Mersch's phrase, we are _filii in Filio,_ sons in the Son.[8] To summarize in his words:

"If we examine St. Paul's reasoning closely, Christians are not sons of adoption so much as members of the Son himself; the grace they have received is not a favour complete in itself, wholly separated from the eternal generation. It is but one aspect of incorporation in this eternal Son who has become incarnate; it is, if we may use the expression, incorporation into his sonship. . . .

"There is only one Son, but in this one Son is included the multitude of poor sinful men; and in him, they, too, are sons, sons by participation in his sonship. This participation is their adoption."[9]

---

[1] Col. i. 15.   [2] Heb. i. 3.   [3] Eph. i. 4, 5.   [4] See, for example, _De Sacramentis_, V, iv.
[5] Liturgy of St. John Chrysostom: Καταξίωσον ἡμᾶς, Δέσποτα, μετὰ παρρησίας, ἀκατακρίτως, τολμᾶν ἐπικαλεῖσθαί σε τὸν ἐπουράνιον θεὸν Πατέρα καὶ λέγειν:
[6] Roman Missal: _Praeceptis salutaribus moniti, et divina institutione formati, audemus dicere:_   [7] Scottish Liturgy.
[8] Cf. the article by Mersch under this title in the _Nouvelle Revue Théologique_, July–Aug. 1938.   [9] _The Whole Christ_, p. 144.

And again:

> "To be a child of God is thus not a mere psychological attitude,
> a mere pious disposition of confidence, humility and love. It is an
> ontological reality, so great as to be of a different order from every
> created magnitude, to overflow our intellectual categories, to be
> truly mysterious, to be capable of definition as regards what it is
> in itself only in terms of that which defines God as he is in himself."[1]

In other words, this adoption as sons of God is not just the concession of certain rights by a legal fiction, a mere imputation, as is
done in the process of adoption in English law; it is a real communication of the sonship of Jesus Christ. "Beloved, now are we
children of God."[2]

"An inheritor of the kingdom of heaven." This is a direct
consequence of our sonship, as our sonship was of our incorporation. "If a son, then an heir through God," writes the Apostle, or,
as another reading has it, "an heir of God through Christ."[3]
"If children, then heirs; heirs of God and joint heirs with Christ."[4]
That is to say, everything that is Christ's in virtue of his sonship
is ours by our adoption into him. We receive—of course in a way
adapted to our mode of existence as creatures, for *quidquid recipitur
recipitur ad modum recipientis*—a real participation in the life of the
Holy Trinity; through our union with Christ we are caught up into
the act whereby he eternally adores the heavenly Father. We are
made, in the New-Testament phrase, "partakers of the divine
nature."[5] As St. Paul told the Ephesians, God "raised us up with
[Christ] and made us to sit with him in the heavenly places, in
Christ Jesus."[6] This does not, of course, remove us from the conditions of earthly existence; it makes us, on the contrary, members
of two worlds at once. We are to "*seek* the things that are above,
where Christ is, seated on the right hand of God"; nevertheless,
St. Paul says to us in the same context, "your life *is hid* with Christ
in God."[7] "The infinite Being," writes Mersch, "has two ways of
giving himself to finite beings: by the former, he gives himself to
them in *their* way, which makes them themselves; by the latter he
gives himself to them in *his* way, which makes them one with
him."[8]

---

[1] Art. cit. *supra*, p. 825. [2] 1 John iii. 2.   [3] Gal. iv. 7.   [4] Rom. viii. 17.
[5] 2 Pet. i. 4.   [6] Eph. ii. 6.   [7] Col. iii. 1, 3. [8] Art. cit., p. 820.

II

It is this participation in the life of God, this sharing in the response which the eternal Son makes to the Father's love, that is the basis of the teaching of both the fathers and the mystical theologians about the "divinization" or "deification" of man in Christ. It is absolutely essential to remember the conditions under which it takes place if we are to avoid serious heresy. It is a result of the threefold bridge of union which, we have seen, spans the gulf between us and the Father. It is through our adoptive union with Christ and the hypostatic union of his human nature with his divine Person that we are caught up into the life of union which he essentially shares with God the Father. And we saw that one of the characteristics of our adoptive union with Christ is that our personal identity is preserved. Even if, in a strictly guarded sense, we can say, with some of the mystics, that Christ and God are *what* we become, we can never say that they are *who* we become.[1] In describing the supreme stage of mystical union in which "all the desires of the soul and its faculties . . . are changed into divine operations" and in which "the soul, having its operations in God, through the union that it has with God, lives the life of God," St. John of the Cross, while he asserts that "the understanding of this soul is now the understanding of God, and its will is the will of God, and its memory is the memory of God, and its delight is the delight of God" and will even go so far as to say that "it is thus God by participation in God," insists that "the substance of this soul . . . is not the substance of God, for into this it cannot be substantially changed."[2] This union is indeed unbelievably

[1] It is the neglect of this fact in certain circles of the Liturgical Movement in Germany that has led to the condemnation in a recent Papal encyclical of those "who, failing to appreciate sufficiently that the Apostle Paul spoke metaphorically on this matter [sc. the doctrine of the Mystical Body] omit to make the necessary distinctions between the several meanings of physical, moral and mystical body, with the result that they introduce a perverse explanation of this union. According to them," continues Pope Pius XII, "the divine Redeemer and the members of the Church are united to form one physical person, and consequently while attributing divine properties to human beings, they make Christ our Lord subject to error and human frailty." (*The Mystical Body of Jesus Christ*, p. 51; cf. J. Hennig on "Trends of Catholic Thought on the Continent," in *Blackfriars*, May, 1944, p. 172 f.)

[2] *Living Flame of Love*, 2nd redaction, II, 33, 34 (*Works*, Peers's trans., Vol. III, p. 157-8). Even a mystic so inclined to "pantheizing" as Ruysbroeck affirms clearly that "we do not become God." (*The Seven Steps of the Ladder of Spiritual Love*, trans. by F. Sherwood Taylor, cf. p. 63 with p. 51, and see Fr. J. Bolland's introduction, p. 8.) For what can be said in defence of Angelus Silesius, see Maritain, *Degrees of Knowledge*, p. 412, n. 2.

It is well to remember in this connection that, according to the scholastic doctrine,

intimate; "the soul now loves God, not through itself, but through himself; which is a wondrous brightness, since it loves through the Holy Spirit, even as the Father and the Son love one another," it "loves God in God";[1] nevertheless, its individuality is not destroyed. Even in the Beatific Vision it will still be the individual soul that it is; and, however deified, it will still remain a creature. Now if this is true of the summits of the Christian life, it must *a fortiori* be true in the lower stages; there is no question of any pantheistic doctrine of "absorption" into God. But when all these necessary cautions have been stated we can then affirm without hesitation that to live as a Christian incorporated into Christ is to live, however haltingly and imperfectly, with the life of God. To quote words that I have written elsewhere, "there is a fundamental continuity between the state of the ordinary Christian and that of the mystic, or even of the saint in heaven who rejoices in the beatific vision, for, as St. Thomas says, 'Grace is nothing else than a beginning of glory in us.'[2]"[3] In the words of Garrigou-Lagrange, "the mystical life is the Christian life which has become in some way conscious of itself."[4] And the New Testament is not speaking loosely when it tells us that our life is hid with Christ in God and that we are partakers of the divine nature.

Two important consequences follow. One is that God dwells in the soul of the Christian in a way far more intimate than that in which he is present to every finite being at its ontological root as its creator and preserver. What ascetic theology calls "the indwelling of the Trinity in the souls of the just" is of an altogether different order from God's "presence of immensity" in all things "by essence, presence and power"; it is on the level of grace, not of nature; it derives from redemption, not just from creation. Its basis is our incorporation into Christ. "If a man love me, he will keep my word, and my Father will love him, and we will come unto him, and make our abode with him."[5] "If that which ye heard from the beginning abide in you, ye also shall abide in the Son and in the Father."[6] In Christ the Christian enjoys an

---

the soul does, in a certain way ("intentionally," not "entitatively"), *become* whatever it *knows*. In this sense a man can even become a cabbage. The difference between our natural knowledge of things and our supernatural knowledge of God is that in the former case the soul is energized by its own vitality, and in the latter by God himself.

[1] *Living Flame*, III, 82 (Vol. III, p. 206).
[2] *S. Theol*, II, II, xxiv, 3 ad 2m.   [3] *He Who Is*, p. 149.
[4] *Perfection chrétienne et Contemplation*, I, p. 149.   [5] John xiv. 23.   [6] 1 John ii. 24.

intimacy with God that exceeds all that a creature could dream of. He is admitted into the very life of the triune God.

> "The meanest man in grey fields gone
>   Behind the set of sun,
> Heareth between star and other star,
> Through the door of the darkness fallen ajar,
> The council, eldest of things that are,
>   The talk of the Three in One."[1]

And the unity which Christians have with one another is nothing less than a participation in the unity of God himself: "That they may all be one," the incarnate Word prayed, "even as thou, Father, art in me, and I in thee, that they also may be in us."[2]

The other consequence is that, in Christ, by our participation in the life of God, we are given a certain transcendence over the time-process. God is, by his very nature, timeless; the eternity which Christian theology attributes to him is not just continuance for an unlimited time, "going on for ever," even though, in virtue of the fact that his creative activity is present to every created being at every moment of its existence, this is how he appears to us. *Aeternitas* in the strict sense is not just *diuturnitas* or *sempiternitas*;[3] it is a mode of life altogether above and independent of time. Eternity is the mode of life proper to God, as time is the mode of life proper to us; we are created, not *in tempore* but *cum tempore*. Eternity is, in Boethius's famous phrase, "the simultaneously whole and perfect possession of interminable life," a definition which St. Thomas, with other Christian theologians, has defended and explained at length.[4] Now we as creatures are inescapably involved in time, and temporality is both a mysterious and a tragic fact, as philosophers and poets have alike maintained. We never cross the same river twice, and the snows of yesteryear are irrecoverable. Through our immersion in time our direct personal experience of the world-process is limited to an exceedingly thin slice of the whole extent of history; our personal acquaintance is confined to our contemporaries, and when we would interrogate the giants of the human race we find only too often, as Mr. E. C. Bentley found at the tomb of Wordsworth, that

> "man is always born too late
> Or else he dies too soon."

---

[1] G. K. Chesterton, *The Ballad of the White Horse*, Book I.
[2] John xvii. 21.   [3] Cf. *S. Theol.*, I, x, 4.
[4] Boethius, *De Consol. Phil.*, v. Cf. *S. Theol.*, I, x, 1. *Aeternitas est interminabilis vitae tota simul et perfecta possessio.*

H

This character of successiveness is part and parcel of our very existence. Even in the Beatific Vision it cannot be altogether removed; although there can be neither increase nor decrease in our final felicity, it will none the less be true that we "go on" enjoying beatitude and that we "used not" to possess it, unimaginably different as the conditions of life *in patria* will be from those that now govern our experience *in via*. To escape altogether from temporality we should have to cease to be creatures; and, as creaturehood is involved in our very nature, that means that we should have to be destroyed. Nevertheless, through the exaltation into the life of God which is the fruit of our incorporation into Christ, we are granted, in a profoundly mysterious manner and in a mode which is strictly conformed to our creaturely nature, a real share in the eternity of God, as we are in everything else that God possesses; we receive, by grace, a created participation in God's own mode of life. What I have just given is nothing else than a statement in philosophical terms of the gift which St. John's Gospel denotes by the term "eternal life," a mode of experience which, as many modern commentators have shown is not just a future blessing but is communicated to us "here and now." "He that believeth hath eternal life"; "He that eateth my flesh and drinketh my blood hath eternal life"; "God gave unto us eternal life, and this life is in his Son."[1] It is true that there are other New-Testament passages in which ζωὴ αἰώνιος is spoken of as something in the future which we have not yet attained;[2] but this only helps to bring out the point, which is precisely that the gift which, considered in relation to the chronological sequence of the natural order, is in the distant future, is, when considered from the standpoint of our elevation into the order of supernature and grace, already in our possession. And, as the Johannine texts tell us, it is "in Christ" that we have it: "this life is in his Son." As I pointed out above, it is only through our incorporation into the manhood of Christ that we are taken up into God's own being, through the bridging of the gulf between us and the Father by the three stages of union which we have already considered. The Christian has thus, as a member both of the order of nature and of the order of grace, a peculiar dual character. In the order of nature, he lives with his own life, a life given him by God in his creation; in the order of grace, he lives with God's life, which is given him by God in his re-creation in Christ. And, the Christian life being a

---

[1] John vi. 47, 54; 1 John v. 11.   [2] E.g., in Matt. xxv. 46; Rom. ii. 7; Gal. vi. 8.

life in which nature, without any destruction of its own proper
being, is progressively supernaturalized, the Christian is, in one
sense, successively *becoming* what, in another sense, he already *is*.
He increasingly makes his own the supernatural and eternal life
which is the life of God. Hence on the supernatural plane he
transcends the separation of past-present-and-future. "All things
are yours, whether . . . things present or things to come; and ye
are Christ's, and Christ is God's."[1]

III

I believe that we have here the clue to the interpretation of that
perplexing body of Biblical ideas and affirmations which goes by
the name of "eschatology"—the doctrine of the Last Things, and
in particular of the Second Coming of Christ and the Final Judgment. It is well known that the early Christians expected Christ
to return in glory within their own lifetime, and that one of the
problems with which St. Paul had to contend was that presented
by the perplexity of the Christians of Thessalonica, who could not
understand how it was that many of them had died and yet the
Lord had not returned. And although the various attempts that
have been made to forecast the date of the Lord's return have not
up to the present been verified, Advent has remained as one of
the great seasons of the Church's year, and Christians have
continued to profess their belief, as they recite the Nicene Creed,
that Christ will come again with glory to judge both the quick
and the dead.

In recent years, however, largely under the influence of the
writings of Sir Edwyn Hoskyns[2] and Professor C. H. Dodd,[3] much
stress has been laid upon the notion of "realized eschatology,"
that is to say, the view that, whatever else it may or may not imply,
the eschatological language of the New-Testament writers signifies
that the Last Day and the Final Judgment are actually present to
Christians now. This conclusion is based primarily upon the study
of the Biblical text; it is shown that the language of Jewish apocalyptic, according to which God would one day break into the
course of human history and vindicate his sovereignty in a great
cosmic cataclysm of mercy and judgment, is frequently used, both

---

[1] I Cor. iii. 22–3.   [2] Cf. the section "Eschatology" in *Cambridge Sermons.*
[3] See, e.g., *The Apostolic Preaching*, Appendix on "Eschatology and History";
History and the Gospel, ch. v.

by our Lord and the Apostolic writers, to describe that which has actually come to pass in the birth, death and resurrection of Jesus Christ. St. Peter, for example, in his first recorded sermon, declared that the descent of the Spirit at Pentecost was the sign that the Day of the Lord had actually come, of which the Prophet Joel spoke.[1] And Christ himself announced that, in the mighty works which he performed, the reign of God—a notion which in the Old Testament is markedly eschatological—had appeared: "If I by the finger of God cast out devils, then is the kingdom of God come upon you."[2] The suggestion is therefore made by the modern eschatological school that it is quite wrong to interpret the eschatological language of the New Testament as primarily concerned with an historical event which is to occur at some unknown future date. Rather it describes what is happening now. It is fulfilled in the life, crucifixion and resurrection of Christ, and the Christian experiences it to-day. "Little children, it *is* the last hour"[3]; we are those "upon whom the ends of the ages are come."[4] "Our Lord's eschatological language," writes Hoskyns,

"as indeed all his teaching and actions, was mainly symbolical. To speak humanly, he felt himself standing on the brink of a new spiritual order, an order which was to come into being as a direct result of his life and death, and which was to be the fulfilment of the longings of the greatest of the Jewish prophets. To express this Gospel he used the traditional language of Jewish expectation of the End, since it provided him with a vehicle to express the significance of his life and death."[5]

And again, with reference to the Pentecost passage in Acts, he writes:

"The coming of the Spirit is the true eschatology, the End, the New Order of God."[6]

Turning now to Professor Dodd, the following passage is typical:

"The myth of a Last Judgment is a symbolical statement of the final resolution of the great conflict. Serious difficulties are raised if we attempt to treat it as a literal and quasi-historical statement that the succession of events in time will one day cease— once again an idea as inconceivable to us as its opposite [the other instance referred to is the story of Creation and the Fall]. Nor, I

---

[1] Acts ii. 14–21. Cf. Joel ii. 28–32. [2] Luke xi. 20. [3] 1 John ii. 18.
[4] 1 Cor. x. 11. [5] *Cambridge Sermons*, p. 31. [6] *Ibid.*, p. 30.

think, is it profitable to rationalize the myth as a prediction that
before man dies out of this earth, or before the earth itself perishes
in some astronomical catastrophe, the good will finally and
manifestly triumph over the evil in human history. Any such
rationalization is beside the true intention of the myth, which says
that the Last Judgment will supervene unexpectedly and unpre-
dictably upon a world showing no indication of its approach,
unless it be that 'the sky grows darker yet and the sea rises higher.'
That seems to imply that there is no moment in the world's history
which by historical necessity leads up to the judgment. Doomsday
simply takes a cut across the time-stream at any point and reveals
the triumph of the divine purpose in it. But this triumph is
something actually attained, not in some coming Day of the Lord,
near or distant, but in the concrete historical event of the death and
resurrection of Jesus Christ. It is significant that Christianity
separated off from the general expectation of Jewish eschatology
this concrete, historical element of 'realized eschatology,' leaving
the residue as a symbolical expression of the relation of *all* history
to the purpose of God. For the essential feature of the Last
Judgment is its universality. It includes 'the quick and the dead,'
i.e. all generations of mankind. It means that *all* history is com-
prehended in that achievement of the divine purpose of which the
coming of Christ, his death and resurrection, is the intra-historical
expression."[1]

Now it is impossible not to be struck by the great element of
truth of the most vital importance contained in this doctrine of
realized eschatology. It brings the Last Day into direct relevance
to every one of us, as something of which we have to take instant
account. And it exposes the superficiality of the type of Pelagian
humanism which looks upon the kingdom of God as an order of
merely human justice and sublunar happiness, to be set up simply
by man's own endeavour and manifested in freedom from world-
war and a vast extension of the social services. Nevertheless, it is
difficult to take it as doing full justice to the facts. We notice even
in Hoskyns a tendency to hedge on the question whether the
Second Coming of Christ is associated, as is his First Coming, with
a definite date in history. And when we come to consider Dodd,
although the matter is obscured by the difficulty of knowing
precisely what is the content given by him to the term "myth," it
seems fairly clear that for him eschatology simply describes the
mode of life and the relation to God upon which Christians have
entered through their incorporation into the crucified and

[1] *History and the Gospel*, p. 170.

ascended Christ; the eschatology is altogether "realized," and the whole of history from the Resurrection onwards is merely a "residue." Now this seems to be very unsatisfactory. For, in the first place, there is a mass of teaching in the New Testament itself which looks upon the Last Judgment as a future historical event, in spite of the difficulties that this raises. St. Paul did not take the simple course of allaying the misgivings of the Thessalonians by explaining to them that the Second Coming was only a vivid description of the state that they had been in ever since their baptism; on the contrary, he went into some very elaborate, rather obscure and not immediately convincing details about a future historical occurrence. Nor does the Book of Revelation suggest an altogether realized eschatology with no reference to the temporal future. And there are some hard things said in the Second Epistle to Timothy about Hymenaeus and Philetus, "men who concerning the truth have erred, saying that the resurrection is past already, and overthrow the faith of some."[1] And, unless we are to dismiss such Biblical passages as the apocalyptic discourse in the twenty-fifth chapter of St. Matthew as mere inventions of the early Church, we shall have, it is to be feared, to convict the incarnate Word of having given to his followers some extremely misleading teaching, which they have consistently failed to understand throughout the centuries. In Christ's own teaching we are told, not only that "the Kingdom of God is within you" —or "among you"[2]—but also that the Kingdom will have its appearance in the harvest which the angels will reap "at the end of the world."[3]

The second difficulty in Dodd's view is that it seems to deprive all human history since the Resurrection of Christ of any real significance. The time before the birth of Christ would indeed be a *praeparatio evangelica*, in which there could be discerned the convergence of manifold currents of the Holy Spirit's working, meeting together and finding their fulfilment in Christ. But all later history would be, in Dodd's phrase, simply a "residue," without any theological significance attaching to the sequence of events, since the Last Day would be already here, and we should be living in it.[4] It therefore seems highly relevant to inquire whether it may not be possible to understand the Second Coming,

[1] 2 Tim. ii. 17, 18.   [2] Luke xvii. 21.   [3] Matt. xiii. 37-43.
[4] See the criticisms of Dodd along these lines by Dr. E. R. Hardy, Jun., in *Theology*, Jan. and Feb. 1940, and by Dr. A. E. J. Rawlinson, in *Theology*, Feb. 1942.

the *Parousia*, of Christ as being, from the point of view of the chronological order which is inherent in the temporal character of the material world, an event which will take place at some future though unknown date through a supernatural act of God, and as being at the same time accessible to Christians as a present reality and as the fact that gives supreme significance to their life. If this is so, we shall not be under the necessity of rejecting either the "Pauline" doctrine of a future Parousia as being due to an over-literal acceptance of the ideas of Jewish apocalyptic, or the "Johannine" doctrine of "eternal life here and now" as being the result of gnostic influence upon the writer of the Fourth Gospel. And we shall be able without reserve to accept the eschatological utterances of our Lord, with their tantalizing inter-weaving of language referring to the immediate and to the distant future, without supposing either that he himself was mistaken about the way in which his victory was to be achieved or that the Gospels contain an altogether unreliable account of his teaching.

Now the view which I have expounded, of the relation of the Christian to the timelessness of God through his adoptive incor-poration into Christ, provides us with the required possibility. From the purely chronological point of view, in relation to the temporal ordering of past-present-and-future which is inherent in our nature as created bodily beings, who are, by their physical constitution, immersed in, and indeed part of, the realm of material existence, the Second Coming of Christ and the Last Judgment are future events whose date, were we granted the necessary fore-knowledge, we could specify as a particular day and year. Of its exact nature we are, of course, ignorant; and we need not take the imagery of the clouds and the trumpet as anything more than a symbolical form of words, providentially provided by God through the medium of Jewish apocalyptic, to give the most adequate expression possible in human language of something lying alto-gether outside the range of our past experience.[1] The Second Coming will, of course, inaugurate a radically different order of existence from that which we know at present; it will mark the end of what, in Dr. Whitehead's term, we might call "the present cosmic epoch."[2] The present order of things will pass away, there

---

[1] A similar use of symbols is, of course, to be found in the Biblical description of the Fall, with the two trees, the serpent, etc. And there too the question of the symbolic nature of the language is an entirely different one from the question as to whether what the language is describing is a past event in human history or merely a universal human experience. [2] *Process and Reality*, p. 126 *et al.*

will be "a new heaven and a new earth," and the New Jerusalem will descend to earth from heaven; *solvet saeclum in favilla*. Nevertheless, it will be an event in the course of history, even if in it history as we know it will come to an end. That is to say, the present chronological course of occurrences will continue until that moment arrives. The great event may, for all we know, put an end to time as we experience it; there may conceivably be nothing "after" it, as there was nothing "before" the temporal process began.[1] This does not deprive it of its character as a temporal event, though it does of course imply that its true significance is derived not from the temporal order but from the eternal. In this sense, then, the Parousia is in time, even if it is at the end of time. It may be, as some writers have said, in "another dimension"[2] than that of time, but if so, this other dimension at least intersects the time-dimension at some definite moment of the latter.

All this is true, but it is not the whole truth. For, as we have seen, by our adoptive union with the human nature of Christ, which is in turn hypostatically united with his divine Person, we are given, in the mode proper to us as creatures, a real participation in the eternity which is one aspect of the life of God. To him all things are present *simul et semel*, in one timeless act by which, existing outside time, he is related to every moment of the temporal process from its beginning to its end. To us, therefore, considered not from the point of view of our first creation but from that of our re-creation into Christ, the whole of history is present in a mysterious but none the less real way, and in particular we are brought into a concrete relation with all that has taken place or will take place in the human nature of Christ. This truth has, as we shall see, many and far-reaching implications; here we are concerned with it only as it brings us into relation with the Second Coming. The point is that, through our participation in the eternity of God, the Parousia is something of which we have a direct experience in virtue of our union with Christ, and the foreshortening of history, which is so marked a feature of the New-Testament writings, represents not merely a vivid psychological anticipation but an actual ontological relationship. Thus,

---

[1] The "beginning" and the "end" cannot, of course, be comparable in all respects, for at the beginning the created order began to exist, whereas the Second Coming and the Last Judgment will involve not our destruction but our transformation.

[2] This particular application of a metaphor from mathematics seems to me to obscure rather than to illuminate the problem.

while in the natural order the eschatological language of the New Testament refers for the Christian, as for everyone else, merely to future events of cataclysmic importance, in the supernatural order which is the possession of the Christian through his rebirth into Christ it describes the very nature of his present experience.

In this way, then, the disastrous antithesis between the two interpretations of the New-Testament eschatology is, I suggest, to be avoided. It enables us to take quite seriously the eschatological content which the Church has always known to be inherent in her nature, without making it necessary for us to eviscerate history by denying the reference of eschatology to a future event in which God's work will be consummated and his sovereignty vindicated. And it will explain the eschatological language which Christians have from time to time applied both to the Church and to the Eucharist. It is well known that the primitive Church saw in the Eucharist not only the memorial of the Passion of Christ but also his Second Coming, and there is a whole cycle of hymns in which the language of the Apocalypse about the New Jerusalem is applied to the Church of Christ. We may recall the noble sixth-or seventh-century poem which has become the office-hymn for the Feast of the Dedication of a Church.

> *Urbs beata Jerusalem dicta pacis visio,*
> *quae construitur in caelis vivis ex lapidibus,*
> *et angelis coronata ut sponsata comite,*
>
> *Nova veniens de caelo, nuptiali thalamo*
> *praeparata, ut sponsata copuletur domino;*
> *plateae et muri ejus ex auro purissimo.*

"Blessed City, heavenly Salem, vision dear of peace and love,
Who, of living stones upbuilded, art the joy of Heav'n above,
And, with angel cohorts circled, as a Bride to earth dost move.

From celestial realms descending, ready for the nuptial bed,
To his presence, deck'd with jewels, by her Lord shall she be led:
All her streets, and all her bulwarks, of pure gold are fashioned."[1]

This, however, takes us into questions which I shall discuss more fully later. It is enough here to note, after the somewhat long digressions into which we have been led, that in this chapter we have been considering the fact, fundamental to a proper understanding of the Christian life, that the Christian is a man or woman

[1] Trans. J. M. Neale.

who has been reborn by a real incorporation of his or her human nature into the human nature of the incarnate Word, and who has thus been taken up into the very life of the triune God. "Your life," wrote St. Paul to the Colossians, "is hid with Christ in God."[1]

[1] Col. iii. 3.

CHAPTER VII

THE MYSTICAL BODY OF CHRIST

I

BECOMING a Christian, as we have seen, means being incorporated into the human nature of Christ, the very human nature which he united to his divine Person in the womb of the Blessed Virgin and which he offered upon the Cross as "a full, perfect and sufficient sacrifice, oblation and satisfaction for the sins of the whole world," the human nature which in his Resurrection and Ascension has been glorified and set free from the spatial limitations of ordinary human existence. This adoptive union with the triumphant Christ is altogether unique in its kind; it involves a real participation in Christ's human nature on the part of the believer and a real communication of it to him. By it the believer's own human nature is not destroyed but is strengthened and perfected by its grafting into the archetypal human nature of the Ascended Lord. There is no destruction of the created person, nor in being supernaturalized is he removed from the natural order. His life as a citizen of Earth continues, but he has a new and greater citizenship in Heaven. He is a new man, because he has been re-created in the New Adam. And because the Christ is both God and man, the Christian, by his incorporation into Christ, has received a share in the life of God himself. He has been made a partaker of the divine nature, the nature of God who is Trinity. His life is hid with Christ in God.

It is this fact of incorporation and adoption that is the onto-logical basis of the Christian Church. Many writers in recent years have pointed out that the New Testament knows nothing of an isolated Christian, a Christian outside the Church. Becoming a Christian and becoming a member of the Church are synonymous; faith and baptism are conjoined. This is not, moreover, a merely arbitrary prescription either of Christ or his followers; it arises out of the very nature of Christian adoption. For if we are each of us really and not merely by imputation united to Christ, we are by that very fact united to one another. If our adoption into Christ's sonship is ontological and not merely legal, so is our brotherhood with one another. If we are each of us members of Christ, then we are collectively his body. So St. Paul writes to the Romans: "We who are many are one body in Christ and severally members one of another."[1] To the Corinthians he says: "Ye are the body of Christ and severally members thereof."[2] And this is no novel doctrine in Anglicanism. Hooker, after insisting that we participate Christ not only by imputation but by "habitual and real infusion," writes as follows:

"From hence it is that they which belong to the mystical body of our Saviour Christ, and be in number as the stars of heaven, divided successively by reason of their mortal condition into many generations, are notwithstanding coupled every one to Christ their Head, and all unto every particular person amongst themselves, inasmuch as the same Spirit, which anointed the blessed soul of our Saviour Christ, doth so formalize, unite and actuate his whole race, as if both he and they were so many limbs compacted into one body, by being quickened all with one and the same soul."[3]

We must therefore take quite seriously the Pauline terminology in which the Church is described as the Body of Christ. This does not, of course, mean that we can find in the Church an exact duplication of the various organs of a physical body; the efforts of some Roman-Catholic writers to particularize the Church's heart and neck seem to be somewhat strained, and to extend the identification to other organs would become rapidly ludicrous and irreverent. Even the description of the Holy Spirit as the soul of the Church requires careful qualification.[4] In St. Paul's writings themselves we find a double conception of the Body. In some passages Christ is spoken of as the Head, and the Church as the Body which belongs to it: "He is the Head of the Body the Church";[5] "Christ also is the Head of the Church, being himself the saviour of the Body."[6] In other places Christ is the Body itself and the

[1] Rom. xii. 5.   [2] 1 Cor. xii. 27.
[3] *Eccl. Pol.*, V, lvi, 11: ed. of 1888, II, p. 254. The passage immediately preceding this has been quoted on p. 83 *supra*.
[4] Among various uses of the phrase, "soul of the Church," the following may be noted: (1) the Holy Spirit (e.g. in Congar, *Divided Christendom*, pp. 57, 82); (2) the inner essence of the Church as contrasted with its outward expression (*ibid.*, p. 80); (3) sincere non-Catholics as contrasted with explicit Catholics (this use appears to occur first in Bellarmine; cf. Congar, *ibid.*, p. 224). In the most immediate and obvious sense the soul of the Church would mean simply the human soul of Christ, which still persists as an element in his human nature in its glorified state.
[5] Col. i. 18.   [6] Eph. v. 23.

individual Christians are his members: "As the Body is one and hath many members, and all the members of the body, being many, are one body, so also is Christ."[1] Furthermore, the word "head" itself, though less strongly in Greek than in English, bears, besides its physiological sense, the suggestion of "governor" or "chief"; it is interesting to note that Mersch in his great work, *Le Corps Mystique du Christ* has to ring the changes on the words *tête* and *chef*[2] in order to bring out the full meaning. Moreover, the word Christ itself, which in English has become to all intents and purposes a personal name of the Saviour, is in the Greek simply the equivalent of the Hebrew *Mashiach* (Messiah), "the anointed one"; and in the Bible it can suggest the anointed people of God as well as the personal deliverer. Mersch refers in this connection to the scholastic discussions of the question whether Christ is himself a member of the Body.[3] The existence of these verbal nuances, however, strengthens the argument. For the relation of Christians to Christ is not one of external juxtaposition; it involves even more intimacy and interpenetration than exist between the head and the body of a man. The Christian is re-created into Christ. Christ's life becomes his life, and Christ's sonship his sonship. In the order of supernature he is identified with the Saviour in every- thing except his indestructible and inconvertible personal indi- viduality; *Christianus alter Christus.* "As the body is one and hath many members, and all the members of the body, being many, are one body, so also is"—not Christians, but—"Christ." St. Thomas, who of all the scholastics has his feet perhaps most firmly set upon the earth, goes so far as to say:

> "Just as a natural body is one whole, composed of many members, so the whole Church, which is the Mystical Body of Christ, is *reckoned as one person with its Head*, who is Christ."[4]

Fr. de Lubac writes as follows:

> "The Pauline metaphor of the body—which in itself was in no way original—does indeed take on a most striking meaning from the fact that Paul does not say merely 'the body of the Christians,' as we might say 'the body of the Greeks' or 'the body of the Jews,' but 'the body of Christ,' and that he comments on it in the

---

[1] 1 Cor. xii. 12.

[2] Part III, ch. vi. The difference does not appear in the English translation, *The Whole Christ.*   [3] *The Whole Christ*, p. 460 f.

[4] *S. Theol.*, III, xlix, 1c. The context is a discussion as to how the death of Christ can avail for his members.

formula which he repeats incessantly, 'in Christ, in Christ Jesus.'
If in St. John the bond between the faithful, as between them and
their Saviour, is suggested as a collection of reciprocal relations
of intense intimacy, in St. Paul Christ appears rather as a medium,
an atmosphere, a world where man and God, and man and man,
are in communion and unity."[1]

I need not attempt to amass the evidence from the New-
Testament writings and from the fathers in support of the contention that, while it contains of course a certain element of
metaphor, the description of the Church as the Body of Christ is
to be taken ontologically and realistically. That has been done
with complete adequacy in the great works of Mersch, Thornton
and de Lubac.[2] But it will be worth while, I think, to observe the
way in which the conception that a man will form of the nature of
the Church is determined by his view of the relation of the
Christian to Christ. Fr. Congar has given an illuminating
demonstration of this by taking the two extreme cases of traditional
Protestantism and Eastern Orthodoxy.

"Extreme Protestants," he writes, "do not believe in the real
and actual gift of the divine life to human nature: they believe
that this life is only promised, albeit truly promised, and it is
regarded as purely eschatological. In this perspective the benefits
of the Covenant are not actually present in the Church under a
form homogeneous to human nature: nature's part as such is non-
existent. Thus the Church in her human and social form may
proclaim and promise; may be, like John the Baptist, the call to,
and the finger pointing out, the Christ, but it is not the incarnation
of the power of God, which under forms connatural to mankind
expresses and effects, in their initial stages, the realities of the new
Covenant and of the heritage of God. Logically, the institutional
Church does not exist for them in the Christian sense; it is only the
community of those who have heard the promise."[3]

I must point out, in passing, that this distinctive feature is to be
seen even when, as has been increasingly the case in the last few
years, Protestant theologians have put the idea of the Church in
the forefront of their doctrinal presentation. Thus, for example,
Mr. D. T. Jenkins, in his important and stimulating book, *The
Nature of Catholicity*, sees the essence of the Church's catholicity to

---

[1] *Catholicisme*, p. 19.
[2] E. Mersch, S.J., *Le Corps Mystique du Christ*: E.T., *The Whole Christ*. L. S. Thornton,
C.R., *The Common Life in the Body of Christ*. H. de Lubac, S.J., *Catholicisme: les aspects
sociaux du dogme*.   [3] *Divided Christendom*, p. 91.

lie in her faithfulness to the apostolic testimony. She is catholic
and apostolic only in so far as she proclaims this testimony; she is
thus constantly under the judgment of the Word of God, as that
Word speaks through the Scriptures, and "reformation according
to the Word of God" is the perpetual condition of her life. In
consequence, the Bible, so far from being her own book which she
is qualified to interpret and expound, is something standing "over
against" her as her judge and in a position of isolation from her.
How closely this view of the Church corresponds to the classical
Protestant doctrine of justification as imputation will be clear;
neither the Christian nor the Church is seen as ontologically
cohering in the glorified manhood of Christ; Christ is "over
against" them both.[1] Mr. Jenkins's book is, however, a healthy
reminder that the Church in her empirical manifestation may often
belie her real essence; there is no Christian body which has not
exhibited the need for reformation in the course of its history.

Turning to the Eastern Orthodox, Fr. Congar remarks that,
with their Platonic leanings, the Easterns look for explanation of
the visible world primarily in terms of formal, where the West
looks for it in terms of efficient, causality. The East thinks about
similitude and participation, the West of creation.

"For the East, man is by nature a similitude of God, albeit an
imperfect one, which grace will make perfect by transforming
him, so to say, into his true self; the Christian life is a progressive
transfiguration into the likeness of God, a realization of the eternal
in time, and of the spiritual in the sensible, a transforming

[1] These remarks do little justice to the worth of Mr. Jenkins's book as a whole.
See Fr. A. G. Hebert's discussion in *The Form of the Church* and Mr. G. B. Bentley's
review-article in *Sobornost*', June 1943.
Mersch remarks that Protestant theologians, even when they speak of the Church
as the Mystical Body, interpret this in a different way from Catholics. "The incorporation in Christ which they prize so highly becomes a nonentity. It seems to be
everything; it seems to give us the whole life of Christ: for he alone is holy; he alone
lives, with an eternal life; we have no life but his, and we have all of that life. Yes,
indeed. But according to their doctrine this life does not vivify. Like justification, of
which it is one aspect, this life remains external to us; the Mystical Body as they
describe it possesses life, to be sure, but a life that is outside the body itself. The body
is dead; it lies in closest proximity to the Living One, but it is a corpse, none the less."
(*The Whole Christ*, p. 504.) Wilberforce has pointed out that the same extrinsicism is
to be found in the Lutheran doctrine of the Eucharist, according to which the presence
of Christ, while it is real, is given not as an instrument of sanctification, but as the most
solemn symbol possible of the justification that has already taken place. (*Doctrine of
the Holy Eucharist*, p. 129 f.) In this latter connection Dom Gregory Dix has remarked
that the sixteenth-century Eucharistic controversies were really only by-products
of the dispute about justification. (*The Parish Communion*, p. 136.) It is, of course,
a matter for gratitude that in practice Protestants do not always adhere to the strict
consequences of their doctrines.

illumination of human nature. For the West, the Christian life is not so much a realization of the divine in humanity as the pilgrimage of man towards God. Less is said of 'deification' (*theosis*) than of 'beatitude.' . . .

"As to the Church," Fr. Congar continues, "for the East it is, above all, the coming of the eternal into time, of the invisible into the visible, the sphere of the deifying transformation of humanity by worship and the sacraments. . . . She is looked upon less as a religious *societas* whose Founder is Christ, and more as a manifestation of him, as his sacrament (*mysterium*), his theophany, or, so to speak, his icon. . . .

"In the West, to be sure, nothing of this is denied. . . . But the West was more apt to consider the Church in its aspect of a society possessed of certain powers, a certain constitution, and certain prerogatives, over against the civil society. The Church was indeed a mystical reality of life with God, by Christ, in the Holy Ghost, but she was also very definitely a Church Militant, a sphere of moral activity for the triumph of the Sovereign Good."[1]

I am far from wishing to suggest that these differences of emphasis are absolute and irreconcilable. Indeed, the increased place which is being given to-day to the doctrine of the Church as the Mystical Body of Christ by Western theologians may offer a new possibility of understanding between East and West. It has indeed been the East rather than the West that has in the past been really explicit about the Mystical Body; the writings of the Russians on *sobornost'*, the Catholicity or "togetherness" of the Church, are the most notable instances of this. I remember hearing it remarked some years ago that a book with the title "The Body of Christ," if it were by an Eastern writer, would almost certainly be a treatise on the Church, while, if it were by a Western, it would be about the Blessed Sacrament; but I am not sure that this remark would be as true to-day. That there are outstanding differences of emphasis is clear, but it is difficult to believe that they are really irreconcilable; and perhaps even the Protestant theologians may come to see that their tremendous conviction of the omnipotent *fiat* of the transcendent God has as its necessary consequence that God does not impute without imparting or

[1] *Divided Christendom*, pp. 201–2. For Orthodox expositions of the Church, see A. Khomiakov's essay in *Russia and the English Church*, ch. xxiii; V. Solovyev, *God, Man and the Church*, Part II, ch. ii; G. Florovsky's essay in *The Church of God*; S. Bulgakov, *The Orthodox Church*, ch. i; F. Gavin, *Greek Orthodox Thought*, lect. iv; S. Zankov, *The Eastern Orthodox Church*, ch. iii.

account a man righteous without re-creating him. Our differences may then be brought vastly nearer reconciliation.

II

In the last chapter, after considering the primary fact of adoption into Christ we went on to discuss the elevation of the Christian into the life of God. Because he was a member of Christ, he was the child of God, and because he was the child of God, he was an inheritor of the Kingdom of Heaven. His life was hid with Christ in God; he was a partaker of the divine nature. For by his adoptive union with the human nature of Christ he was taken up into that eternal act of loving response with which the Son ever regards the Father in the interior life of the Holy Trinity. Now just as the doctrine of man's incorporation into Christ has its analogue in the sphere of the Church, so has the doctrine of man's participation in the divine nature. In Congar's phrase, the Church is not only *Ecclesia ex hominibus* and *in Christo*; she is also *Ecclesia de Trinitate*.[1] The life of the Church is the life of the Trinity imparted to men; if we may say with Bossuet that the Church is *Jésus-Christ répandu et communiqué*, we may also say with Congar that "the Church is not merely *a* Society, men associated with God, but the divine *Societas* itself, the life of the Godhead reaching out to humanity and taking up humanity into itself."[2] The life by which the Church lives is nothing less than a created participation in the life by which God himself lives, in which the three divine Persons are knit together in complete mutual interpenetration and love. In the words of a Russian theologian, "the Church is the likeness of the existence of the Holy Trinity, a likeness in which many become one."[3] The Church's unity, therefore, is not just the empirical unity that is set up by the common activity of Christians through ecclesiastical organizations, necessary as those organizations are. Organization itself, even Church organization, is something on the natural level, not the supernatural, though like all else on the natural level it can be supernaturalized. The manifestation of common activity and mutual co-operation among Christians is the *result* of the Church's unity, not its essence. The unity of the Church is the Church's participation in the unity of God the Holy Trinity. And the bond of the Church's unity is the same as

---

[1] *Divided Christendom*, ch. ii.   [2] *Ibid.*, p. 48.
[3] Metropolitan Antony Khrapovitsky, quoted by Florovsky, *The Church of God*, p. 61.

I

the bond of unity of the Godhead, namely the Holy Spirit. We are therefore praying in strict accordance with theology when we sing :

> "As thou in bond of love dost join
> The Father and the Son,
> So fill us all with mutual love
> And knit our hearts in one,"

or when the time immediately before Whitsunday is devoted to prayer for Christian unity.

"Thus therefore we see," writes Richard Hooker, in a passage of remarkable eloquence,

"how the Father is in the Son, and the Son in the Father; how they both are in all things, and all things in them; what communion Christ hath with his Church, how his Church and every member thereof is in him by original derivation, and he personally in them by way of mystical association wrought through the gift of the Holy Ghost, which they that are his receive from him, and together with the same what benefit soever the vital force of his body and blood may yield, yea by steps and degrees they receive the complete measure of all such divine grace, as doth sanctify and save throughout, till the day of their final exaltation to a state of fellowship in glory, with him whose partakers they are now in those things that tend to glory."[1]

Through her elevation into the life of God, the Church, like the individual Christian, participates in God's timelessness in a created mode. "In the life and existence of the Church," writes Dr. Florovsky,

"time is mysteriously overcome and mastered, time, so to speak, *stands still*. It stands still not only because of the power of historical memory, or of imagination, which can 'fly over the double barrier of time and space'; it stands still, because of the power of grace, which gathers together in catholic unity of life that which had become separated by walls built in the course of time. . . . *The Church is the living image of eternity within time*."[2]

I shall point out later the significance of this for Eucharistic theology. Here we need only recognize that the transcendence of time which the individual possesses as a member of Christ is equally the possession of the Church as the Bride of Christ. And it

---

[1] *Eccl. Pol.*, V, lvi, 13: ed. of 1888, II, p. 255. He adds the caution: "As for any mixture of the substance of his flesh with ours, the participation which we have of Christ includeth no such kind of gross surmise."

[2] *The Church of God*, p. 63 (italics mine).

receives a most moving expression in the great solemnities of the Church's liturgical action. The Church's worship, as Professor Sergius Bulgakov has remarked,

"is not only the commemoration, in artistic forms, of evangelical or other events concerning the Church. It is also the actualization of these facts, their re-enactment on the earth. During the service of Christmas there is not merely the memory of the birth of Christ, but truly Christ is born in a mysterious manner, just as at Easter he is resurrected. It is the same in the Transfiguration, the Entry into Jerusalem, the mystery of the Last Supper, the Passion, the burial and the Ascension of Christ, and also of all the events of the life of the Holy Virgin, from the Nativity to the Assumption. *The life of the Church, in these services, makes actual for us the mystery of the Incarnation.* Our Lord continues to live in the Church in the same form in which he was manifested once on earth and which exists for ever; and it is given to the Church to make living these sacred memories so that we should be their new witnesses and participate in them."[1]

The quotations which I have just cited are from Eastern theologians. This sense of timelessness is not, however, confined to the Eastern Church, though it is there that its penetration of the forms of worship is fullest. We see it in the canon of the Latin Mass, in the reference to the sacrifices of Abel, Abraham and Melchizedek, but perhaps its most eloquent expression is in the great rite of Holy Saturday. In the chant with which the paschal candle is blessed, the faithful are declared to be actually present at the great redemptive acts of Old-Testament history in which the supreme redemptive act of Christ's Passion was prefigured.

"This is the paschal feast wherein the true Lamb is slain, by whose blood the doorposts of the faithful are consecrated. This is the night wherein of old thou didst lead forth our fathers, the children of Israel, out of Egypt and madest them to pass on dry land through the Red Sea. This is indeed the night that with the pillar of fire purged away the shades of sin. . . . This is the night wherein, having broken the bonds of death, Christ ascendeth victorious from hell."

Then, after the singing of the Prophecies, whose range extends from the Creation and the Fall, through the Flood, the Story of Abraham and Isaac, the Exodus, the Passover and the other great moments of Jewish history to the mysterious presence of the Son of

[1] *The Orthodox Church*, p. 150 (italics mine).

God with the three heroes in the fiery furnace, the water is blessed for the baptism of the catechumens in words of universal import:

"I bless thee, O creature of water, by the living God, the true God, the holy God, by God who in the beginning separated thee from the dry land by his word, whose Spirit moved over thee; who made thee to flow from the fountain of Paradise, and commanded thee to water the whole earth with thy four rivers; who in the desert, when thou wast bitter, bestowed upon thee sweetness and made thee into drink, and brought thee forth from the rock for a thirsting people. I bless thee also through Jesus Christ his only Son our Lord, who by his power in Cana of Galilee changed thee in a wondrous miracle into wine; who walked upon thee with his feet, and was baptized in thee by John in Jordan; who brought thee forth together with blood from his side, and commanded his disciples that those who believe should be baptized in thee. . . ."

In words such as these the Church has given expression to her sense of the timelessness which is hers by her union with her Lord.

III

We must now notice two properties which the Church, as the Mystical Body of Christ, shares with other living bodies. The first is that she is in process of growth. In a purely geographical sense this is obvious; as the centuries have passed since the first Whitsunday, so the Church has, though not without such notable setbacks as the extermination of the great Christian bodies of North Africa and Persia, progressively increased the area of her conquest and the number of her earthly members. But there is a deeper significance than this. For Christians do not cease to exist when they die, and the Church of Christ is not confined to those who are now on earth. The relevant fact is not that there are more Christians in England now than there were in the reign of Queen Elizabeth or that the Christian Church is now active in lands that were unknown to Gregory the Great or Francis of Assisi. Each generation of Christians is taken up into an already existing unity, not in order to take the place of its past and present members but to enter into a perpetual fellowship with them. Thus, even if only six converts were made to Christianity in the course of a century, the Church would nevertheless be greater at the end of that century by precisely half a dozen members. It is not a question of succession but of incorporation; by his baptism a man enters into the communion of the saints. The Church is thus antecedent to the individual Christians, first of all because Christ is antecedent to them and entry into the Church means entry into Christ, and secondly because the Church embraces in her unity all those who have become already hers. "We are sometimes asked to think," said Archbishop Frederick Temple, in a famous sermon,

"that the Church only exists in the union of believers, and has no reality of its own. Now, it is perfectly clear that in the New Testament the idea of the Church is not that. Men speak as if Christians came first, and the Church after; as if the origin of the Church was in the wills of the individual Christians who composed it. But, on the contrary, throughout the teaching of the Apostles we see that it is the Church that comes first, and the members of it afterwards. Men were not brought to Christ and then determined that they would live in a community. Men were not brought to Christ to believe in him and in his Cross, and to recognize the duty of worshipping the Heavenly Father in his name, and then decided that it would be a great help to their religion that they should join one another in that worship, and should be united in the bonds of fellowship for that purpose. In the New Testament, on the contrary, the Kingdom of Heaven is already in existence, and men are invited into it. The Church takes its origin not in the will of man, but in the will of the Lord Jesus Christ. He sent forth his Apostles; the Apostles received their commission from him; they were not organs of the congregations; they were ministers of the Lord himself. He sent them forth to gather all the thousands that they could reach within his fold; but they came first, and the members came afterwards; and the Church in all its dignity and glory was quite independent of the members that were brought within it. Everywhere men are called in; they do not come in, and make the Church by coming. They are called in to that which already exists; they are recognized as members when they are within; but their membership depends upon their admission, and not upon their constituting themselves into a body in the sight of the Lord. . . . In the New Testament the Church flows out from the Lord, not flows into him. In the New Testament the life and the power which constitute the Church begins above, and not here on earth. In the New Testament the ministers are sent forth to bring the children of men within the fold, and are not simply selected by the members of the Church to help them in their spiritual life."[1]

[1] Sermon preached when Bishop of London on the Consecration Day of Truro Cathedral. (*Twelve Sermons . . .*, p. 17.)

If, therefore, the Whole Christ consists of both Head and members, the point of the great Pauline passage in the fourth chapter of Ephesians becomes clear:

> "He gave some to be apostles; and some, prophets; and some, evangelists; and some, pastors and teachers; for the perfecting of the saints, unto the work of ministering, *unto the building up of the body of Christ*: till we all attain unto the unity of the faith, and of the knowledge of the Son of God, unto a full-grown man, *unto the measure of the stature of the fullness of Christ*: that we . . . may grow up in all things into him, which is the head, even Christ; from whom all the body fitly framed and knit together through that which every joint supplieth, according to the working in due measure of each several part, maketh the increase of the body unto the building up of itself in love."[1]

Here, we see, Christ is the Head of the Body and we are his members; and the Body is still, through the labours of the Apostles and the other ministers, being built up. And what it is being built up into is not a mere aggregation of individuals, but "a full-grown man," "the fullness of Christ." In other words, while Christ as Head of the Body is perfect, Christ as Body-and-Head (*Totus Christus, membra cum capite*) is incomplete. In his natural body there is no imperfection of any kind, and the natural body is the very principle of life of the Mystical Body. In one sense he is perfect without us; in another, he needs us for his perfection. For, as St. Paul wrote elsewhere, we "are all *one man* [εἷς] in Christ Jesus."[2]

We may sum this up in the glowing words of Augustine:

> "Our Lord Jesus Christ, like a whole and perfect man, is Head and body. . . . His body is the Church, not simply the Church that is in this particular place, but both the Church that is here and the Church which extends over the whole earth; not simply the Church that is living to-day, but the whole race of saints, from Abel down to all those who will ever be born and will believe in Christ until the end of the world, for all belong to one city. This city is the body of Christ. . . . This is the whole Christ: Christ united with the Church."[3]

Closely connected with this fact of growth is the second characteristic which the Church shares with other living bodies, namely that of possessing a structure. Even in the biological realm it is true that to be recognizable as a genuine organism it is

---

[1] Eph. iv. 11–16.   [2] Gal. iii. 28.
[3] *In Ps. xc* (P.B.V., xci), *Sermo* 2, no. 1; quoted by Mersch, *The Whole Christ*, p. 415.

necessary for a living substance to possess a certain differentiation of parts and a certain organization of the various functions which they serve. If all the cells that go to make up the body are precisely similar in structure and function, it is difficult to know whether the aggregation of cells can properly be described as a multicellular individual at all and should not rather be considered as a colony of unicellular individuals. Now, with regard to the Church, whose life is a supernatural and sacramental life and whose unity is a supernatural and sacramental unity, this differentiation too must presumably be of the supernatural and sacramental order; the need cannot be met by any humanly imposed ordering, as for example a ministry owing its form and authority merely to ecclesiastical organization. We are concerned with something more than churchwardens, incumbents, archdeacons and so forth. Now the ministry as it is conceived in Catholic theology meets this requirement in every respect. It exists indeed not apart from the Church, but *in* the Church and *for* the Church; it is an organ of the Church's very life. But it does not come *from* the Church, but from Christ who is the Church's Head; and one of the truths that recent New-Testament study has brought into prominence is that the Apostolate, no less than the Church itself, is inherent in the evangelical deposit.[1] That the Church is itself priestly, that there is a "priesthood of all believers" and that this priesthood is nothing

---

[1] Cf. A. M. Ramsey, *The Gospel and the Catholic Church*, chs. v, vi. Cf. the words of Dr. William Temple in his Presidential Address to the Convocation of Canterbury on May 25th 1943:

"When we go back to the first records of the Church we find neither a Ministry which called people into association with it, nor an undifferentiated fellowship which delegated powers to a Ministry: but we find a complete Church, with the Apostolate accepted as its focus of administration and authority. When the Lord's earthly ministry was ended, there was found in the world as its fruit and as means of its continuance this Body, in which the distinction of Ministry and Laity is already established. The Apostles were in no sense ministers of the Laity; they were ministers of Christ to the laity, and to the world waiting to be won. They took steps for the perpetuation of the ministry, and it has descended to ourselves. So when I consecrate a godly and well learned man to the office and work of a Bishop in the Church of God, I do not act as a representative of the Church, if by that is meant the whole number of contemporary Christians; but I do act as the ministerial instrument of Christ in his Body the Church. The authority by which I act is his, transmitted to me through his apostles and those to whom they committed it; I hold it neither from the Church nor apart from the Church, but from Christ in the Church."

It may be added that the commonly heard description of the ordained minister as "representing" the Church, while it can be given a legitimate meaning, only too often seems to be based upon a degenerate medieval doctrine, which has persisted through the Reformation and is as widespread among Protestants as among Catholics to-day, according to which the minister was a kind of substitute who did things "instead of" the people. The primitive view was, of course, that clergy and laity had each their different, organically related and equally necessary parts in the action of the one Body of Christ. See the description of the early Eucharist below.

other than a participation in the one and only self-sufficient priesthood, which is that of Jesus Christ the Great High Priest, we may well admit. This does not destroy the possibility that this priesthood may be participated in different modes, in order that the priestly action of the Church may be not merely a loose association of isolated "atomic" acts, but shall be the united and unified activity of an organism, whose one life permeates all the parts and is lived in each of them. The true function and nature of the Christian ministry is most clearly seen in the performance of the Eucharistic Liturgy, especially in the form which it had in the earliest days, before the vicissitudes of the Church's history had contributed, together with much enrichment and beautification, to a certain blurring of outline and loss of primitive purity. In the Eucharist of the second century, as Dom Gregory Dix has described it in his essay in *The Parish Communion*,[1] the true organic nature of the Church as the Body of Christ is manifest. The Bishop, as the local representative of the Fatherhood of God and the Priesthood of Christ, sits or stands behind the altar flanked by the presbyters and closely attended by two of the deacons, and faces over the altar towards the rest of the deacons and the laity. He is the central figure in the household of God and the priestly Body of Christ, which is assembled for its Liturgy, its *common work*. The laity are the λαός τοῦ θεοῦ, the People of God, and there is no exclusion of the Lord's People from the sanctuary, as will be necessary in later days when the Church has become swamped with half-converted baptized heathen; there is no expression of fear or abasement, for these are the children of God in their Father's house. The oblations are their offering, and they bring them themselves to the deacons, who place them on the altar. And when, through the lips of the Bishop, "the cup and the bread receives the Word of God and becomes the Body and Blood of Christ,"[2] the faithful approach to partake of the Holy Gifts, and the Mystical Body is fed with the Sacramental Body.[3] The Bishop is by no means a mere delegate of the people. He stands in their midst as the representative of Christ; to the Mystical Body he is the visible embodiment of its invisible Head. But he is among them as he that serveth, not as lording it over the flock of Christ.

The doctrine of the Apostolic Succession is thus entirely coherent with the Christian Gospel. If the Church were nothing more than

---

[1] This description is based mainly upon the *Apostolic Tradition* of Hippolytus.
[2] Irenaeus, *Haer.*, v, 2, 3.   [3] See p. 163 f. *infra*.

a society formed by the voluntary association of those individual Christians who are now on earth, then its ministry, if indeed a ministry were then necessary at all, might be sufficiently conferred in any way that they themselves might contrive. But if the Church is rooted in the concrete historical events of the incarnation, death and resurrection of Christ, and if we who are now on earth are only the last of sixty or so generations of Christians who have each in its turn made up the earthly Church, then surely it is most significant that the Bishop who exercises the pastoral care and government of the faithful in each place has received his commission and his sacerdotal character not merely from that small and struggling part of the Church which is now militant on earth, but, by a kind of spiritual and sacramental inheritance, from the generations of the past. There is a fine phrase in which tradition has been described as "the democracy of the dead," and in this sense the apostolic succession is truly democratic. But, since Christ has overcome death and opened unto us the gate of everlasting life, the Church which was once militant here upon earth in the past is the Church which is now triumphant and expectant beyond the grave. This is therefore not just the democracy of the dead but of the living, as God himself is not the God of the dead but of the living. The Bishop is therefore not merely the organ of the earthly Church, whether of the past or of the present, but of the whole Church of Christ, here and beyond the grave. And the sinful man on whom priestly character is conferred in ordination receives the Holy Ghost for the office and work of a priest not only in the Church of England or even in the Church militant, but, as the Anglican ordinal itself says in its ordination-formula, "in the Church of God."[1]

One thing more must be added to make this consideration complete. The common phrase, "apostolic succession," is quite correct if it is used to describe the relation of the bishop to the earthly Church. It is in virtue of their consecration that bishops conse-

[1] A tacit assumption that the Church through which a bishop or priest receives his consecration or ordination is merely the earthly Church seems to underlie the discussion of the Ministry given by the late Dr. Quick in his book, *The Christian Sacraments* (ch. vii); it leads to the conclusion that "in a divided Church the validity of orders becomes inevitably a matter of degree" (p. 145). If, however, the Church by which and in which a man is ordained is not just the empirically manifested Church now militant on earth, but the archetypal Church which is nothing less than Christ's own manhood into which generations of Christians have been incorporated, the conclusion fails. It is not the "black" imperfect empirical Church that is the source of the priestly character, but the "comely" Church, of which the empirical Church is but the local and passing manifestation and which is itself the Body and Bride of Christ.

crate other bishops and that bishop succeeds bishop in his see. In relation, however, to the whole Church of Christ, here and beyond the grave, the *Totus Christus* which is *membra cum capite*, there is no succession because there is no demise. Instead, there is incorporation into the apostolic college by the communication of the apostolic character. The Apostolate receives a new member, who is then part of it as the first apostles were. Just as baptism takes a man or woman up into an already existing unity, so consecration takes a man up into an already existing unity, a unity which exists within and for the sake of the former one. And so, in lesser mode, does ordination to the diaconate and to the priesthood; and so, it may be suggested, in a lesser mode still does confirmation. The Christian ministry is thus the means by which the priestly activity of Christ is perpetuated in his Church, and through it the Church's structure as not merely an aggregation of priestly individuals, but a coherent and differentiated priestly organism—"a spiritual house, a holy priesthood . . . an elect race, a royal priesthood, a people for God's own possession"[1]—is maintained and preserved.[2]

IV

In the New Testament, side by side with the conception of the Church as Christ's Body there appears the conception of the Church as his Bride. There is indeed one great passage in the Epistle to the Ephesians in which, basing his teaching upon the Old Testament doctrine that a man and his wife are "one flesh"—a doctrine which Christ himself endorsed[3]—St. Paul sees these two truths as implied in each other:

"The husband is the head of the wife, as Christ also is the head of the Church, being himself the saviour of the Body. But as the

---

[1] i Pet. ii. 5, 9.

[2] I have assumed what would appear to be the primitive view, that it is the bishop who possesses the plenitude of the priestly office, and that the presbyterate enjoys a partial and delegated (i.e., sacramentally, not merely juridically delegated) share in this. But the essential point is not lost if it is held that the presbyterate is the fully priestly order, the episcopate possessing something *more* than priesthood, though the centrality of the bishop will then become rather less sacramental and rather more jurisdictional. Dom Gregory Dix holds (see his articles on "Jurisdiction in the Early Church" in *Laudate*, 1937–8, and his edition of the *Apostolic Tradition*) that in primitive times, while the priestly function was concentrated in the bishop, the jurisdictional power was exclusively vested in the *presbyterium*: cf. Jalland on "The Government of the Church," in *Thy Household the Church*, p. 24, and in *The Church and the Papacy*, p. 143, *et al.*, for some discussion of this question.

[3] Gen. ii. 23, 24; Matt. xix. 5; Mark x. 7.

Church is subject to Christ, so let the wives also be to their husbands in everything. Husbands, love your wives, even as Christ also loved the Church, and gave himself up for it; that he might sanctify it, having cleansed it by the washing of water with the word, that he might present the Church to himself a glorious Church, not having spot or wrinkle or any such thing; but that it should be holy and without blemish. Even so ought husbands also to love their own wives as their own bodies. He that loveth his own wife loveth himself: for no man ever hated his own flesh; but nourisheth it and cherisheth it, even as Christ also the Church; because we are members of his Body. For this cause shall a man leave his father and mother, and shall cleave to his wife; and the twain shall become one flesh. This mystery is great: but I speak in regard of Christ and of the Church."[1]

This nuptial relationship of the Church to Christ has been traced out in detail by Mr. Claude Chavasse in his book, *The Bride of Christ*, which, if not altogether exempt from criticism on certain points, is nevertheless of the greatest value. He shows that the basis of the doctrine is the Old-Testament figure of the marriage of Jehovah to his people Israel, a marriage which is sealed by a covenant; it follows in consequence that apostasy or idolatry is a form of adultery. That this conception is fulfilled in the person of Christ is, he argues, shown by the title of the Bridegroom by which Christ is designated and by the repeated use in the Gospels of the image of the wedding-feast.[2] Mr. Chavasse attractively urges that in all probability we ought to think of the Last Supper as not only the Passover meal but also the marriage-feast of the Bridegroom. "Essentially," he writes,

"the Passover itself was nuptial. The foundation of the marriage between Yahweh and his People was the Covenant between them. That Covenant was made and ratified by the Passover. It is therefore no playing with words, but the sober truth, to say that Jesus, if not enacting *a* marriage at the Last Supper, was solemnizing *the* Marriage between himself and his Church in this, the New Covenant."[3]

---

[1] Eph. v. 23–32. It is interesting to note how, both in Scripture and the fathers, important theological passages often occur almost accidentally. Here St. Paul's tremendous doctrine of the Church is brought in to illustrate his teaching about human marriage. It has been remarked concerning 1 Cor. xi that, if someone had not come to the sacrament at Corinth the worse for drink, there would be no evidence whatever that the Eucharist was known to St. Paul. And the passage from Tertullian quoted below occurs quite in passing, in a discussion of sleep as one of the functions of the soul.

[2] *The Bride of Christ*, ch. ii.   [3] *Ibid.*, p. 60.

He points out how the Last Supper itself was like a Jewish wedding-feast:

> "Outwardly, too, the ceremonies of the Last Supper suggest a marriage of those days. The house was prepared as for the reception of the bridegroom who had absented himself with his friends; at a given signal, he and his party returned to find the room prepared for the wedding-feast. The feast itself began with the prescribed hand-washing and benediction. Then the great winecup was filled, and the principal personage, taking it, and holding it, recited over it the prayer of bridal blessing. Then the men seated themselves. Only the men sat at the marriage-supper. After the supper the bridegroom left the feast with the bride. . . .
>
> "There is no lack of evidence that throughout his Ministry our Lord was preparing the minds of his disciples for the Marriage-Feast of the Eucharist. The 'beginning of his signs,' his first enacted parable, was the turning of water into wine at a wedding. *His* hour was not yet come, but he made use of a human marriage to illustrate it; he turned the common water of purification into the wine of Marriage; he kept the best, the great Marriage, for the end of his ministry, and in his doing so St. John saw that he manifested forth his glory."[1]

So the Bridegroom goes forth from the Marriage-Feast to take his Bride to himself:

> "From the Marriage-Feast to the Consummation of his Marriage went the Bridegroom, with the words 'Arise, let us go hence.' That consummation was the Sacrifice of Calvary; but it is strange to see how the various nuptial traditions of the Old Testament converge and meet on Good Friday."[2]

Mr. Chavasse's exposition has been accused of over-fancifulness in some respects,[3] but his main point seems to be assured. It is confirmed by Fr. Thornton in the chapter on "The Consecration of the Church," in his great work, *The Common Life in the Body of Christ*. "The prophets," says this last writer,

> "taught that Israel is the wife of Jehovah. Her children are his children. Jehovah chose their mother to be his bride, an act of condescending grace of which Israel was not worthy. This marriage-covenant is not represented as being based upon a community of nature between God and man in virtue of creation. . . . Its whole significance depends upon the contrast between a

[1] *The Bride of Christ*, pp. 61–3.   [2] *Ibid.*, p. 64.
[3] As, e.g., by Dr. D. Stone in *J.T.S.*, Jan. 1941, p. 86.

holy God and the sinful people whom he has chosen. . . . Nature-worship offered a community of nature between gods and worshippers as its great attraction. The 'desire' of Israel was naturally towards these lovers. . . . But if Israel returns to her first espousals 'it shall be at that day, saith the Lord, that thou shalt call me Ishi (my husband); and shalt call me no more Baali (my master).' It is as though the relationship in Genesis iii. 16 has been replaced once more by that of the 'help-meet' greeted by Adam in the previous chapter. One thing is lacking—the 'one flesh.' That was provided by the Incarnation.

"Accordingly in the New Testament our Lord appears in the role of the bridegroom, which in the Old Testament belonged to Jehovah. For the Messiah exercises divine functions as the author of the new creation. 'Thy maker is thy husband' is a statement which becomes wholly true as applied to the Christian Church."[1]

It is thus not surprising to find the fathers teaching that it was upon the Cross that the Christian Church came into full being as the Bride, in her espousal to Christ. Thus Tertullian writes in the third century:

"As Adam was a figure of Christ, Adam's sleep shadowed out the death of Christ, who was to sleep a mortal slumber, that from the wound inflicted on his side, might, in like manner [as Eve was formed], be typified the Church, the true Mother of the living."[2]

Dr. Christopher Wordsworth, perhaps the most Patristic of all modern commentators, brings out this same point in commenting on the fact that both the Book Genesis and the Gospel of St. John open with the words, "In the beginning":

"May we not venture to suppose," he writes, "that the Holy Spirit by this verbal identity intended to give us a hint and intimation that we may trace an analogy between the Cosmogony of Nature and the Cosmogony of Grace; and between our first Creation in the Divine Image in Adam and our second Creation and restoration to the Divine Image in Christ, whom St. John has taught us to recognize as no other than the Creator himself? Are we not thus led gently onward to recognize a mysterious parallel between the formation of Eve, his Bride, from the side of the first Adam as he slept (who, we know, was a type of Christ, and is so called by St. Paul), and the formation of the Church, the Bride of Christ, from the side of the Second Adam, as he slept the sleep of death, to which the Church owes her life, and by which she became the Spiritual Eve—'the Mother of all living'? "[3]

[1] Op. cit., p. 223. The whole chapter should be read.
[2] *De Anima*, xliii. [3] *Commentary on the Pentateuch*, p. xviii.

We find the same teaching in Hooker:

"The Church is in Christ as Eve was in Adam. Yea by grace
we are every of us in Christ and in his Church, as by nature we
are in those our first parents. God made Eve of the rib of Adam.
And his Church he frameth out of the very flesh, the very wounded
and bleeding side of the Son of man. His body crucified and his
blood shed for the life of the world, are the true elements of that
heavenly being, which maketh us such as himself is of whom we
come. For which cause the words of Adam may be fitly the words
of Christ concerning his Church, 'flesh of my flesh, and bone of my
bones,' a true native extract out of mine own body. So that in
him even according to his manhood we according to our heavenly
being are as branches in that root out of which they grow."[1]

To quote Thornton again:

"Our Lord, once a victim on the Cross, but also then and now
our high-priest, solemnly consecrated the Church to be his own
bride. The *ecclesia* which he so consecrated was the true Israel
which had always existed since the promises - were first given,
notwithstanding the apostasy of 'Israel after the flesh.' . . .

"The Messiah was 'Israel, my servant'; but also the *ecclesia*
was Israel, the bride of Jehovah. Israel is the Messiah and his
community, neither without the other. So both together passed
through the crisis in which Israel became new. Nevertheless the
Messiah administered baptism to his bride. He was the high-
priest and she the neophyte. . . .

"Christ and his bride passed through the crisis together. Yet
this 'togetherness' includes a contrast. She was, and ever remains,
in dependence upon him. What happened to him has consequences in her. He gave himself up in order that he might cleanse
and consecrate her. His self-donation constitutes her cleansing
and consecration. Yet it is also the ground of her ever-renewed
initiation."[2]

It is thus not strictly true to describe the Church as beginning
with the descent of the Spirit at Pentecost. In a very real sense the
Church had existed from the first appearance of man upon the
earth. "It is difficult," writes the Russian theologian, Sergius
Bulgakov,

"to point to a time when the Church did not exist in humanity,
at least in the state of previous design. According to the doctrine
of the fathers, a primordial Church already existed in Paradise
before the Fall, when the Lord went to speak with man and put

[1] *Eccl. Pol.*, V, lvi, 7: ed. of 1888, II, p. 250.   [2] *The Common Life*, pp. 227-8.

himself into relation with him. After the Fall, in the first words about the 'seed of the woman' the Lord laid the foundation of what may be termed the Church of the Old Covenant, the Church wherein man learned to commune with God. And even in the darkness of paganism in the natural seeking of the human soul for its God, there existed a 'pagan sterile Church,' as some of the songs of the Church call it. Certainly the Church attained the fullness of its existence only with the Incarnation, and in this sense the Church was *founded* by our Lord Jesus Christ and realized at Pentecost. On these events, the foundation of the Church was laid, but its fulness is not yet attained. It is still the Church militant, and it must become the Church triumphant, where 'God shall be all in all.' "[1]

We shall consider later on the relation of the Church of God to the whole process of history. Here I will only summarize our discussion of the Church's dignity as the Bride of Christ in the words with which Christopher Wordsworth began his History of the Christian Church:

"There is one Church of God, from the beginning of the world to the end. In Paradise, after the Fall, under the Patriarchs, under the Levitical Law, after the Incarnation of the Son of God, even to his Second Advent, the Church has been, is, and ever will be, one. Holy men before his coming believed in Christ to come; holy men after his coming believed in him having come. The times of the Church have changed; her faith is always the same.

"At the Incarnation of the Son of God the Church acquired universality in time and space, and became partaker of the divine nature by her mystical union with him as his Bride, and as Queen at his right hand, and was admitted to an inheritance and partnership in that kingdom which will never be destroyed. . . .

"For this Church, his Bride, he died upon the Cross: he cleansed her and purchased her with his own blood. Almighty God in Paradise formed Eve, the Bride of Adam, from the side of Adam as he slept, and she became '*the mother of all living.*' So the spiritual Eve, the Church, the Bride of the Second Adam, 'who is the Lord from heaven,' and the Author of the new, regenerate race, was formed from Christ, the Second Adam, sleeping in death on the Cross, and she owes her life to the sacramental streams of blood and water which then flowed from his side; and by her union with him, and by the ministry of the Word and Sacraments instituted by him, she imparts the life to all which she receives from her Lord."[2]

[1] *The Orthodox Church*, p. 15.   [2] *Church History*, Vol. I, pp. 1, 3.

V

We have seen that the nuptial language of the Old Testament finds its fulfilment in the New-Testament doctrine that the Christian Church is the Bride of Christ. It has, however, in the course of Christian history, received two other interpretations. Sometimes it has been applied to the soul of the individual Christian in his union with Christ, sometimes to the Blessed Virgin. Mr. Chavasse, in the book from which I have already quoted, characterizes both these applications as deviations from the authentic norm. The modern theologian, he tells us, has been

"inclined to dismiss this doctrine as a mere metaphor; and it is largely this that in the popular devotions of Christians has raised the historic, human person of the Virgin Mary to that position of Queen of Heaven, on the right hand of our Lord, which in the classical ages of theology had been occupied by the Bride-Church. . . .

"Even," he adds, "while the Church's title to be the Second Eve was being assigned to the Blessed Virgin, her fundamental theological claim of being the Bride of Christ, which expresses her part in the Incarnation, was, all unnoticed, being given to another. This was the individual soul, at first of virgins and widows; then of all celibates, male and female; then of every devout Christian; and finally of certain specially privileged souls."[1]

St. Bernard of Clairvaux, writing in the early twelfth century, is perhaps the theologian in whom the individualistic interpretation of the Song of Songs reaches its height, and it must be admitted that the piety of the Middle Ages tends, as we see later on in the great fourteenth-century English mystics,[2] to let the conception of the Church as the Mystical Body and Bride fall very much into neglect in favour of a concentration upon the union of the individual soul with its Saviour. I cannot, however, see that there is any fundamental contradiction between these various interpretations. Wordsworth himself, while agreeing with the Authorized Version of the Bible in giving to the Song of Songs the ecclesiastical interpretation, also applies it to the individual soul, for, he says,

"every soul in the Church is, as it were, in a certain sense, a Church in itself. . . . We would not indeed," he says, "bring down

1 *The Bride of Christ*, pp. 161, 169.   2 See, e.g., David Knowles, *The English Mystics*.

the Canticles from the lofty elevation of its comprehensive
Catholicity, and represent it only or mainly as a picture of the love
of the individual soul for Christ; but while we maintain, with the
great body of Ancient Expositors, that this book represents the
mutual love of Christ and his Church Universal, we would also
affirm, that each individual soul of every member of the Church
may see herself reflected here as in a mirror, and may learn what
her own privileges and duties are."[1]

And although Wordsworth is very reluctant to see Mariological
references in Scripture, we can hardly deny that what applies to
every member of the Church must apply a fortiori to that member
of it who has been most highly favoured by God. As Canon
Balmforth has said, "we can go all the way with Mr. Chavasse in
stressing the thought of the Church as the Heavenly Queen and
Bride of Christ. But we need not therefore reject as perversions the
further developments which speak of the Christian soul as the
bride of the divine Spouse or of our Lady, in Bulgakov's words, as
the centre and personal embodiment of the queenly Church."[2]
And indeed there is reason to suppose that the Blessed Virgin has
a very definite place in the act by which the divine Bridegroom
espoused his Bride the Church.

I have already quoted the passage in which Tertullian refers to
the Church as the Second Eve. But even earlier than Tertullian,
Justin Martyr was writing that

---

[1] *Introduction to the Song of Solomon*, p. 126. Cf. de Lubac on the interpretation of
Scripture:
"This social exegesis, which discovers everywhere the whole human race in its
relation to the Saviour, and which is almost obsessed by the contrast of the Church
and the Synagogue, is not less interested in the individual soul. But these are not two
separate objects, and their very order—the order of doctrine and of 'practice'—is not
indifferent. For if everything that happens to Christ happens also to the Church,
'everything that happens to the Church happens to each Christian in particular.'
Pascal, in this famous maxim from his letter to Mlle de Roannez, expresses the
unanimous tradition. The soul which is concerned is the *anima in ecclesia*. . . .
"Whether it is a matter of the Old Testament, or of the Gospel, and especially the
parables, the Tradition maintains side by side a twofold mystical meaning, one
element in which refers to the collective destinies of the human race, and the other
the intimate history of the soul. Thus, in the last resort, everything that Scripture
tells us finds its fulfilment in each one of us. The Paradise which is the Church with its
saints is also the interior of each one of these saints with its virtues. In every man there
is a Church and a Synagogue, an Abel and a Cain, an Esau and a Jacob, a Hagar
and a Sarah. . . . The great Easter night recalls the crossing of the Red Sea by the
Hebrews and brings to mind the conclusive passage to the life of the Risen Christ: in
it is signified in the first place the passage of the whole world to the 'dignity of Israel,'
but then also the passage of each convert to the divine life by baptism. . . .
" . . . As there is a correspondence in the Body of Christ between the Head and the
members, so there is also a correspondence between each one of these members and
the whole Body." (*Catholicisme*, pp. 151–3.)
[2] In a review in *Christendom*, March 1941, p. 62.

K

"Eve, being a virgin and undefiled, conceiving the word which was from the serpent, brought forth disobedience and death; but the Virgin Mary, taking faith and joy, when the Angel Gabriel told her the glad tidings, . . . answered, Be it unto me according to thy word."[1]

Irenaeus is even more explicit:

"Mary the Virgin is found obedient, saying, 'Behold the hand-maid of the Lord; be it unto me according to thy word.' But Eve was disobedient; for she did not obey when she was yet a virgin. . . . And thus also it was that the knot of Eve's disobedience was loosed by the obedience of Mary. For what the virgin Eve had bound fast through unbelief, this did the Virgin Mary set free through faith."[2]

"If the former did disobey God, yet the latter was persuaded to obey God, in order that the Virgin Mary might become the advocate of the virgin Eve. And thus, as the human race fell into bondage to death by means of a virgin, so is it rescued by a virgin: virginal disobedience having been balanced in the opposite scale by virginal obedience."[3]

The thought of these passages is beautifully summed up in the ninth-century office-hymn:

> Sumens illud Ave
> Gabrielis ore,
> Funda nos in pace,
> Mutans Evae nomen.

Are we then to conclude that, since both the Church and the Blessed Virgin are described as the Second Eve, one of these attributions must be rejected as nothing more than a pious fancy? Let us see what Sir Edwyn Hoskyns has to say.

"At the time of our Lord's death," he writes, "a new family is brought into being. If the unity of the Church is symbolized by the seamless robe, the peculiar nature of that unity is indicated here [that is, in the Third Word from the Cross: "Woman, behold thy Son.—Behold thy mother."] The Church proceeds from the Sacrifice of the Son of God, and the union of the Beloved Disciple and the Mother of the Lord prefigures and foreshadows the charity of the *ecclesia* of God. Mary the Mother of the Lord, becomes the mother of the faithful."[4]

And in the fact that, while the other evangelists describe the Lord's death by the quite ordinary phrases, "He gave up the ghost" and

---

[1] *C. Tryph.*, 100.   [2] *Adv. Haer.*, III, xxii, 4.   [3] *Ibid.*, V, xix, 1.
[4] *The Fourth Gospel*, p. 631.

"He yielded up his spirit," St. John uses the very strange phrase, "He handed over the spirit," Hoskyns sees an indication that for St. John the death of Christ is the first outpouring of the Holy Ghost upon the Catholic Church.

> "If it be assumed that the writer intends his readers to suppose that the Beloved Disciple and Mary the Mother of Jesus remain standing beneath the cross, the words *He bowed his head* suggest that he bowed his head towards them, and the words *He handed over the Spirit* are also directed to the faithful believers who stand below."[1]

So Hoskyns heads this section of his Commentary with the words, *Christus mortuus est: emittit Spiritum Sanctum et vivificantem.* He thus discerns three successive outpourings of the Spirit upon the infant Church, each being more inclusive than the one before. The other two are the breathing of Jesus on the disciples in the closed room on the day of the Resurrection and the descent of the Spirit in fire on the Day of Pentecost.

In another place Hoskyns has dealt with this even more fully. Commenting on our Lord's words at the wedding-feast at Cana— "Woman, what have I to do with thee? Mine hour is not yet come," he says:

> "Because Mary is the mother of Jesus, she will become the mother of those who believe in him. This second motherhood of Mary is anticipated, whose hour will come when the sacrifice on the cross has been offered. 'Woman' is a far better translation than 'Lady.' When, therefore, the fathers say that Mary is the new Eve, they have caught the meaning of the passage far better than modern commentators; for, while Eve was the mother of a sinful people who ceased to have real contact with God, Mary is the mother of believers, who, redeemed from sin, are reborn and abide (μένειν) with God. . . ."

Referring to the passage in Justin Martyr he says:

> "There is no reason to suppose that such a comparison was first drawn in the second half of the second century, and we may even suggest further that the mother of Jesus was historically of far more importance within the community of original believers than modern critics have allowed. . . .
>
> "The idea of re-creation and new birth therefore underlies St. John's account of the death on the cross, and Mary herself, as the mother of the faithful, shares in this rebirth. If this be accepted

[1] *The Fourth Gospel*, p. 633.

we can hardly dismiss as fantastic the allusion implied in the account of the reclining of the head of Jesus in sleep, followed immediately by the rebirth of Mary from his side. The account suggests Genesis ii. 21–22 . . . , and Tertullian's comment, *De Anima* 43, represents real insight, 'For as Adam was a figure of Christ, Adam's sleep shadowed out the death of Christ, who was to sleep a mortal slumber, that from the wound inflicted on his side, might, in like manner [as Eve was formed], be typified the Church, the true mother of the living.' "

So sure is Hoskyns of the inseparable connection between the Blessed Virgin and Mother Church that he sees in the woman of the twelfth chapter of the Apocalypse a direct Marian reference, and not merely a symbol of the Church to which Catholics have given an unwarrantable Marian interpretation. After the passage quoted above about the wedding at Cana, he writes:

"The same allusion is found in the twelfth chapter of the Revelation, where the Γυνή-Μήτηρ [the Woman-Mother] is also referred to. There the woman is first the mother of the child, who is caught up to God and to his throne, xii. 5, and then also the mother of the Christians, who are called 'the remnant of her seed, who keep the commands of God and have the testimony of Jesus' (a phrase which incidentally is Johannine). Both the mother and her seed fly to the desert, where they are persecuted by the great dragon, the old serpent, called in *v.* 15 simply 'the serpent.' The Mother of the Messiah is also the mother of the believers, and is persecuted by the serpent, but in contrast to Eve protects her seed from the serpent's power. The suggestion is that the mother of the Lord and of those who believe in him is the new Eve, still persecuted by the serpent; but, where Eve failed by handing her seed over to death, the new Eve is victorious by bearing children who possess eternal life."[1]

It thus seems to be possible to hold, without any forcing of the facts, that the interpretations of the Church and the Virgin Mary as the Second Eve, so far from being contradictory, are implied in each other. Christ was born from the womb of Mary, and Mary was born again from the side of Christ. By the former birth she is the mother of Christ's natural body; by the latter she is the mother of his Mystical Body. And as her motherhood of the natural body was given her by the overshadowing of the Spirit at Christ's annunciation, her motherhood of the Mystical Body was given her by the breathing forth of the Spirit at his death.

[1] "Genesis i–iii and St. John's Gospel," in *J.T.S.*, April 1920, p. 210 f.

CHAPTER VIII

THE RESTORATION OF UNITY

I

THE Church is, as we have seen, the sphere of the New Humanity, of human beings remade by incorporation into Christ. "If any man is in Christ, he is a new creature: the old things are passed away; behold, they are become new."[1] We must not, however, look upon this renovation of man as being merely a communication to man of something that he never possessed before. Rather it is a restoration of man to his primeval innocence and union with God, to the state from which he fell through the transgression of God's law. Dom Anselm Stolz, in his book, *The Doctrine of Spiritual Perfection*, has shown how the early Christian writers sometimes show an almost materialistic realism in their teaching that through union with Christ man is restored to the Paradise from which he has been excluded since the Fall. It is indeed true that, in the thought of most Christian theologians, redemption in Christ has been held to have brought with it even greater blessings than man lost by his sin: "greater good because of evil, larger mercy through the Fall."[2] The Church has not been afraid even to acclaim the sin of Adam as a "happy fault," since it was found worthy to have so great a redeemer,[3] and the Thomist tradition has tended to the view that the Incarnation itself, which is the very foundation of man's incorporation into Christ and elevation into the life of God, would not have occurred but for human sin.[4] This does not alter the fact that the Church has consistently looked upon redemption as a *renewal*, a renewal first perfected by Christ in his own self and then progressively communicated to the rest of the human race and indeed to the whole of creation. This note is most forcibly struck

---

[1] 2 Cor. v. 17.　　　[2] F. W. Faber, *English Hymnal*, No. 499.
[3] *O felix culpa, quae talem ac tantum meruit habere redemptorem!*—Blessing of the Paschal Candle in the Latin rite.
[4] *S. Theol.*, III, i, 3. Cf. the *Dies irae*:
　　　　　　　　Recordare, Jesu pie,
　　　　　　　　Quod sum causa tuae viae.

in the liturgical services of the Latin Church for Holy Saturday, wherein Christ's own redeeming act and its impartation to the newly baptized are in closest juxtaposition. The new fire is struck and hallowed, and the new water is blessed for the new birth of baptism. The priest, having prayed that "the power of the Holy Ghost may descend upon the fulness of this font and make the whole substance of this water fruitful unto regeneration," goes on to implore:

> "Here may the nature which was formed in thine image be restored to the honour of its first estate and cleansed from all the filthiness of its old condition; that every man who comes to this sacrament of regeneration may be born again into the new childhood of true innocence."

And earlier in the rite, after the second of the Old-Testament prophecies, in which there is related that story of the preservation of Noah and his family from the Flood which the First Epistle of Peter tells us is a type of baptism,[1] there is chanted the thrilling prayer, of Gelasian origin:

> "O God, who art might unchangeable and light eternal, look down in mercy upon the wondrous mystery of thy whole Church, and, by the operation of thy continual providence, accomplish in tranquillity the work of man's salvation; and let the whole world see and know that things that were cast down are being raised up, that things that had grown old are being made new, and that all things are returning to their perfection through him from whom they took their origin, Jesus Christ thy Son our Lord."

Indeed, in the Jewish Passover ceremonies this fact of renewal was expressed in the law which ordered the use of unleavened bread for the seven days of the festival. No doubt for the Jews of our Lord's day the unleavened bread was primarily a reminder of the haste in which their forefathers had left the Land of Egypt; and the Christian Church has seen the Jewish Exodus as a type of the greater Exodus which the Christ accomplished at Jerusalem.[2]

---

[1] 1 Pet. iii. 20, 21.

[2] I cannot resist quoting the splendid words of Christopher Wordsworth in which this truth is expounded. Referring to the conversation of our Lord with Moses and Elijah at the Transfiguration, he writes:

"St. Luke . . . says that the subject of that conversation with Moses and Elias was Christ's 'Exodus.' [Luke ix. 31.] (This is the only place in the Gospels, where the word ἔξοδος is used for death.) And thus he appears to suggest that the death of Christ was the great moral and spiritual End, to which the Law and the Prophets, represented by Moses and Elias, looked. He says that they spake of his Exodus, which he should accomplish at Jerusalem. Did not the Holy Spirit thereby intend us to infer, that the Exodus, which was begun by Israel at the Red Sea, was accomplished by Christ at

Modern commentators, however, have laid stress upon the affinity of the Paschal celebration with the ceremonies in which the Semitic peoples greeted the first-fruits of the harvests, and here too the Church has anticipated them. She has seen the break with the past which is involved in the prohibition of the mixing of leaven with the newly prepared dough as a sign of the new life brought to us in Christ, as well as of the purity of his offering to the Father. Thus, in the Eastertide office-hymn, *Ad coenam Agni providi*, we find the stanza :

Jerusalem? Did he not intend us to bear in mind, what he has taught us by St. Paul, that Christ's *Exodus* is the *substance*, of which Israel's Exodus was the *shadow*;—that Christ is the true Passover [1 Cor. v. 7. Cf. John xix. 36 with Exod. xii. 46] ; that his passage through the Red Sea of his own blood, by which we come forth out of our spiritual Egypt, and in which our spiritual Pharaoh and his host are overwhelmed, and from which we march forward to the Canaan of our Rest, was prefigured by the Exodus of Israel from Egypt; and that in reading the Book of Exodus, we are not only reading a true history of a past event, but have there a prophetical Gospel, a typical delineation of Christ himself, and of Mankind summed up in him [1 Cor. x. 1–11]—of Mankind dying in his death, and rising again to life in his resurrection?" (Comm. on Pentateuch, p. xx.)

Again, after describing the significance of the Exodus as the great redemptive act of God for his people the Jews, he writes :

"The Exodus was all this; but it was something more.

"It was the type and figure of the greatest event which the world has ever seen; it was a preparation for an event which concerns all mankind in every nation of the Earth, until the end of time, and through the countless ages of eternity. It was the type and figure of the World's Exodus; it was the type and figure of Mankind's deliverance by the Death and Passion of him who is no other than the Lord Jehovah himself, and who took our nature and became incarnate, and passed through the Red Sea of his own Passion, and overwhelmed Satan in its abysses, and marched through that Sea, and carried the World with him, and led it forth in triumph from the house of spiritual bondage—from the Egypt of Satan, Sin, and Death,—and conducted it in a glorious career toward the Canaan of its heavenly rest.

"The Holy Spirit, in the New Testament, teaches us to regard the Exodus in this light. He teaches us that Israel, God's 'firstborn,' was a figure of Christ [Matt. ii. 15] ; and that all things in the Exodus of Israel were τύποι ἡμῶν, *figures of us*; that they were figures of Christ's Church, whose members are united together under him their Head, who has engrafted them into his own body, and has made them partakers of his own Death and Resurrection by the Sacrament of Baptism, which was fore-shadowed by the Passage of Israel through the waters of the Red Sea. Israel's Exodus was Christ's Exodus. It was the Exodus of his Church in him. Their wanderings are ours. Christ has taught us to see himself in the Manna from Heaven [John vi. 49], and in the Brazen Serpent [John iii. 14] lifted up by Moses in the wilderness. St. Paul has taught us to see him in the smitten Rock gushing with water in the desert. The history of the Israelites is our history; it is the history of the Church Universal. It was written for our sake, as the Holy Spirit teaches, when he says by St. Paul, 'All these things happened unto them τυπικῶς,' so as to have a figurative meaning, and 'are written for our admonition, upon whom the ends of the world are come' [1 Cor. x. 11]." (Ibid., pp. xiii, xiv.)

One can see the relevance of passages such as these even if one holds a more "critical" view of the Bible than Wordsworth held. The point is that the whole ideology of the Old Testament is the presupposition and framework of the thought of the New. Thornton's great work, *The Common Life in the Body of Christ* makes this abundantly plain. It is interesting to compare the following references to it with the passages from Wordsworth just quoted: pp. 246 f., 195, 363. Cf. also de Lubac, *Catholicisme*, p. 119 f.

Jam Pascha noster Christus est,	"Now Christ our Paschal Lamb is slain,
qui immolatus agnus est;	The Lamb of God that knows no stain,
sinceritatis azyma	The true Oblation offered here,
caro ejus oblata est.	Our own unleavened bread sincere."[1]

and this is, of course, an echo of the words of St. Paul which replace the *Venite* in the Anglican morning-office on Easter Day:

"Our passover also hath been sacrificed, even Christ: wherefore let us keep the feast, not with old leaven, neither with the leaven of malice and wickedness, but with the unleavened bread of sincerity and truth. . . . But now hath Christ been raised from the dead, the first fruits of them that are asleep. . . . For as in Adam all die, so . also in Christ shall all be made alive."[2]

And this same note of novelty is expressed in the great Eucharistic sequence of St. Thomas:

In hac mensa novi regis	"Lo, the new King's table gracing,
novum Pascha novae legis	This new Passover of blessing
phase vetus terminat.	Hath fulfilled the elder rite:
Vetustatem novitas,	Now the new the old effaceth,
umbram fugat veritas,	Truth revealed the shadow chaseth,
noctem lux eliminat.	Day is breaking on the night."

We may note also that the very words with which the first book of the Old Testament opens in the Septuagint version—ἐν ἀρχῇ, "In the beginning"—are also the first words of the Gospel of St. John; and while the account of creation in the second chapter of Genesis begins with the words, "This is the book of the genesis —ἡ βίβλος γενέσεως—of heaven and earth," the Gospel of St. St. Matthew begins with the words, "The book of the genesis of Jesus Christ." The implication is clearly that in the redemptive work of Christ the world is created anew.

Hoskyns has remarked on the significance of the fact that it was in the garden that the Risen Lord met with Mary Magdalene.[3] It was in a garden that the first Adam fell; it was in a garden— Gethsemane—that the Second Adam, by his resolution to drink the cup of obedience, reversed the first Adam's disobedience; it was in a garden that he rose from death to glory. But, asks Hoskyns, why did Christ appear in a form that could be mistaken for that of the gardener? The answer is, because he *was* the

---

[1] Translation of J. M. Neale. Cf. the sequence of Adam of St. Victor, *Zyma vetus expurgetur.* [2] 1 Cor. v. 7, 8; xv. 20, 22 (R.V.).
[3] Art. cit., *supra.*, *J.T.S.*, April 1920, p. 214 f.

Gardener: the Adam placed in the garden by the Father in order
that it should bring forth its fruits, and also the supreme and
original Gardener, the Lord Jehovah, who had planted the garden
eastward in Eden.[1] And as, after the Fall, the Lord God walked
in the garden in the cool of the day in the evening of man's defeat,
so, after man's redemption, he walks in the garden in the cool of
the day in the morning of man's victory.

And the day of the Lord's Resurrection is the day in which he
triumphs with the Church which is his Bride:

> "Rise up, my love, my fair one, and come away.
> For, lo, the winter is past,
> The rain is over and gone;
> The flowers appear on the earth;
> The time of the singing of birds is come,
> And the voice of the turtle is heard in our land:
> The fig tree ripeneth her green figs,
> And the vines are in blossom,
> They give forth their fragrance.
> Arise, my love, my fair one, and come away."[2]

II

Deeply connected with this renovation of man by re-creation in
Christ is the restoration of unity.[3] This unity has three aspects:
man's unity with God, man's unity with himself, man's unity with
his fellow-men; though it is the first and third of these with which
we are mainly concerned here. In all these aspects unity has been
lost by sin and is restored in Christ.

First, then, man's unity with God. The story of man's primeval
state, as it is described in the early part of Genesis, is one in which
man is living in a state of childlike innocence and obedience, and
of perfect fellowship with God. Man fell through disobedience
and lost this fellowship. What precisely was the nature of the
sin which Genesis describes as the eating of the forbidden fruit of
the tree of the knowledge of good and evil it may be difficult to
determine: Mr. Charles Williams has interpreted it as the desire

---

[1] John xx. 15. Gen. ii. 8.
[2] Cant. ii. 10–13. (Lesson for Evening Prayer on Wednesday in Easter Week in the Revised Lectionary.)
[3] Reference should be made to Fr. de Lubac's fine work, *Catholicisme: les aspects sociaux du dogme*, for a thorough patristic and systematic discussion of this theme. Cf. also Ramsey, *The Gospel and the Catholic Church*, ch. iv.

to know both good and evil from the inside, as it were, and therefore as the deliberate contravention of the will of God in order to gain this interior knowledge of sin,[1] Mr. C. S. Lewis describes it as "the act of self-will on the part of the creature, which constitutes an utter falseness to its true creaturely position."[2] Both these writers agree with the Christian tradition in taking it as the result of pride culminating in disobedience. However that may be, the outcome is clear. Man is no longer able to speak with God face to face as God walks in the garden in the cool of the day. He is cast out of the garden and is excluded from the tree of life. Between him and God there is now a barrier which he is unable to pierce; the glorious and uninterrupted fellowship has departed, and the changeless divine perfection which in man's state of innocence appeared to him under the form of God's love now, in his changed condition, appears to him as wrath and curse. There is no change in God; the change is in man. God's wrath is God's love as it appears to the sinner.[3] In his unfallen state, man lived in complete union with God in a life in which the interchange of love for love was complete and uninterrupted. But through sin, man's love for God has been lost; he has become wrapped up in himself, and God's love for him—the love of the God who is Love itself—so far from attracting him, repels and appals him by the demand which it makes upon him for a response which he is no longer prepared to give. Love itself has become hateful. This is the explanation of our misery; and it is the explanation of hell. For in hell, intensely and irrevocably as nowhere else, the love of God is hated by those in whom love is no more. "I am one," said an evil spirit to St. Catherine of Genoa during an exorcism, "in whom there is no love."[4]

Now this loss of union with God, which goes hand in hand with man's loss of love, is repaired in man's restoration in Christ. I have already discussed this in some detail, and shall therefore now

---

[1] *He came down from Heaven*, ch. ii.
[2] *The Problem of Pain*, p. 68; cf. the more extended discussion in *A Preface to Paradise Lost*, chs. x, xi.   [3] See the additional note at the end of this chapter.
[4] It is, I would suggest, probably a mistake to distinguish too sharply between the *poena damni* and the *poena sensus*. The words of Mephistophilis in Marlow's *Doctor Faustus* may be quoted:

> "Think'st thou that I, who saw the face of God,
> And tasted the eternal joys of heaven,
> Am not tormented with ten thousand hells
> In being deprived of everlasting bliss?"
> —Scene iii.

pass on briefly to consider the second point, the restoration of man's union with himself.

St. Bernard uses a most expressive term to describe the effect of sin upon the sinner. It places him in the *regio dissimilitudinis*, the "Land of Unlikeness"; that is to say, it makes him unlike his real self, since it makes him unlike the God in whose image and likeness he was made. It introduces into his very being an element of disintegration, incoherence and self-contradiction. "Man," writes Professor Gilson, summarizing St. Bernard's teaching on this point,

"is an exile. He no longer inhabits the land of his birth. We might say, in terms but slightly different, that he lives in a climate that is not his. As God made him, he was a noble creature—*nobilis creatura*—and he was so because God created him to his own image. Disfigured by original sin, man has in fact exiled himself from the Land of Likeness to enter into the Land of Unlikeness: *Regio dissimilitudinis*. There we have the first inversion of order from which all the evil has arisen. Conversion reversed, conversion for ever 'execrable,' by which man exchanged the glory of the divine image for the shame of the earthly image, peace with God and with himself for war against God and against himself, liberty under the law of charity for slavery under the law of his ownself-will. We might go still further and say that man, by that conversion, has exchanged heaven for hell; a word in which all the foregoing is summed up, for hell is at once self-will, and its consequence, unlikeness to God, and war set up between creature and creator."[1]

The immediate effect upon man of this loss of his true likeness is a loss of unity within the self, a condition whose classical description has been given by St. Paul in his famous passage about the two laws in the Epistle to the Romans:

"That which I do, I know not: for not what I would, that do I practise; but what I hate, that I do. . . . But if what I would not,

<hr/>

[1] *Mystical Theology of St. Bernard*, p. 45. Gilson is summarizing a passage from Bernard, *De Diversis, Sermo* 42, 2 (*De quinque negotiationibus et quinque regionibus*). The phrase, *regio dissimilitudinis*, occurs in Augustine, *Conf.* VII, x (16). We may compare the words of a modern Russian Orthodox: "The purpose of human life was conceived [in Russian Orthodoxy] as approximation to the divine prototype. The Russian language powerfully expresses this conviction; people who show the example of a better and purer life are called *prepodobnye*, which, literally, means 'most like.' In other words, holy men and women are those who approach nearest to the original picture of man. On the contrary, every form of ugliness, violence and disorder is branded by the word *besobrazie*, 'that which lost its image,' or unseemliness." (Zernov, *Three Russian Prophets*, p. 32.)

that I do, it is no more I that do it, but sin which dwelleth in me. I find then the law, that, to me who would do good, evil is present. For I delight in the law of God after the inward man: but I see a different law in my members, warring against the law of my mind, and bringing me into captivity under the law of sin which is in my members. . . . So that I myself with the mind serve the law of God; but with the flesh the law of sin."[1]

The Christian ascetic tradition has discerned in this disintegration two chief elements: namely, the escape of the sensitive level of the soul from its proper subordination to the rational level, and as a result a disharmony in the sensitive level itself through which the various passions of the soul conflict and compete with one another. All that need be said here is that the disintegration is repaired through union with Christ, for in him the likeness of perfect manhood is unspoilt: "The law of the Spirit of life in Christ Jesus made me free from the law of sin and of death."[2] As we shall see in a later chapter,[3] the Christian character is nothing less than the character of Christ progressively communicated to his members. For Christ is the Father's own image, and in this image and likeness man was made.[4]

III

In our consideration of the Church, however, it is the restoration of the third kind of unity with which we are most directly concerned, namely the unity of man with man. After the phase of individualism through which, in the Middle Ages to some extent but far more in the post-Reformation period, Christian thought and piety have passed, theology is beginning at the present day to recover its sense of the corporate nature of both sin and redemption. The credit for this must very largely be given to the three French writers, Mersch, Congar and de Lubac. The last of these authors writes as follows:

"Whereas to-day we seek almost exclusively within the interior of each individual nature to find its secret wound, and, so to speak, the slipping of the springs which has caused the machine to go wrong . . . , it used to be natural to regard the setting up of individuals as naturally hostile centres as being, not of course the

[1] Rom. vii. 15–25.   [2] Rom. viii. 2.   [3] Ch. xii. *infra*.
[4] For some remarks on the traditional distinction between "image" and "likeness," see p. 222 *infra*. St. Bernard's doctrine on the question is discussed by Gilson, *Mystical Theology of St. Bernard*, p. 46 f.

Mascall, E. L.

Corpus Christi

The One Church. M. distinguishes with Aquinas between numerical unity and ontological unity. The unity of the Church is numerical but also organic. Christians are one because of a common participation in the life of God himself thru incorporation into Christ' humanity. Christ' human nature is both universal and particular (both extreme realism and nominalism must be avoided) in the question of universals). The Church's unity is not based merely jurisdictional (Roman) or invisible (Protestant) but sacramental. The visible organ by which the Church's unity is expressed is the apostolate, instituted by Christ in the twelve and expanded into the universal Episcopate. Mascall argues that it is foolish to advocate acceptance of episcopacy as a practice without meaning on any particular episcopal theory. Quoting Dr. Bragg: "To urge the acceptance of an institution without meaning on any reasoned meaning of it reduces it to something like mumbo-jumbo." To accept the historic Episcopate without meaning on a theory of Episcopacy is to advocate the acceptance which the institution has come to take and that is to destroy the hope of uniting the churches which may have myself it. You can only reform an institution by applying to it in its actual condition some theory about its essential nature and so bringing it into closer conformity to that pattern. The unity of the Church is sacramental; the visible expression of the unity in the Episcopate for the episcopal character is conferred by a sacramental act. "And this is why it is impossible to locate the organ of the Church's unity in the Papacy; for the Papal character is not conferred by a sacramental act at all, but by the purely administrative and organisational process of election." M. does not deny that the Pope is the successor of Peter but he feels Post-Tridentine Roman Catholicism has made Peter not merely the Prince of the Apostles but the only Apostle. A newly consecrated bishop, says M., is not in the strict sense a successor of the apostles; he is simply a new apostle. "Ordination is an act by which the universal Apostolate, most of whose members are not on earth, acting thru its earthly heart incorporates a new member into itself." M. insists that the Episcopate continues in the Triumphant Church. (Although the sacraments will cease in heaven the Liturgy will not).

first or only fruit of sin, but at least the second fruit 'equal to the first.' "

And he quotes some remarkable passages from the early Christian writers to bring out his point:

> "Maximus the Confessor considers original sin as a separation, a breaking up; we might even say, individualization, in the bad sense of the word. While God acts unceasingly in the world to make everything work in unity, by sin (which is man's deed) 'the one nature was broken into a thousand pieces,' and humanity, which ought to constitute a harmonious whole with *mine* and *thine* unopposed, became a dust of individuals with violent discordant tendencies. 'Now,' Maximus concludes, 'we tear one another like wild beasts.' 'Satan has scattered us,' Cyril of Alexandria used to say in explaining the Fall and the need for a Redeemer. And in a curious passage, in which there can still be heard the echo of an ancient myth, Augustine gives symbolically an analogous explanation. After associating the four letters of the name of Adam with the four points of the compass in their Greek form, he adds: 'Adam therefore hath been scattered over the whole world. He was in one place and fell, and as in a manner broken small, he filled the whole world.' "[1]

The conception of redemption as the gathering together of the scattered elements of the human race can be found most prominently in the Bible itself. "I will bring thy seed from the east and gather thee from the west. I will say to the north, Give up, and to the south, Keep not back. Bring my sons from far, and my daughters from the end of the earth."[2] The High Priest, St. John tells us, unwittingly "prophesied that Jesus should die for the nation, and not for the nation only, but that he might also gather together into one the children of God that are scattered abroad."[3] The prayer of the Christ himself on the night before his crucifixion was that "they may all be one."[4] And in the Epistle to the Romans St. Paul develops this same thought under the metaphor of the olive tree which represents the Israel of God, and into which are to be grafted both the wild olive-branches which stand for the Gentiles and the branches broken off from the tree itself which stand for the apostate Jews.[5]

---

[1] *Catholicisme*, pp. 11, 10. The reference to Augustine is *In Ps. xcv* (P.B.V., xcvi), no. 15; the four letters stand for *Anatole, Dysis, Arctos* and *Mesembria*, and the association is found in the Greek Anthology, Bk. I, Epig. 108. The quotation continues: "But the mercy of God gathered together the fragments from every side, and forged them by the fire of love, and made one what was broken."

[2] Isa. xliii. 5, 6.   [3] John xi. 51, 52.   [4] John xvii. 21.   [5] Rom. xi. 13–32.

From the Incarnation onwards the history of the world is the history of the Christian Church, and the end to which the whole process is moving is the remaking and gathering together of the whole human race through incorporation into Christ. It does indeed appear that there will be at the end of time some human souls who have rejected finally and irrevocably the gift of eternal life. In admitting this, I do not mean to imply that I find the doctrine of hell anything but terrible to consider; but, while we cannot say that any particular person is in hell, loyalty to the plain teaching of the Gospel[1] compels us to recognize that the final separation of a human soul from God is a very genuine possibility. We need not hesitate to acknowledge that in the popular mind, as moulded by the stories of nursemaids of the last generation but one and the sermons of the less scrupulous type of preacher, the doctrine of hell has been so conceived as to make religion a matter of fear rather than of love, and that the torments of hell have sometimes been depicted in crude and even ridiculous ways. But, in its essence, hell simply means that a man's ultimate destiny is determined by his own decision, and in this sense we must surely agree with Mr. Eric Gill that the doctrine of hell "implies the most stupendous compliment to man humanly conceivable." To-day, he says, "the doctrine of hell is not disbelieved because kind people have persuaded us that a kind God would not be so unkind, but because we have slipped down from the proud eminence upon which, with great pain and labour, religion had placed us—an eminence upon which we stood as men meriting to receive the uttermost praise or the uttermost blame— . . . into an easy place where we can grovel comfortably."[2] Hell does not, it must be repeated, imply a denial of the love of God; what marks it off from heaven is not anything in God, but the condition of the human soul. The joys of heaven, the joys and pains of purgatory, and the pains of hell all proceed from the love of God—in heaven from love returned to its fulness; in purgatory from love returned, but as yet only in part; in hell, from love rejected. "It is terrible," writes Maritain, "to fall into the hands of the living God, for those hands give to each man what his will has settled on."[3]

We are not concerned here to consider fully the doctrine of hell, but we are concerned to recognize that it is not incompatible with the truth of the Church's final perfection, the *pleroma* which will

---

[1] E.g., the dominical discourse in Matt. xxv.   [2] *The Necessity of Belief*, pp. 135, 183.
[3] "The Mystery of Israel," in *Redeeming the Time*, p. 133.

THE RESTORATION OF UNITY

be achieved when, after "all things have been subjected unto him, then shall the Son also himself be subjected to him that did subject all things unto him, that God may be all in all"[1]; the *apocatastasis*, or restitution of all things[2]; the *anakephalaiosis*, or recapitulation of all things in Christ.[3] For it is of the essence of the notion of hell that the damned are altogether excluded from the community of the redeemed. They do not form a kind of fringe or slum of the heavenly Jerusalem, whose presence is a perpetual reproach to it, as the depressed areas in England were a reproach to the national honour; they are not in it at all, they have ceased to count. And if it be urged that heaven will be numerically incomplete by the number of the damned, the answer must be that the perfection of heaven is not a numerical perfection anyhow. For even heaven is composed of created beings, and is therefore finite: to demand that it should be so perfect that nothing more perfect were conceivable is in effect to demand that it should not be finite at all; in fact, that it should be just God himself.[4] There can be no *a priori* calculation of the number of the redeemed; that is a secret hidden with God. As de Lubac writes:

> "The Church is, in fine, nothing else than humanity itself, vivified, unified by the Spirit of Christ. She was willed by God to animate creation.' Woe then to him who separates himself from her! If schism is the sin unto death, death itself, damnation, is a schism: the supreme schism, the 'total' alienation, the decisive severance; and one which can be the lot of those who are to all appearance the most ardent enthusiasts for unity: for if 'many are within who seem to be without,' some can be without who pass for the guardians of that which is within. *Novit Dominus qui sunt ejus*. But, whatever may be in this respect revealed at the Last Day, one thing is certain: the Church will not enter the kingdom mutilated. In the Jewish legend, when Lot's wife had been changed into a pillar of salt, one limb after another was successively torn from her; however, by a miracle of immediate restoration, she

---

[1] 1 Cor. xv. 28.   [2] Acts. iii. 21.

[3] Eph. i. 10. For the fulness of meaning that is comprised in this term, see Mersch on its use by Irenaeus: "a résumé, a taking up of all since the beginning, a recommencement, a return to the source, restoration, reorganization, and incorporation under one Head." (*The Whole Christ*, p. 230.)

[4] A similar fallacy underlies Leibnitz's demand that this must be the best of all possible worlds: see my *He Who Is*, p. 105. Cf. de Lubac: "We must, with Augustine and the Gospel, distinguish the world, the terminus of creation, which must be saved, from the *mundus perditionis* which, however vast it may be, does not impair the organic integrity of the former.... Those who cut themselves off from the body are no longer truly members, but must be compared to noxious matter, which the body must reject for its health." (*Catholicisme*, p. 213.)

always remained whole. So also the Church, the 'salt of the earth,' is often maimed, but finds her limbs again. And so humanity itself: all its defections leave no void in it. They can do nothing against its fulness. As in our fleshly body the members are jointly involved in one another, so humanity will share in the destiny of him who took it as his body. Since the Head has triumphed, the whole Body, the *Pleroma*, will be saved."[1]

IV

Closely connected with all this is the doctrine, traditional in Christianity, that the reunion of soul and body, which is necessary for the full restoration and resurrection of human beings, will not take place for each individual man immediately after death—although his final fate will then be made evident to him in the Particular Judgment—but will take place for all men together at the Last Day, when Christ will return as Judge with the angels, who will reap the harvest and separate the wheat from the tares.[2] The point is that a man's final state of union with God will not be achieved in isolation from his fellow-men; the heavenly worship is not to be conceived of as a competitive rendering of simultaneous solos by spiritual individualists, but rather as a great symphony in which each has his part to play, but all unite and blend in the great corporate hymn of praise to the Father who made them all.[3] The Resurrection of the Body will thus be the Resurrection of the Mystical Body, the Resurrection of the Church; and even if we hold, with the generality of theologians, that the Beatific Vision of the Holy Trinity may be achieved by individuals before the Last Day,[4] the fact remains that it will receive a great access of plenitude in the General Resurrection, for it will then be the property not of disembodied individuals, but of the Church as a whole. It is Christ himself, the Perfect Man, that is, in his ascended glory, the archetypal possessor of the

[1] *Catholicisme*, p. 211 f. Cf. the New-Testament notion of "the elect" (ἐκλεκτοί).
[2] Matt. xiii. 24–30, 36–43.   [3] Cf. Mersch, *Morale et Corps Mystique*, p. 138.
[4] There was a vigorous discussion about this in the Middle Ages. Pope John XXII (pope from 1316 to 1334) preached that the Beatific Vision could not be enjoyed before the final resurrection. This opinion was condemned by his successor, Benedict XII, in 1336 (Denzinger, *Enchiridion*, 11th ed., No. 530). Cf. Christopher Wordsworth's well-known hymn:

> "Love and peace they taste for ever,
>   And all truth and knowledge see
> In the beatific vision
>   Of the blessed Trinity."
>   (*E.H.*, 198.)

Beatific Vision, and when his Church is reconstituted by the resurrection of her members into the unity of his no longer stained and incomplete, but glorious and perfect Mystical Body, the members will severally and corporately share in his enjoyment of the Vision through their incorporation and union in the re-assembled Body of which he is the Head. St. John of the Cross gives this truth the most exquisite expression in his *Spiritual Canticle*, commenting on the line, "Let us go to see ourselves in thy beauty." "This," he writes,

"is the adoption of the sons of God, who will truly say to God that which the Son himself said through St. John to the Eternal Father: All my things are thine, and thy things are mine. He by essence, being the Son by nature; and we by participation, being sons by adoption. And thus he spake, not only for himself, who is the Head, but for his whole mystical body, which is the Church, and which will share in the very beauty of the Spouse in the day of her triumph, which will be when she sees God face to face; for which cause the soul here entreats that she and the Spouse may go to see themselves in his beauty."[1]

And in this final and indefectible glorification of man, the whole created universe, with the exception of the reprobate, will have its part. Among other reasons, this is demanded by the mere fact of bodily corruption after death, as a result of which it is quite impossible, in the world as it is, to determine precisely which atoms and electrons belong to which human being. In the ordinary processes of physical metabolism, there is a constant interchange of matter between different human bodies, so that any given particle of matter may belong at different times to different human bodies, while the same body may at different times consist of different matter. Indeed, it is commonly said that the matter in a human body almost entirely changes in the space of seven years, so that a man of fifty has "owned" enough matter to make seven complete human bodies. If there were not a radical transformation of the material order at the Resurrection the plight of the woman who had had seven husbands would be nothing compared with that of the man who had had seven bodies. For the fact is that, through his bodily constituent, a man has a real and inescapable affinity both with other men and with the whole material order; and his full restoration as a unity of soul and body involves nothing less than a transformation of the entire physical

---

[1] *Spir. Cant.*, 2nd red., xxxvi, 5 (Peers's Trans., Vol. II, p. 381).

L

world. Not only man, but the universe, will be transfigured and glorified, and in this transfiguration the great mystery of the Resurrection of the Body will be brought about. As the Apostle tells us, God purposed in Christ "unto a dispensation of the fullness of the times, *to recapitulate all things in Christ, the things in the heavens and the things upon the earth.*"[1] St. Thomas writes: "Not only the nature of men but that of all the world will be restored by the resurrection."[2] "The glorified state," writes the Archpriest Bulgakov, "inherent in the body of the risen Christ, will be communicated to the whole of creation; a new heaven and a new earth will appear, a transfigured earth, resurrected with the Christ and his humanity."[3] Thus the Resurrection of the Body is not only the Resurrection of the Mystical Body; it is also the Resurrection of the World.

Christianity, therefore, is a religion which generates a philosophy of history, and in this respect, with the Judaism of which it is the fulfilment, it stands out from all the other religions of the world. It does not merely affirm a dogma about the nature of existence; it asserts that, at certain moments and in specific ways, God has himself acted. It therefore sees the time-process as essentially heterogeneous. To live before and after the birth of Christ are two different things. The Incarnation is a decisive act which gives to history a centre, as the Second Coming is a decisive act which gives history an end. We are expressing more than a convention when we date our letters with the Year of the Lord. It is not an accident that the first real attempt to write a philosophy of history was made by a Christian, Augustine of Hippo, writing concerning the City of God. What Gerhard Kittel has called "the scandal of particularity" is inherent in the Christian Religion. Christ was crucified, as the ancient baptismal creed asseverates, at a particular moment of history, "under Pontius Pilate," and Christ crucified is "unto Jews a stumbling-block and unto Gentiles foolishness; but unto them that are called, both Jews and Greeks, Christ the power of God, and the wisdom of God."[4] "Human life in the ancient world," wrote Bernard Manning, was "at its best a comic tragedy played in a picturesque and dignified cemetery"[5]; for the Christian, on the other hand,

---

[1] Eph. i. 10.
[2] *In III Sent.*, d. 19, q. 1, a. 3, sol. 2. Cf. *S. Theol.*, Supp., xci, 1c; 3 *sed con.*: "At the one same time the world will be renewed and man will be glorified. . . . The whole world will be renewed for the better."
[3] *The Orthodox Church*, p. 210.   [4] 1 Cor. i. 23.   [5] *Essays in Orthodox Dissent*, p. 68.

it is a Divine Comedy, the comedy of the Re-creation of the World.

V

Since the very essence of the Church is the human nature of Christ communicated to men by adoption and incorporation, it follows that the sole channel of grace[1] to the world is the Church. Christ and his Bride are one flesh. In this sense it must be said that, in the famous phrase of St. Cyprian, "there is not salvation outside the Church."[2] But it must also be asserted that this refers to the channel or instrument of grace, and not primarily to its objects. It is not, I think, always realized that traditionalist theologians, even of the Roman Communion, have been very ready to give full weight to the manifestations of grace which can be discerned outside the borders of the visible Church as they understand it. This may be seen, for example, in the condemnation by Pope Alexander VIII of the view that "pagans, Jews, heretics and the like receive no influx of grace whatever from Jesus Christ,"[3] in the discussion by Otto Karrer of Salvation and Revelation outside the visible Church,[4] in the writings of Maréchal and Maritain on non-Christian mysticism,[5] and in the whole attitude to the non-Christian world of so influential a student of missionary problems as the Jesuit Père Charles, who has shown a largeness of outlook towards the heathen world which is in marked contrast with the exclusiveness of such Protestant thinkers as Dr. Kraemer.[6] Fr. de Lubac expounds this thesis, with a wealth of patristic illustration, in his chapter on "Salvation through the Church"[7]; he remarks on the general recognition by theologians of his communion that "the grace of Christ is universal and that the concrete means of salvation—in the full sense of the word— are not lacking to any soul of good will. There is not one man," he writes, "not one 'infidel' whose supernatural conversion to God is not possible from the very threshold of his rational life."[8]

---

[1] That is, of all grace that is to be described as "the grace of our Lord Jesus Christ." Theologians distinguish between *gratia Dei*, which is conferred by God independently of the merits of Christ, and *gratia Christi*, which is conferred in view of them.

[2] *Salus extra ecclesiam non est* (Ep. lxxiii. 18). The phrase actually occurs in an argument against the validity of heretical baptism!

[3] Denzinger, *Enchiridion*, 11th ed., No. 1295. [4] *Religions of Mankind*, chs. xii, xiii.

[5] Maréchal, *Studies in the Psychology of the Mystics*, chs. v, vi; Maritain, *Redeeming the Time*, ch. x.

[6] See, e.g., G. Phillips on "The Missionary Principles of Pierre Charles, S.J." in *Intern. Rev. of Missions*, Oct. 1943; Kraemer, *The Christian Message in a Non-Christian World, passim.* [7] *Catholicisme*, ch. vii. [8] *Ibid.*, p. 161.

It is clear that a man's practical attitude to non-Christian religions, and indeed to the virtuous acts and habits of all who are not within the visible economy of the Church will depend very largely upon his attitude to this question of the universality of grace. It will also depend upon his view of the extent to which, and the manner in which, man's nature itself has been affected by sin. For when we are confronted with some remarkable act of self-sacrifice and heroism or with some extraordinary state of union with God in mystical prayer, on the part of someone who is not visibly a member of the Church, it is, in general and in principle, possible to explain this in either of two ways. We may, on the one hand, say, "This is an effect of grace, and therefore grace must be active beyond the visible limits of the Church," or we may, on the other hand, say, "This is an effect of nature, which therefore cannot be as corrupted as one might have expected." Or we may, of course, combine both explanations. In a particular concrete case we may be able to choose one alternative with fair confidence, in another we may find it almost impossible to discriminate; this is a question of the practical order, which does not involve any matter of theological principle.[1] There are, however, two points which it is important to stress. One is that it is most unwise to lay down *a priori* the degree to which human nature is itself corrupted. The other is that we can hold with perfect firmness to the doctrine that salvation and grace are mediated only through the Church and still see their effects manifested throughout the human race, even in those who have never heard of Christ; we may indeed see the effects of the Incarnation in a gradual supernaturalization of the whole created order. For the Incarnation was not only something happening to Christ; it was something happening to the world itself, inasmuch as God the Word united to himself the nature of man, in whom the created order reaches its culmination and in whose praise and service towards God the purpose for which the world was created—the glory of God—reaches its rational and articulate expression. We shall indeed expect to find obscurity, error and confusion, to a greater or less extent, where grace is operating without the guidance of the Church's visible preaching of the Word and administration of the Sacraments; nevertheless, grace will be there, and who shall dare to set limits to its effects? In the coming of Christ, everything that was good in the fallen world was claimed

[1] Cf. Maritain on Buddhism and Hinduism, *Redeeming the Time*, p. 248 f.

by him to whom it belonged and was brought beneath the radiance of his redeeming activity. The Creator of the world is also its Redeemer. This does not, of course, mean in the least that membership of the Church is optional or unnecessary, for her human members have their part to play in making salvation available to their fellows, and it is God's purpose that ultimately the visibility of the Church shall be complete. I am not expounding some doctrine of an invisible Church; the Church has a visible structure, a visible ministry, visible sacraments. But, however anomalous such a condition may be, it is possible to belong to this visible Church in an invisible way; and it seems far better to use this form of words·than to speak of a "soul" and "body" of the Church.[1] The point is, I hope, clear. It is that with the Incarnation something new has begun to be, namely human nature hypostatically united to the Person of the Word of God; and, while the organic communication of this re-created human nature to men and women as their personal possession is (at any rate normally) brought about by baptism, its radiance and healing power are shed upon the whole of the created order. The rejoicing in all that is good in the natural order which is so attractive a feature in the lives of such saints as St. Francis of Assisi does not, it must be emphasized, imply that nothing is wrong with the world. On the contrary, Christianity demonstrates that the world is far more evil than had ever been suspected, since it has crucified incarnate Love itself. But, just because the Creator came to be the Redeemer, the evil is declared to be the corruption of a good that is still lovable and redeemable, and the Cross itself becomes the Tree of Life, whose leaves are for the healing of the nations. It may be true that Eastern Christianity has been so conscious of the cosmic effects of the hypostatic union as sometimes to suggest that the kingdom of the world has already become the Kingdom of God and of Christ and to imply that the personal incorporation and sanctification of individual men and women is secondary and almost unimportant. It may also be true, at the other extreme, that the Christian West has sometimes laid such stress upon individual sanctification and justification, whether, with Catholicism, it has seen its chief instrument in baptism and the sacramental life, or with Protestantism, in the act of faith in Christ, as

[1] The statement that it is possible to belong to the "soul" though not to the "body" of the Church seems to go back no further than to Bellarmine. See Congar, *Divided Christendom*, p. 224 f., and cf. de Lubac, *Catholicisme*, p. 175 f. See also p. 110, n. 4 *supra*.

to treat the world outside the Church as altogether excluded from the influence of the Incarnate Lord. At their truest, however, neither East nor West has fallen into these exaggerations. For the truth is that the Light of Christ has already shone out upon the darkness of the world, although the world's re-creation into Christ is far from its completion.

"It is not man alone," writes a member of the Russian Church,

"who is affected by the redemption and the joy of victory; with the joy over our resurrection is linked also joy over the redemption of the whole world, over the ending of the dominion of corruption, over the redemption of all creation and the dawn of the kingdom of life. And the eye of the spirit gazes fervently out towards the glory to come—that 'splendid freedom of the children of God,' of which all creation shall partake. The resurrection is thus an event of cosmic significance, and the world, equally with man, is thereby already permeated by the radiance of the celestial glory, although as yet in hidden form, and has attained to a new and high worth; for it has already taken into itself the germ of immortality. Christ, so sings the Eastern Church, is 'risen as God from the grave in glory and hath thereby raised the whole world with him'. . . . Therefore is the whole world, the whole creation, summoned to rejoice and sing praises to the Lord. . . ."[1]

VI

I must touch on one further point before we leave this chapter. In the discussion which I have just given of the state of the world outside the Church, I have made considerable use of the writings of Roman-Catholic theologians. Now, it may be objected, to a Roman Catholic the visible Church simply means those Christians who are in communion with the Holy See; can you therefore transpose their views into a context in which the Church is not so defined? I believe that, in all relevant respects we can, and for this reason. It is, no doubt, true that, according to the modern Roman theory, obedience to the Papal See is materially necessary to salvation, whatever exceptions there may be in practice for those whose schism is in good faith and not, in the technical sense, "formal." But, even so, membership of the Church must be seen to be primarily not jurisdictional or moral, but sacramental; for

---

[1] N. Arseniev, *Mysticism and the Eastern Church*, p. 35. There is an illuminating discussion of the senses in which, through its union with the Person of the Logos, the human nature of Christ is and is not omnipresent, in Hooker, *Eccl. Pol.* V, lv: ed. of 1888, II, p. 238 f.

presumably any Roman theologian will assert, with Congar, that every baptized child, even of dissident parents, is "truly incorporate in Christ and in the Church—the True Church,"[1] even while he will add that it is a duty, when the child attains the age of reason, for it consciously to accept the Papal jurisdiction. And, after the stress of the Reformation upheavals, during which, by the very force of circumstances, the attention of controversialists of all parties was concentrated upon questions of jurisdiction and organization, the signs are beginning to be seen to-day of a marked reaction on the part of Roman theologians, to give their main attention, in discussing the doctrine of the Church, to the fundamental fact upon which the fathers laid so much stress, namely, that, whatever may be the truth about jurisdiction and obedience, the Church in her inner nature is not so much an organization as a supernatural and sacramental organism. There is thus an increased readiness to recognize that, in Fr. Victor White's words, "membership of the Church is an analogical concept which admits of many manners and degrees, [and] so correspondingly is privation of membership"[2]; this is, incidentally, altogether in line with the teaching of St. Thomas.[3] It is not part of my purpose here to enter into a discussion of the Papal claims, though it will be clear that the view which I have expounded of the Church is one which sees her structure as subsisting primarily through the sacramental acts of baptism and the conferring of Holy Orders, rather than by such moral or juridical acts as, for example, the election of a Pope.[4] All I have tried to show is that, with obvious necessary modifications, the discussions which modern Roman theologians give of questions such as those of the possibility and character of revelation and salvation outside the visible limits of the Church are not devoid of relevance and usefulness to Anglicans simply on account of the differences between them as to what those visible limits are, and that it should be possible therefore for us gratefully to make use of their work without causing embarrassment either to them or to ourselves.

---

[1] *Divided Christendom*, p. 230.
[2] "The Effects of Schism," in *Blackfriars*, Feb. 1942, p. 49. See the same author on "Membership of the Church," *ibid.*, Sept. 1941. Cf. Congar on "The Status of our Separated Brethren, in *Divided Christendom*, ch. vii; Mersch, *The Whole Christ*, Part III, ch. viii.   [3] *S. Theol*, III, viii, 3.
[4] It is true, of course, that a bishop is elected too. But his election is succeeded by consecration; a Pope's, if he is already in episcopal orders, is not.

ADDITIONAL NOTE TO CHAPTER VIII
(*See page* 140)

THE FALL AND ORIGINAL SIN

We are not directly concerned in this book with the precise interpretation that is to be given to the Fall-Story in Genesis, but a few remarks may not be out of place. We may agree with many of the fathers in seeing in the story a certain element of allegory. But I do not think that we can take it as being nothing more than a symbolic description of what happens in every human sin; it professes to be an account of the first entry of sin into human affairs, and the inheritance of that moral and spiritual perversion which theology calls original sin is too widespread and drastic for us lightly to discard the main clue which the Bible gives as to its origin. Still less can we afford to reject the story altogether, as an obsolete relic of primitive mythology; whatever may be the source of the material out of which it is composed, its presence in the Bible guarantees that it is written for our learning. And the late Dr. N. P. Williams's famous theory of the fall of a world-soul[1] seems to raise more problems than it solves and to be the one weak feature of an erudite and brilliant work.

The essential features of the story are: (i) that man was created in fellowship with God and endowed with special gifts of union with God, of supremacy over the lower creation, and of personal felicity; (ii) that he was tempted by an evil extra-human agency to pride and disobedience and yielded to this temptation; (iii) that, in consequence, he found himself excluded from his previous union with God, subjected to the very beings which were originally subject to him, and under the rule of pain and death; (iv) that these consequences have been inherited by subsequent generations as permanent disabilities under which they labour; (v) that there is a mysterious promise of restoration through the "seed of the woman." Among modern discussions of the Fall, which adhere to the traditional teaching while taking full account of recent research and criticism, I would specially mention Mr. T. M. Parker's small work, *The Re-creation of Man*, as well as the books of Mr. Charles Williams and Mr. C. S. Lewis, which have been referred to in the text; while Dr. F. J. Hall's *Evolution and the Fall*, though

---

[1] *The Ideas of the Fall and of Original Sin*, lect. viii.

written as long ago as 1910, is far from valueless to-day. Mr. Lewis's two novels, *Out of the Silent Planet* and *Perelandra*, utilize the doctrine for the purposes of imaginative writing in a way which perhaps brings out its real significance better than any merely academic discussion. The following further points seem to be relevant:

(1) Any view, like that of Berdyaev,[1] which asserts that "the Fall could not have taken place in the natural world, because this world is itself the result of the Fall,"[2] runs perilously near to making God responsible for evil.

(2) To avoid this, it is essential to distinguish clearly between God's creation of the world and the world's disobedience to God. Niebuhr has remarked that in Barthianism "the emphasis upon the difference between the holiness of God and the sinfulness of man is so absolute that man is convicted, not of any particular breaches against the life of the humanity community, but of being human and not divine. Thus, to all intents and purposes, creation and the Fall are practically identified."[3]

(3) It will hardly do to say with Dr. J. S. Whale that "the Fall refers not to some datable aboriginal calamity in the historic past of humanity, but to a dimension of human experience which is always present—namely, that we who have been created for fellowship with God repudiate it continually; and that the whole of mankind does this along with us."[4] This ignores the problem of the origin of human sinfulness and understresses our corporate solidarity in it. And it is open to the grave charge that it implies that God has made man intrinsically evil; neither Tillich[5] nor even Niebuhr,[6] who both take this general line, seems altogether to avoid this charge; or if they do it is at the cost of unintelligibility.

(4) Orthodox doctrine does not compel us to believe that Adam was created in a state of advanced intellectual or moral development, but that he was *innocent*; Mr. Lewis's *Perelandra* gives a vivid picture of what this might mean. We have not to hold, with Robert South, that "an Aristotle was but the rubbish of an Adam, and Athens but the rudiments of Paradise."

(5) There is nothing "unscientific" about belief in a historical

---

[1] See, e.g., *Freedom and the Spirit*, ch. i.   [2] *Ibid.*, p. 22.
[3] *Moral Man and Immoral Society*, p. 68.
[4] *Christian Doctrine*, p. 52. Cf. Brunner, *Man in Revolt*, p. 85 f.
[5] *The Interpretation of History*, *passim*.   [6] *The Nature and Destiny of Man*, Vol. I, *passim*.

Fall, nor is it contradicted by the fact that, in certain respects, man has steadily "risen." The Fall was a single moral act of a type that is inherently inaccessible to scientific investigation, and it is at least striking that man's steady "rise" so consistently bears within itself the seeds of its own frustration.

(6) Belief that human mortality is a consequence of the Fall is in no wise contradicted by theories of man's evolutionary affinity with other animals, to which death is natural. Orthodox theology has never taught that man was physically immortal *by nature*, but that bodily immortality was a *donum superadditum* conferred on man in Paradise.[1]

(7) "Original sin" is not the same as "actual sin"; the word "sin" is analogical. In some respects original sin is like the disgrace which one member of a family may bring on the others; in other respects it is like the personal disgrace which a sinner brings upon himself. It has a greater element of personal responsibility in it than the former, and less than the latter. But there is nothing *precisely* like it except itself, so any comparison will fail somewhere; it is "what it is, and not another thing."

(8) One of the great problems is to know how the effects of the first sin can be "transmitted." The description of original sin as an "entail" is a convenient metaphor from the realm of law, but it does not *explain* anything. If, however, the chief effect is a destruction of unity, as is suggested in the text, the problem is somewhat eased, for no mechanism is needed to transmit the *absence* of something. It is presumably original righteousness rather than original sin that would require a *mechanism* for its transmission; and since the Fall that mechanism is no longer there. To put this in different words, if it is objected that the human race has not such a close-knit unity that the sin of one man immediately affects everyone else, the reply may be that the unity with which the human race was endowed by God was destroyed by the first sin and therefore cannot be discerned any longer. Traditional theology has always seen the primary effect of the Fall as a privation, a *spoliatio gratuitorum*, and has seen the positive wound, the *vulneratio naturalium*, as consequent on this.[2] I would add, however, that Verrièle[3] asserts that the generic unity of the human race and the transmission of human nature by procreation are insufficient to propagate either original righteousness or its privation, and that

[1] Cf. *S. Theol.*, I, xcvii, 1. [2] *Ibid.*, II I, cix.
[3] *Le Surnaturel en nous et le Péché originel*, p. 135.

we must add to this an entirely free positive determination by God himself. He makes great use of the notion that the Fall must not be viewed as an accident which took God as it were by surprise, but that there is an organic unity, in God's foreknowledge, embracing in one great sweep creation, Fall and redemption.[1]

(9) The universality of original sin agrees most easily with monogenism (the view that the human race is descended from one biological origin), but it would not necessarily be irreconcilable with polygenism. Even if the elevation from the animal to the human level occurred independently in more than one place, it might still be the case that the affinity and coinherence that existed through the common possession of manhood was so radical that one sin would produce its effects in mankind as a whole. As we have already observed, the universal "manhood" is of a unique and very puzzling kind.[2] Monogenism seems, however, to be the theory favoured by most biologists.

(10) The uniqueness of Adam's sin consists not in any extraordinary moral obloquy, but in the fact that it is the *first* sin of a material being. With it, for the first time, the material realm violated the law of its being by action from within itself and so planted within itself the principle of self-contradiction. It may have been previously interfered with from without by sin in the spiritual realm on the part of its "guardian angels," but that would presumably be far less drastic in its consequences and its significance than interference from within its own being. It may be added that the occurrence of sin in the angelic realm may be the most satisfactory explanation of the evil (if any) that was in the world before the appearance of man.

Some very interesting discussions of these questions by a theologian who is also a trained scientist will be found in Dr. F. H. Smyth's *Manhood into God*, ch. iii *et al.* And one of the best purely theological works on the Fall and its effects is the work of the Abbé Verrièle to which reference has been already made.

---

[1] *Le Surnaturel en nous et le Péché originel*, p. 108.   [2] See p. 71 f. *supra*.

CHAPTER IX

THE SACRAMENT OF UNITY—I

I

IN his brilliant essay on "The Idea of 'The Church' in the Primitive Liturgies," which should be studied by anyone who wishes to understand fully the real nature of the Church and her liturgical action, Dom Gregory Dix opens the exposition of his theme as follows:

> "The mystery of the Church is the mystery of 'Christ in us, the hope of glory,' and this indwelling is in them that 'eat his Flesh and drink his Blood' and so 'have eternal life.' There is a necessary, intimate and obvious relation between the doctrines concerning the Mystical and the Sacramental Body of the One Christ, which finds its profoundest expression in the Liturgy. In the eucharistic rite of the pre-Nicene Church when its outlines were still uncomplicated by the later decorative additions of piety, that relation was expressed with a classic simplicity and truth, not only in the formulae, but in the very substance and structure of the Liturgy.
>
> "In the primitive view the *raison d'être* both of the Church and Eucharist is ultimately one thing only—λατρεία, worship, offered to God. That 'God *seeketh*' worshippers 'in spirit and in truth' is the Divinely-given reason for the Incarnation, which holds good of its extensions in the Church and the Eucharist. This worship is both the result of and a participation in a divine action, into which the Church and its human action are taken up. The Church's worship is effective, it absolutely glorifies God, because the Church 'is one with (ἀνακεκραμένη) Jesus Christ as Jesus Christ is with the Father.' "[1]

It will thus be fitting to begin our discussion of the Eucharist by considering the nature of worship itself. We may first note that "worship" is a good old English word, which in its essence does not necessarily mean anything particularly religious. Worship is just worth-ship, and it signifies the rendering to any person or body of persons of that to which their "worth"—their worthiness—

---

[1] *The Parish Communion*, p. 97. The closing quotation is from Ignatius, *Eph.* v, 1.

entitles them. So a magistrate on the bench is referred to as "Your Worship," the bridegroom in the Marriage-Service promises to worship his bride with his body, and one of the London livery companies is called the Worshipful Company of Spectacle-Makers. Neither the magistrate, the bride nor the master-opticians are entitled to the reverence which is due to Almighty God; they are, however, each of them *worthy*, because of the importance of the offices which they fulfil, and each of them therefore is entitled to worship, though the worship will be of a different kind in each case, and will in each case be finite.

When, however, we turn from creatures to consider God, the question of worship appears in a different light. God, the self-existent, self-sufficient, all-perfect Being, who depends upon nothing outside himself for his existence, while all other beings depend entirely upon him for *theirs*, God the all-holy, all-wise and all-loving, is of *infinite* worth, and therefore is entitled by his very nature to a worship that knows no limits. It is not simply that his creatures owe him gratitude for his love in creating them, though this is, of course, perfectly true, but that his own nature, what he *is* quite apart from what he *does*, is supremely worthy and so supremely worshipful. In something of the same way as a beautiful picture, just because it is beautiful, has a claim upon our admiration regardless of any benefit that we may have received from its existence, so God has a supreme claim on our worship just because he is infinite perfection, regardless of the benefits—boundless as those of course are—which he has showered upon us. We realize, therefore, the duty of worship, not by reflecting on God's goodness towards us and then trying to decide what we owe him in return, but by reflecting on what he is in the perfection of his Being and then realizing—or vainly striving to realize—what such perfection is entitled to receive. And this supreme type of worship, which is due to God and God alone, is what theology describes by the Greek word *latreia* and what we usually know as *adoration*.

Once, however, we begin to recognize what kind of worship God's infinite worth demands, we can hardly fail to be conscious of our total inability to give it to him. Even the most devoted human being who has ever lived, even the whole human race from the beginning to the end of time, even the angelic hosts of heaven cannot render to God that infinite honour to which his perfection entitles him. So we find in all, or almost all, the races of mankind a profound consciousness that we can make a worthy offering to

God only if, before we offer it to him, he has taken it and trans-formed it into something that is good enough for him. This is, I would suggest, at least one of the roots of the universal institution of *sacrifice*, in which, under a bewildering variety of forms, men offer to God different kinds of gifts which are consecrated to this use by some priestly ritual act.

Non-Christian sacrifice, however, is a recognition of the existence of the problem rather than a solution of it; none of the sacrificial acts of the pre-Christian religions were adequate offer-ings from man to God. The various acts of consecration did not, as a matter of fact, bring about the required change in the gifts offered; all they could do was to testify to man's consciousness of the fact that his offerings were unfit and his sacrifice powerless to render to God that worship to which God's worth entitles him. For here is the paradox: God's infinite worth merits from his creatures an act of infinite homage; but an act of infinite homage could be given him only by an infinite being. In fact, only God himself could render the worship which man is called upon to give, and this quite apart from the fact that man's universal sinfulness has debased to an unknown degree even that limited worship which a finite being might by its nature offer. Are we then to conclude that no adequate act of worship can ever be offered to God?

We might indeed be tempted to think so, were it not for the fact that God is not a bare monad but the ever-blessed Trinity. In the eternal and incomprehensible fulness of the life of the divine Being, God the Son is ever making to the eternal Father that complete and infinite act of love and homage which the Father's perfection can justly claim. In the life of the Holy Trinity, then, a perfect and adequate worship is unceasingly performed: God is offering God to God. But still a question remains. Granted that the one perfect worshipper is God the Son, so that from him the Father does receive his due worship, is there still no *human* worship that has been or can be offered which is adequate to God?

At this point there appears the relevance of the doctrine of the Incarnation, of the fact that, by taking human nature from a pure Virgin, God the Son, the eternal adorer of the heavenly Father, was made man and lived a human life. And in that human nature he not only made atonement for the sins of men; he also offered to the Father the only adequate offering of adoration that any human being has ever made. For, since he was man, it was a human offering, and since he was God it was an infinite one; furthermore, since he was sinless, it was an unspoilt offering.[1] So in the life of perfect human obedience which God the Son lived upon earth, he offered to the Father one coherent, adequate and unimpaired act of adoration, the only sufficient worship that had ever been offered by man to God. And as his earthly work drew near its close, he could say, "I have glorified thee on the earth; I have finished the work which thou gavest me to do."[2]

And because in the Ascension Christ's manhood was not destroyed but was taken out of this visible realm into the heavenly places, this perfect act of human worship has not ceased. It is going on for ever in heaven, Christ having, as the Epistle to the Hebrews puts it, entered in once for all into the Holy Place.[3] So also in the Apocalypse St. John describes how, when the door was opened in heaven, he saw not only the eternal Father seated on his throne and surrounded by all the hosts of heaven, but also the Lamb as it had been slain, who alone was worthy to open the sealed book.[4]

There is, then, a perfect and adequate human worship of God going on at this moment; it is going on in the heavenly realm, and it is being offered by the ascended Christ in his glorified human nature. However, this still does not solve our problem. How are we imperfect sinful creatures living here on earth to make the offering which *we* owe to God?

The answer is amazingly simple, but almost incredible in the manifestation which it gives of the condescension of God. It is that Christ unites our human nature to his, so that we may be able to offer his offering or, rather, that he may be able to offer it through and in us. For, as we have seen, it is not a mere metaphor, but the literal truth, that the Church is the Body of Christ. Christ has only one Body, that which he took from his mother the Virgin Mary, but that Body exists under various modes. As a natural Body it was seen on earth, hung on the Cross, rose in glory on the first Easter Day and was taken into heaven in the Ascension; as a mystical Body it appeared on earth on the first Whitsunday and we know it as the Holy Catholic Church; as a sacramental Body it becomes present on our altars at every Eucharist when, by the operation of the Holy Ghost and the priestly act of Christ, bread and wine are transformed into, and made one with, the glorified

---

[1] There are two points here: the offering was unspoilt by sin; it was also infinite. If we accept the traditional belief in the personal sinlessness of the Blessed Virgin, we should have in her case as well an unspoilt offering, but it would not be an infinite one, for her person is that of a finite creature.
[2] John xvii. 4.   [3] Heb. ix. 12.   [4] Rev. iv, v.

Body which is in heaven. Now we were made members of the Mystical Body in our baptism, whereby we were incorporated into Christ. So our whole life as members of the Christian Church is an act of worship, simply because we have been incorporated into the manhood of Christ and made parts of his Body. And just as the Incarnation, while appearing to us as a coming down of God the Son from heaven, is in its essence a taking up of manhood into God,[1] so the consecration of the Eucharist, while appearing to us as a coming down of the ascended Christ from heaven on to our altars, is in essence the taking up of this, that and the other portion of bread and wine to become identified with the Body in heaven. Each Eucharist is thus, to borrow the phrase of the Apocalypse, a door opened in heaven,[2] so that it is not a repetition of Christ's sacrifice but is identical with it. And because, as we have just seen, Christ has not three bodies but one Body which exists in three modes (natural, mystical, sacramental), in offering the Eucharist we offer ourselves, or, to express it more accurately, Christ offers us as members of his Body. So we may see the force of St. Augustine's famous words: "The mystery of yourselves is laid upon the table of the Lord."[3]

So, then, the Eucharist is the one perfect act of worship that we can offer to God. And far from Eucharistic worship being a matter merely of the sanctuary and the sacristy, it is of direct relevance to the world in which Christians live and work and love and die. For the Body which appears in its sacramental form upon our altars is the same Body which in its mystical form is at work in the world and of which we are members. In a quite true sense, therefore, what Christians do in the world, in their work and in their play, is identical with the offering made upon the altar and with the act of worship made by Christ in heaven. That is to say, for the Christian as a member of the Body of Christ, his whole life is liturgical and there is real point in the motto which was used by the young Catholic working-men of the French Jocist movement: "My bench is my altar, my factory is my Church, my work is my Mass."

There is an all too common view of the relation of worship to life whose falsehood should now be evident. I mean the view that the main value of worshipping in church is that it enables one to do God's will more thoroughly in one's daily life. It cannot be too strongly emphasized that the Eucharist—as indeed every act of worship—is its own justification. It is the rendering to God of

---

[1] See p. 42 f. *supra.*   [2] *Rev.* iv. 1.   [3] *Serm.* 272.

that of which he is worthy, and in that its whole reason lies. It would, however, as we have just seen, be wrong to suppose that the Eucharist has no relation to life, for both life and liturgy are activities of the Mystical Body and, as we have seen, the Mystical and the Sacramental Body are in their essence one.

I will carry this thought a little further. If the one perfect act of worship is being offered by Christ in his glorified natural Body in heaven and if the Mystical Body and the natural Body are identical, might it not seem that we make our perfect act of worship simply by being devout members of the Mystical Body without there being any need for the Sacramental Body and the Eucharistic rite? To answer this question, it is necessary to recognize one great and fundamental difference between the sacramental and mystical aspects of the Body of Christ.

The Sacramental Body is, in a quite definite sense, perfect, while the Mystical Body is not. All the sinlessness of Christ's glorified human nature is manifested in the Eucharist, wherein he communicates himself to us and unites us to himself in the integrity and splendour of his spotless humanity. The offering of himself to the Father which he makes there is unsullied by any flaw. The Mystical Body, in contrast, is made up of sinful human beings, whose incorporation into Christ, while in the truest sense a new birth and a communication of Christ's own life, has not restored at one stroke all that sin had destroyed. In addition, the Mystical Body is woefully incomplete, for many who will one day belong to it are not members of it as yet. In consequence, while, on the side of him who is its Head, the Mystical Body is perfect and entire just because it is his, on the side of those who are its members it is maimed and undeveloped. It needs therefore, for its healing and its growth, to be brought into repeated relation with the glorified Body which is its archetype; and this is done in the Eucharist, which is, as we saw above, the door opening from earth into heaven, the link between the natural and the Mystical Body of Christ. It is by the Eucharist that the Church lives, and on it that she feeds; as Dom Dix has pointed out, the Eucharist is not, as people so often say, primarily the *expression* of the Church's unity, but its *cause*.[1] In the Eucharist, Christ, the great High Priest, offers his

---

[1] *The Parish Communion*, p. 122. Cf. the inspiring exposition of this theme by Dr. A. M. Farrer in his essay in the same work (pp. 78–83). "The Glorified Body," he writes, "*is* the Mystical Body—that is, the second has no reality that is not the reality of the first. . . . And what the Eucharist means is the creation of the Mystical Body by partaking in the glorified Body—not yet in the fullness of Resurrection-being, but in that spiritual anticipation of it that we have tried to set forth." (p. 83.)

M

Body under its sacramental aspect, perfect and complete, not having spot or wrinkle or any such thing, holy and without blemish, through that same Body under its mystical aspect which is the Church, weak, sinful and unfinished. "I am black, but comely," speaks the bride in the Song of Songs,[1] and the Bride of Christ may repeat the same words. She is black with the sins and failures of her members, but the mystery of herself is laid upon the table of the Lord, comely and fair and holy.

For the Christian, then, in the Mystical Body, life and worship are but two elements in one great act, the self-offering of Christ the God-man to the Father in heaven. Life itself is liturgical, for whether the Christian serves God or whether he sins against him, he is acting as a member of the Body, and it is in the Eucharist that his life is given its true interpretation as not merely his life but the life of Christ in him: "I live; and yet no longer I, but Christ liveth in me."[2]

I cannot better summarize the thought of this discussion than by quoting three Latin phrases which have recently been widely used in this connection. As Christians we are *filii in Filio*, sons in the Son, sons of God by adoption, through our real incorporation into him who is the Son of God by nature. The Church is *Totus Christus*, the Whole Christ, for, while in its natural aspect Christ's Body is perfect and complete as he took it from his Virgin Mother, in its mystical aspect it consists not only of Christ but also of us. And lastly, the Church's offering is made, not just by us who are its members or just by Christ who is its Head, but by Head and members together, *membra cum Capite*, to the glory of God the Everlasting Father.

II

It is not, however, merely the human part of the created order that receives redemption and makes its true self-offering to God by joining "with angels and archangels" in the heavenly worship. The whole material realm is involved, for man is "nature's priest." There are in the Bible mysterious suggestions that not only man but the sub-human creation also has fallen under the dominion of sin and needs to be redeemed. In Genesis, man, as God's vice-gerent who bears on himself the divine image, is given supremacy over the creatures that lie beneath him in the hierarchy

---

[1] Cant. i. 5.   [2] Gal. ii. 20.

of God's handiwork. He is placed in the Garden of Eden to cultivate it so that it may bring forth its fruit to perfection, and the Lord God brings to Adam the beasts of the field and the fowls of the air to receive their names, "and whatsoever the man called every living creature, that was the name thereof."[1] And, after the Fall man is not only driven out of the Garden and excluded from the tree of life; the very earth itself turns against him. "Cursed is the ground for thy sake; in toil shalt thou eat of it all the days of thy life; thorns also and thistles shall it bring forth to thee."[2] This same conception is expressed by St. Paul in the Epistle to the Romans:

> "The earnest expectation of the creation waiteth for the revealing of the sons of God. For the creation was subjected to vanity, not of its own will, but by reason of him who subjected it, in hope that the creation itself also shall be delivered from the bondage of corruption into the liberty of the glory of the children of God. For we know that the whole creation groaneth and travaileth in pain together until now."[3]

Let us follow this thought out. The lower creation is meant to find its fulfilment through the use made of it by man. Through the powers with which God has endowed both him and it—powers of intelligence and craftsmanship in the one case, the physical properties that are summed up in the laws of nature in the other— it is meant to minister to man's true happiness as it is used by him in the life of praise and worship by which he glorifies God. Left to itself it can glorify God only passively and dumbly, by continuing to be what God has made it. This, of course, is itself a great privilege, as Addison declared in his hymn concerning the orbs of heaven:

> "What though in solemn silence all
>   Move round the dark terrestrial ball;
>   What though no real voice nor sound
>   Amid their radiant orbs be found;
>   In reason's ear they all rejoice,
>   And utter forth a glorious voice;
>   For ever singing as they shine,
>   'The hand that made us is divine.' "

But in being rightly used by man, who is God's vice-gerent in the material realm, they achieve an even greater destiny, for they are taken up as an element in the "rational service," the λογικὴ λατρεία

[1] Gen. ii. 19.   [2] Gen. iii. 17–18.   [3] Rom. viii. 19–22.

which man is able to offer to God. (We can see the literal truth of this if we reflect that man is a being of a double nature, material and spiritual, and that, in becoming his food, material things are taken up into the actual physical organism in which he serves the Creator.) Now because of man's sinful condition his service is partial and maimed. Hence, through his sin man not only fails to achieve his own fulfilment; he prevents the sub-human realm from receiving its fulfilment too, for its highest end is to be rightly used by man in the service of God. There is therefore great significance in the fact that the raw material of the Eucharist is bread and wine, for these elements are provided by the joint co-operation of the material realm and man. The bringing of the bread and wine to the altar involves a combination of human activities whose range and complexity elude the grasp of the human imagination. There is the labour of the men who have ploughed the wheatfield and sown and reaped and milled the grain, of those who have planted and harvested the vine, of those who have baked the bread and fermented the grape-juice, and of all the vast mass of human beings who have directly or indirectly, and knowingly or unknowingly, been concerned with the making of the eucharistic elements and their conveyance to the place where the Sacrament is to be celebrated. It is a natural and laudable sentiment that has frequently entrusted to religious orders the manufacture of sacramental wine and altar-breads, in order to ensure the utmost care and reverence in their production, but it is literally impossible to exclude anyone from *some* share, remote or proximate, in this activity, and the elements as they are offered on the altar focus into themselves this unimaginably complex human co-operation, with all the sin, as well as all the virtue, that is implicated in it. The bread and wine of the Offertory are the tokens or first-fruits of the material order, in which it is exalted to the highest function of which, by the power of God, it is capable, namely of becoming the sacramental Body and Blood of Christ; but their manufacture and transportation are the work of man as "nature's priest," performing his sacerdotal function in the natural order, and through this they concentrate into themselves all the pain and joy, all the virtue and sin of which man's life is made up. And it is right that this should be so, for sin is what the Eucharist, as the "continual remembrance of the sacrifice of the death of Christ,"[1] is concerned with. Just as Christ took his natural Body from the

---

[1] Prayer-Book Catechism.

very race which had fallen, so he takes the material for his sacramental body from the hands of the same sinful human race. And
just as the immediate channel of the natural body was the "pure
Virgin"[1] who had "found favour with God,"[2] so the immediate
channel by which the Eucharistic elements are brought to God is
the Virgin-Church which is the Bride of Christ. There are thus
three stages in the making of the Eucharistic offerings: what is
placed upon the altar is the fruit which the earth has brought forth,
it is the product of the labour of man, it is taken within the context
of redeemed humanity in the Church of Christ. The next step is
not man's but God's; in the words of St. Irenaeus, "the cup and
the bread receives the Word of God and becomes the Body and
Blood of Christ."[3] And through the reception of the Sacrament
the Mystical Body is fed and bound together in unity, and the one
full, perfect and sufficient sacrifice, oblation and satisfaction for
the sins of the whole world is once more brought before God.
As Nicholas Arseniev writes:

"It is not only for the individual that the sacrament of the
Lord's Supper has a central, living, mystic meaning, but for the
whole community, the whole Church, yes, for all mankind. For
here the divine mingles with the human, the terrestrial; here in
the Eucharist praise and sacrifice are offered to the Lord for the
whole world and by the whole world . . . , and the whole cosmos
is hereby potentially ennobled and sanctified in that earthly
elements of wine and bread become the glorified body and blood
of the Son of God. That is why the idea of all creation assembled
in spirit round the eucharistic altar so constantly recurs in the
old liturgies of the East. For through him, through his death, and
through the glorification of his risen body, here mystically represented, creation partakes of the glory of the redemption."[4]

III

We have seen, then, that in the Eucharist the earthly Church
is given a share in the continual offering which the glorified Christ
perpetually makes before the Father's throne in heaven. And
indeed some eminent Anglican theologians have seen the sacrificial
character of the Eucharist to consist entirely in this. Thus the late
Dr. F. E. Brightman held—or at any rate was believed to hold[5]—
that the death of Christ was only the initial act in his sacrifice and

[1] Prayer Book, Collect for Christmas Day.   [2] Luke i. 30.   [3] *Haer.*, v, 2, 3.
[4] *Mysticism and the Eastern Church*, p. 58.   [5] See p. 169 *infra*.

that the essential sacrificial act is performed in heaven, where, as the Epistle to the Hebrews tells us, he has "through his own blood entered in once for all into the holy place . . . into heaven itself, now to appear before the face of God for us."[1] The Eucharist is therefore, on this view, a true sacrifice because it is directly related to this heavenly offering.

A somewhat similar view is found in the great work of the late Bishop of Lincoln, Dr. F. N. Hicks, *The Fullness of Sacrifice*. There it is argued that the equation of sacrifice with death, which has been common to all Christian theologians, both Catholic and Protestant, for centuries, is erroneous and has consistently vitiated Eucharistic theology, introducing the most lamentable confusions on every side. A careful study of the Biblical text, it is asserted, shows that the essentially priestly and sacrificial act in the Jewish sacrifices was not the slaying of the victim, which might be (and in most cases was) done by a lay person, but the offering upon the altar of the blood which to the Jews was identical with, or at least a divinely ordained symbol of, the victim's life; the slaying was merely an indispensable preliminary by means of which the blood was released. This being so, the argument runs, Catholics and Protestants have simply been at cross-purposes. The Catholics have said, in effect, "The Eucharist is a sacrifice, therefore Christ must in some way be slain in it," while the Protestants have as often retorted, "Christ cannot be slain afresh, therefore the Eucharist cannot be a sacrifice"; and both have assumed that sacrifice is identical with death. But, says Dr. Hicks, "the Sacrifice is not the Death alone; nor the pleading with the blood alone; nor the offering upon the altar 'in heaven'; nor the act of Communion alone. . . . Each stage is sacrificial. All together make the One Sacrifice."[2]

A very subtle theory of this type is found in the *magnum opus* of the Jesuit writer, Père de la Taille, which excited so violent a controversy in his own communion and so much admiration in ours. According to him there are three elements in a sacrifice, namely a ritual oblation, an immolation, and a divine acceptance; in the case of the one true Sacrifice, these are realized in the Last Supper, on Calvary, and in the Resurrection and the entrance into the heavenly places respectively. What then is the Mass? It cannot be a new *immolation*, for Christ cannot die again; and if he could, the Mass would be a different sacrifice from that of Calvary,

---

[1] Heb. ix. 12, 24.   [2] Op. cit., p. 251.

whereas it is actually the same. It must therefore be a new *oblation*, one made by the Church after the immolation, as the Last Supper was the oblation made by Christ before the immolation. The Mass involves no change in Christ himself; he is a victim, but a glorified victim, and as such he is present in the Mass.[1]

A very similar theory to this was elaborated independently by Sir Will Spens; it appears in his essay on "The Eucharist" in *Essays Catholic and Critical*, where it is combined with an original philosophical doctrine of the nature of the Eucharistic presence. According to him, "the Last Supper and the Eucharist are not separate sacrifices from that of Calvary, but supply a necessary element in the sacrifice of Calvary, by expressly investing our Lord's death before God and man with its sacrificial significance."[2] He adopts a slightly different terminology from that of de la Taille, referring to the three elements as oblation, immolation and consecration respectively.

Now in spite of their differences these theories have certain common features. They all (with the possible exception of Brightman's) view the Eucharist as being in some sense a *constituent* of the Sacrifice of Christ, and they all (though this is less obvious in Spens) tend to see it as related primarily to the heavenly priesthood of the ascended Christ rather than to Calvary. (De la Taille, who is a master of subtlety, is difficult to convict altogether on these points, but his general emphasis lies in the way indicated.) Brightman's view was elaborately controverted in Dr. A. G. Mortimer's book, *The Eucharistic Sacrifice*, and this last writer amassed an enormous quantity of material to prove, from both Scripture and tradition, that, whatever we may believe about a "heavenly altar," it is clear that Christ's sacrifice is complete on Calvary, and that it is from the Cross that the Eucharist derives its character as a true, though not an absolute, sacrifice.[3]

[1] The large Latin work *Mysterium Fidei* was published by Beauchesne of Paris (2nd ed., 1924); an E.T. of the first part was published by Sheed and Ward in London in 1941. The shorter work, *The Mystery of Faith and Human Opinion*, appeared in E.T. in 1930; the first essay was also issued separately. A similar line to that of de la Taille was followed by Dr. Alexander Macdonald, the Roman Catholic Bishop of Victoria, B.C., in his book, *The Sacrifice of the Mass*. He says flatly that "without the ceremonial offering in the Mass, the Sacrifice finished on Calvary would have been ritually incomplete. . . . Our Lord's Sacrifice of himself attained its *actus primus*, or complete essence, on Calvary; it attains its *actus secundus*, or complete operation, on our altars." (pp. 105, 108.)
[2] Op. cit., p. 436. Spens was criticized by Canon O. C. Quick in *The Christian Sacraments*, and replied in *Theology*, Jan.–Mar. 1929.
[3] Mortimer has, however, been accused of misrepresenting Brightman; see F. L. Cross, *Darwell Stone*, p. 70.

Dr. Hicks's work, while receiving general approbation as calling much-needed attention to an aspect of the Eucharist that has too often been overlooked, has been criticized as regards its main assertion that the blood simply represents the life. Dr. A. M. Farrer has argued that, while this suggestion contains an element of truth, to identify blood with life simply, to the exclusion of the death through which it has passed, is theologically unsound and does not represent the main Old-Testament tradition.

> "Blood," he writes, "expresses death on its sacrificial side, and not life; and whether our Lord used little premeditation or much in adding the cup to the loaf in his institution, it was precisely this emphasis on death which gave it separate value for the Church, according to the foreordaining providence of God. It is this element which forbids us to forget that not only do we communicate with the Lord's Glorious Body in the sacrament, but equally we declare the Lord's death until he come."[1]

The obvious objection to theories such as de la Taille's and Spens's is that, by making the Eucharist one element in the whole sacrificial act, they tend to depreciate the evangelical fact that, in whatever way it may be, it is the Passion itself with which we are concerned in the Eucharistic Sacrifice and not something additional to it. The Passion *is* the Sacrifice, and the Eucharist is not something extra to it; the Eucharist is the "memorial"—that is, the *anamnesis*, the making present[2]—of the true Paschal Lamb who is the Christ. Indeed the Church's sole warrant for celebrating the Eucharist at all is that, in obedience to Christ's command, she is doing, as his representative and instrument, what he himself did *pridie quam pateretur*, "in the same night that he was betrayed." As St. Thomas says, in his magnificent Eucharistic hymn:

Quod in coena Christus gessit	"What he did at supper seated
Faciendum hoc expressit	Christ ordained to be repeated,
In sui memoriam.	His memorial ne'er to cease:
Docti sacris institutis,	And, his word for guidance taking,
Panem, vinum in salutis	Bread and wine we hallow, making
Consecramus hostiam.	Thus his sacrifice of peace."

It may be added that the exposition of the Eucharistic Sacrifice in the *Responsio* which the English Archbishops issued in 1897 in

---

[1] "Eucharist and Church in the New Testament," in *The Parish Communion*, p. 90.
[2] For the argument that this is the true meaning of *anamnesis*, see G. Dix in *The Parish Communion*, p. 120 f.

reply to the Papal condemnation of Anglican Orders is given
without any reference to the Heavenly Session. "We continue,"
they say,

> "a perpetual memory of the precious death of Christ, who is our
> Advocate with the Father and the propitiation for our sins, accord-
> ing to his precept, until his coming again. For first we offer the ✓
> sacrifice of praise and thanksgiving; then next we plead and ✓
> represent before the Father the sacrifice of the cross, and by it
> we confidently intreat remission of sins and all other benefits of
> the Lord's Passion for all the whole Church; and lastly we offer ✓
> the sacrifice of ourselves to the Creator of all things which we have
> already signified by the oblations of his creatures."[1]

(It is, however, only right to add that this statement was made in
direct reply to the accusation that the English Church teaches that
the Eucharist is only a "nude commemoration of the Cross," and
would therefore naturally tend to concentrate upon the relation of
the Eucharist to Calvary.)

The Eucharist then is primarily related to Calvary and the
Cross; yet we have already agreed that it *is* related to the Ascended
Christ, that the Sacramental Body is the link between the glorified
and the Mystical Body of Christ, that it is the means by which the
Christ who lives for evermore feeds his Church with his own
immortal life. Are we then faced with a choice between a
"Gospel" doctrine which would give us a dead Christ at the altar
and a "Hebrews" doctrine which would give us a living Christ
who is perhaps our food but is no longer really our sacrifice? And
must we return to the Reformation dilemma : either a real sacrifice
and therefore a repetition of Calvary, or no repetition of Calvary
and therefore no real sacrifice? If we remember what is the true
nature of the Church and of adoption into Christ, we shall, I think,
see that the Eucharist is both a feeding upon the ascended Christ
and at the same time a real re-presentation of Calvary.

We must revert to the fact, which I have already expounded,[2]
that, through her inherence in the human nature of Christ, which
is itself hypostatically united with the Person of the Word of God,
the Church has herself a participation in that eternity of God to
which the whole course of the world's history is compresent *simul
et semel*. Her life is hid with Christ in God, and therefore, while
on her human side she lives in the order of time and change—
sponsa Christi quae per orbem militas ecclesia—in her inner divine

[1] *Responsio*, XI (printed in *Anglican Orders (English)*).   [2] See p. 116 *supra*.

reality she has a real experience of, and presence at, not only the things that are but also those that have been and shall be. And this experience is at its height[1] in the Eucharist, for there, as we have seen, the identity of the Mystical Body of Christ with his glorified natural body is most fully manifested and maintained. Hence there is real justification for the conviction of the early Church that in the Eucharist the *Parousia*, the Second Coming, of Christ is really to be found, and for the general Eastern-Orthodox conception of the Eucharist as being the mystery of redeemed humanity in which the whole created order is transfigured and fulfilled, an actual epiphany of the deliverance of the creation itself "from the bondage of corruption into the liberty of the glory of the children of God."[2] In the Eucharist there is a real presence of the Last Day. But if the future is present in the Eucharist, so is the past as well; the whole mystery of man's creation, fall, redemption and restoration is, as it were, focused into one moment of time. And in this Eucharistic participation of the timelessness of God, the Church experiences both the Last Supper and the Crucifixion; there is the *anamnesis*—the "bringing into the present"—of the Upper Room and Golgotha.

But now, it will be objected, we have proved too much. Our original problem was how Calvary, a past event, could be present to us to-day. But now the problem presents itself how, among all the past and future events which are made present to us in the Eucharist, Calvary can stand out as unique among the others. By passing, so to speak, through the human nature of Christ into the timelessness of God we have gone too far. We are mysteriously present at Bethlehem and Cana and Bethany as well as at Calvary; more, we are present at the Fall of Troy, the Battle of Salamis, the discovery of America, and the Gordon Riots. What has this to do with the Eucharist being "a continual remembrance of the sacrifice of the death of Christ"? The consideration of this question will be the main concern of our next chapter.

[1] Need I add here "ontologically, not necessarily psychologically"? It is not what the Christian *feels* is taking place at the Eucharist, but what *is* taking place, that matters.   [2] Rom. viii. 21.

CHAPTER X

THE SACRAMENT OF UNITY—II

I

I HOPE to show in this chapter that, by the very nature of the Eucharist, there is one particular event, among all the events of history, which it makes present to us in a quite unique way. In order to see this, we must consider more closely what is involved in the fact that the Eucharist is a sacrament, and moreover a sacrament constituted by Christ in a certain historic act. In expounding this, I shall make reference to Dom Anscar Vonier's book, *A Key to the Doctrine of the Eucharist*, a work which, although it is much briefer in its compass and has received much less attention from Anglicans than has that of Père de la Taille, is, I believe, theologically of not less importance. I shall, however, follow out the train of thought in my own way, and shall not necessarily confine myself to his exact form of presentation.

The learned Abbot of Buckfast started from the fact, which has received all too little recognition, that, whatever else the Eucharist is, it is a sacrament, and that a sacrament is a *sign*, albeit a sign of a very special kind. Now the purpose of a sign is to represent, and the purpose of that particular kind of sign which is a sacrament is to re-present, to make present, to effect that which is symbolized; as one of the Anglican Articles reminds us,[1] sacraments are not mere "badges or tokens"—*non tantum sunt notae professionis Christianorum*—not, that is to say, *mera signa*, but "effectual signs of grace"—*efficacia signa gratiae*—that is, signs having effective causality, signs that bring about that which they represent. Now—and this is Vonier's main point—sacramental efficacity is an altogether unique type of effective causality and must not be confused with other types. It is, of course, supernatural, for, as another of the Articles says,[2] it is "because of Christ's institution and promise" and not because of any activity of created beings, that sacraments "be effectual"; nevertheless, not all supernatural causality is sacramental. "If," writes

---

[1] Article xxv.   [2] Article xxvi.

Vonier, "the priest at the altar brought down Christ from heaven in his natural state as a full-grown man, this would not be a sacrament in the least, as it would lack the very essence of the sacrament, representative signification."[1] And again :

> "The sacramental world is a new world created by God, entirely different from the world of nature and even from the world of spirits. It would be bad theology to say that in the sacraments we have here on earth modes of spiritual realities which resemble the ways of the angels. We have nothing of the kind. If we spoke with the tongues of angels and men it would not help us in the least to express the sacramental realities. Sacraments are a new creation with entirely new laws."[2]

The Eucharistic presence of Christ, then, is entirely real but it is of an altogether different type from his presence on earth before his ascension and from his presence in heaven after it. Those presences are, so to speak, presences in their own right, while the Eucharistic presence exists because and only because Christ by his institution and promise has attached it to certain material signs. Now it is clear that, whatever this is, it is not that "transubstantiation" which Article xxviii condemns as "overthrowing the nature of a sacrament." For according to this view the presence exists simply because it has a "visible sign ordained by God" and through no other cause whatever. In Vonier's words, "the sacramental sphere is an unknown world with a well-known inhabitant"[3]; we must never lose that sense of something outside the realm of our normal experience and thought which is suggested by the Greek word for a sacrament, *mysterion*.

Vonier quotes St. Thomas in support of the doctrine that Christ is present in the Sacrament in a particular mode of being. "Christ," writes the Angelic Doctor,

> "has not the same *esse* in himself which he has under this sacrament, because when we speak of his *esse* under this sacrament there is signified a relation of himself to this sacrament."[4]

---

[1] *A Key to the Doctrine of the Eucharist,* p. 32. It should be noted that "signify" is here used throughout in its ordinary sense "to be a sign of something," not in the sense which its etymology (from *signum facere*) might suggest, "to make something into a sign." And "re-presentation," when I write it, as I usually shall except in quotations, with a hyphen, will mean not "to be a sign of something which is absent" but "to make something present again." On the whole question of signification, reference may be made to Maritain's difficult but important essay on "Sign and Symbol" in *Redeeming the Time*.

[2] *A Key to the Doctrine of the Eucharist,* p. 35. R. I. Wilberforce writes to a similar effect in *The Doctrine of the Incarnation,* p. 289.

[3] *A Key to the Doctrine of the Eucharist,* p. 92.   [4] *S. Theol.,* III, lxxvi, 6.

And whether we accept or not St. Thomas's exposition of transubstantiation as a true description of the Eucharistic change, we cannot but recognize that he spares no effort to make it plain that not only the means by which the presence is brought about but also the mode of the presence itself is altogether different from that by which things exist outside the sacramental sphere. He says indeed that the substance of the bread is changed into the substance of the Body of Christ and therefore no longer exists, but he adds that every action which bread could perform can still be performed by the sacramental species; in his thought the accidents seem to remain without their proper substance somewhat as the human nature of Christ subsists without a human person, though of course St. Thomas would not say that the accidents of bread inhere in the substance of the Body in the same way as Christ's human nature inheres in the Person of the divine Word. They do not, for him, strictly *inhere* in anything, though the accident of dimensive quantity acts as a subject to the other accidents; hence the change is really a miracle. Now, whether this explanation is satisfactory or not, what is really important in the present connection is not what he says about the bread but what he says about the Body. For he insists that it is not present by way of quantity or dimension or circumscription, but simply by way of substance; otherwise one part of Christ would be in one part of the bread and another in another, whereas in fact the whole Christ is present in every part of it.[1] The Body, he says, is present not "as a body in a place" but "in a certain special way which is peculiar to the Sacrament." It is "not locally in the Sacrament of the altar."[2] Such remarks as this make it quite plain that, in St. Thomas's view,

---

[1] Cf. St. Thomas's hymn:

A sumente non concisus,	"Whoso of this food partaketh
Non confractus, non divisus,	Rendeth not the Lord nor breaketh:
Integer accipitur.	Christ is whole to all that taste.
Sumit unus, sumunt mille,	Thousands are, as one, receivers;
Quantum isti, tantum ille,	One, as thousands of believers,
Nec sumptus consumitur.	Takes the food that cannot waste.
Fracto demum sacramento,	"When the sacrament is broken,
Ne vacilles, sed memento	Doubt not in each severed token,
Tantum esse sub fragmento	Hallowed by the word once spoken,
Quantum toto tegitur.	Resteth all the true content:
Nulli rei fit scissura:	Nought the precious Gift divideth;
Signi tantum fit fractura,	Breaking but the sign betideth;
Qua nec status nec statura	He himself the same abideth,
Signati minuitur.	Nothing of his fullness spent."

[2] St. Thomas's doctrine, which is given in *S. Theol.*, III, lxxiii–lxxxiii, is conveniently summarized in Darwell Stone's *History of the Doctrine of the Holy Eucharist*, I, p. 322 f.

the Body of Christ is present in an altogether different way from that in which substances are ordinarily present in space; it is present not through its own proper occupation of an extended volume of space, but solely through its association with the species of bread which *is* extended, and this association is that of sacramental signification; the Body is there *because* the species of bread is an *effectual sign* of it. And the species of bread *is* an effectual sign because of Christ's institution.

It is, I suspect, a very similar thought to this that underlies Article xxviii, which asserts that "the Body of Christ is given, taken and eaten in the Supper, only after an heavenly and spiritual manner." It is the word "manner" that is important here. There is no denial that what is "given, taken and eaten" is the Body of Christ; on the contrary this is plainly affirmed. But it is asserted that the Body is there not in the ordinary natural mode of existence but after "an heavenly and spiritual manner," or, in the words which I have already used, by the mode of sacramental signification, *per modum sacramenti*. Nor does the so-called Black Rubric contradict this if we may suppose that what it means when it says that "the Sacramental Bread and Wine remain still in their very natural substances and therefore may not be adored" is what St. Thomas means when he insists that every effect which the bread and wine could produce can still be produced by the sacramental species; that is to say, that he and the Rubric are not using the word "substance" in precisely the same sense. It is certainly true that "the natural Body and Blood of our Saviour Christ are in heaven and not here; it being against the truth of Christ's natural Body to be at one time in more places than one," if we are thinking of the local presence which a body has "in its own right"; we are not, it is to be hoped, Lutheran ubiquitarians. But the Revisers of 1661, in substituting a denial of "any corporal presence of Christ's natural Flesh and Blood" for the denial of "any real and essential presence" which the Rubric had contained in its original (and ecclesiastically unauthorized) form, do implicitly affirm that there is a real and essential presence, though it is not a corporal one. Now "corporal presence" must mean "presence *after the manner of* a body"; it cannot mean "presence *of* a Body," for it is precisely the presence of the Body of Christ that is being discussed. In other words, what the Black Rubric, as we have it now in our prayer-books, implies is that there is a real presence in the Eucharist, though it is not what we should to-day describe as a materialistic one.[1] We shall see later on that the Catechism lends support to this view.

II

In asserting the importance of recognizing that the Eucharistic presence of Christ takes place by this unique mode of sacramental signification, I am far from suggesting that this has always been put in the forefront of their teaching by either Anglican or Roman theologians. But I do suggest that its recognition would do much to reconcile their divergences. Indeed the study of such material as is contained in Dr. Darwell Stone's monumental *History of the Doctrine of the Holy Eucharist* leads one to suspect that the remarkable tendency of many, though not all, of the great Anglican divines towards a virtualist or receptionist position without, on the whole, a clear and definite acceptance of it,[2] may be explained as the result of an imperfectly articulated desire to avoid, on the one hand, views of a real presence of the Body of a type that would deprive the external forms of bread and wine of any function other than that of acting as a kind of veil and, on the other hand, of denying that the Eucharistic bread and wine are the Body and Blood of Christ at all. For it must be emphatically repeated—and neither Roman nor Anglican theologians seem to have taken sufficient account of this—a presence of the Body under the species of bread is not necessarily a sacramental presence; it is so only if it obtains in virtue of signification. For a sacrament is, above all else, a *sign*, and unless the mode by which the presence is brought about is the altogether unique mode which I have attempted to expound above, then we may have a real presence but it will not be a sacramental one, and we shall not have a sacrament. An outward *part* is not necessarily an outward *sign*.

There has, however, been at least one Anglican theologian to whom the point at issue was altogether clear, namely, Robert Wilberforce. When he comes, in his treatise on *The Doctrine of the Holy Eucharist*, to discuss the manner of the Eucharistic presence, he makes three statements about it: it is supernatural, it is sacramental, it is real. With the first of these we are not directly

---

[1] This interpretation is confirmed by the passage from Burnet, quoted by Stone, *History of the Doctrine of the Holy Eucharist*, II, p. 319 f.

[2] Hooker is, of course, one of the most conspicuous examples of this tendency; see *Eccl. Pol.*, V, lxvii; ed. of 1888, II, p. 348 f. Cf. Pusey as quoted in Tuckwell's *Reminiscences*, p. 149.

concerned here—the assertion is made that "the *natural* presence of our Lord's humanity is in heaven," while "the presence of his humanity in the Holy Eucharist is not accordant with the ordinary conditions which belong to man's nature . . . it is peculiar and *supernatural*."[1] The important point is that Wilberforce does not think it is sufficient to say simply that the presence is supernatural; he must add that it is *sacramental*:

> "The Subject and Predicate in our Lord's words of Institution were united together by a *sacramental identity*. For this was shown to imply that the Holy Eucharist consisted of two parts, a *sacramentum* and a *res sacramenti*[2]—the first an object to the senses, the second an object only to faith and to the mind. And further, it was shown to be the purpose of consecration, to unite these two together, so that they might have that peculiar relation to one another which belongs to this sacrament."[3]

Wilberforce goes on to remark that this solves the problems of the spatial characteristics of the Eucharistic presence:

> "It is a sacramental presence—the presence, that is, of a *res sacramenti*, which is not, in itself, an object to the senses of men. . . . There is a connection between the *sacramentum* and *res sacramenti*, and form and place belong to the first, though they do not belong to the second. So that though the *res sacramenti*, in itself, has neither place nor form, yet it has them in a manner through the *sacramentum*, with which it is united."[4]

It is then argued that the presence is *real*, and not merely symbolical or virtual.

Wilberforce is thus quite explicit that the presence is a presence of a sacramental type, a presence which exists not in the natural mode but in the mode of signification. The only difference between his exposition and that which I have given is that he does not go out of his way to point out that the presence not only *exists* in a sacramental *mode*, but is also actually *produced* by sacramental *causality*; this last point is, however, plainly implied by his insistence upon the necessity of the formula of consecration—"This is my Body"—with its clear declaration of sacramental signification, as the indispensable means by which the presence is brought about. "The word *is*," he writes,

---

[1] *The Doctrine of the Holy Eucharist*, p. 162.
[2] Elsewhere Wilberforce recognizes the third element, the *virtus*: *The Doctrine of the Holy Eucharist*, pp. 21, 120, 293.
[3] *The Doctrine of the Holy Eucharist*, p. 163.   [4] *Ibid.*, p. 164.

"expresses the *identity* of the Subject and Predicate. . . . But identity is of various kinds, and what is the nature of the identity here intended? . . . It is plainly a peculiar principle—*sui generis*; which, being without parallel in the world around, is entitled to a specific appellation. For it depends upon that mysterious law of consecration, of which we have no other example; and by virtue of this act, the Subject and Predicate make up together a real, but heterogeneous whole. . . . So that since the relation between the Subject and Predicate in our Lord's words of Institution cannot be resolved into any more general idea, it can derive its name only from itself, and the union can be described as nothing else than a *sacramental identity*."[1]

Is it too much to claim that, in all essentials, Vonier was anticipated by seventy years by Wilberforce?

It may here be remarked that, so recently as 1937, the Province of Canterbury committed itself to a definite assertion of the real objective presence of the Body and Blood of Christ in the Eucharistic elements, and so, by implication, ruled out the receptionist and virtualist doctrines. On January 20th of that year both Houses of Canterbury Convocation resolved that the Report of the Conference of Anglican and Rumanian theologians, held at Bucarest in June 1935, was "a legitimate interpretation of the faith of the Church as held by the Anglican Communion" and approved the Report. Now in the Report there occurs the following passage:

"In the Eucharist the bread and wine become by consecration (*metabole*) the Body and Blood of our Lord. How? This is a mystery.

"The Eucharistic bread and wine remain the Body and Blood of our Lord as long as these Eucharistic elements exist.

"Those who receive the Eucharistic bread and wine truly partake of the Body and Blood of our Lord."

III

I have digressed from our immediate theme into matters which we shall consider more fully later. It is time to return to our main line of argument. We were investigating the relation of the Eucharist to Calvary, and in doing this, we were led to consider the fact that, whatever else it is, the Eucharist is primarily a sacrament. The relevance of this lies in the fact, some of the

---

[1] *The Doctrine of the Holy Eucharist*, pp. 116–17.

implications of which we have followed out, that a sacrament is an efficacious sign, a sign which actually effects what it symbolizes. Now we have previously seen that, in the context of the Church, through that partaking of the divine nature which the Church enjoys as the organic whole of those who have been adopted into the sonship of Christ, there is a transcendence of time in which past and future events are made mysteriously, but none the less really, present. If, then, we can show that what is efficaciously signified in the Eucharist is the Sacrifice of Calvary, we shall be able to see that, among all other past and future events, the event which is directly and primarily implicated in the Eucharist *in its essential character as a sacrament* is the death of Christ. We must therefore now go on from our consideration of sacramental signification in general to consider the particular sacramental signification of the Eucharist.

"Jesus Christ . . . in the same night that he was betrayed, took bread; and, when he had given thanks, he brake it, and gave it to his disciples, saying, Take, eat, this is my Body which is given for you: Do this in remembrance of me. Likewise after supper he took the cup; and, when he had given thanks, he gave it to them saying, Drink ye all of this; for this is my Blood of the New Testament, which is shed for you and for many for the remission of sins: Do this, as oft as ye shall drink it, in remembrance of me."[1]

We need not go into the many questions that can be raised as to the precise significance, considered in the light of the ritual of later Judaism, of the New-Testament narratives of the institution of the Eucharist and of the relation of the Last Supper to the actual Jewish Passover-meal. These matters are discussed in all the commentaries. I shall merely assume that, whether by anticipation or not, the Last Supper was, for those who took part in it, their Passover-gathering, and that our Lord did at that meal what the Gospels and St. Paul say that he did.[2] There, in the context of the great annual sacrificial rite and ceremony wherein was made the *anamnesis* of the redemption of the Jewish people from its bondage in Egypt, and wherein the supreme sacrificial element was the consecration, slaying and eating of the passover-lamb, Christ took bread and wine, and declared the bread to be his Body, given for his disciples, and the wine to be his Blood, shed for

---

[1] Book of Common Prayer: Consecration-prayer in the Order for Holy Communion.
[2] Cf. Dr. N. P. Williams on "The Origins of the Sacraments," in *Essays Catholic and Critical*.

them and for many for the remission of sins. If any further indication of sacrificial import is needed, we shall find it in the declaration, "This is my blood of the New Covenant" (or, as another account gives it, "This cup is the New Covenant in my blood"), for here there is an obvious reference to the sacrificial sealing of the Old Covenant with blood by Moses which is described in the twenty-fourth chapter of Exodus. For our present purposes we need assume no more than that, in giving us the narrative of the Institution, the Church was not misinterpreting the intention of her Redeemer and the nature of the rite which he initiated.

Now the institution of the Eucharist under the two species of bread and wine, respectively identified with Christ's Body and Blood, makes it, by the mode of sacramental signification, a re-presentation of his death. At the Last Supper, by his natural mode of existence, Christ was in the Upper Room, alive and speaking to his apostles, just as to-day by his natural mode of existence he is glorified and reigning in heaven. But by the mode of sacramental signification, he was then, and he is in our Eucharists to-day, present under the form of death, with Body and Blood separated, Body broken and Blood poured out. The point must be made quite clear. It is a living, not a dead, Christ who is present on our altars and whom we receive in communion. There is no room for theories, such as have been held by some post-Reformation Roman writers,[1] which conceive the immolation in the Mass as consisting in some kind of "lowering" of the glorified Christ. "Christ being raised from the dead dieth no more; death no more hath dominion over him."[2] But the *sacramental mode* under which he is present is that of his death. And there is food for much reflection in the fact that, in a world which, in spite of the coming of the Kingdom of God in the Person of the Messiah, still lies "in the evil one," the glorified Christ is to be seen only under the figure of his death. Not until the Second Coming will Christ be "all in all"; and then sacraments will cease.

If what I have said is true, the contradiction sometimes alleged between the views which relate the Eucharist to Christ's heavenly offering and his death respectively rests upon nothing but a

---

[1] E.g., Cardinal de Lugo. See Stone, *History of the Doctrine of the Holy Eucharist*, II, p. 373 f. As Vonier points out: "Humiliation and exaltation are not sacramental notions, but ethical notions. The sacrament is a representation of an historic fact, not an ethical deed which has new meritoriousness." (*Key to the Doctrine of the Eucharist*, p. 57.)   [2] Rom. vi. 9.

misunderstanding, for the Eucharist is related in different and definite ways to both. Since he who is present is the living Christ, whose members we are and whose Body and Bride is the Church, the Eucharist admits us into the worship of heaven itself and knits us into the perpetual intercession and impetation of the great High-Priest. But since he is present not in a natural mode, but by a sacramental signification of his condition on Calvary, it is the *anamnesis* and the pleading of his death. The Eucharist is not a different sacrifice from that of Calvary, but the same sacrifice; in it Calvary is not repeated, nor is it added to, but it is re-presented; and it is re-presented not as a meaningless judicial murder but as the act through which God's victory over the powers of evil was won and man's redemption achieved, the act whose outcome was Christ's Resurrection and Ascension and the Descent of the Spirit at Pentecost. As Vonier says:

> "Christ's natural sacrifice and Christ's Eucharistic sacrifice stand to each other in a relationship which is truly wonderful, and of which there is no other instance in the whole realm of revealed truth; one represents the other, but one does not complete the other."[1]

And again:

> "It is the very nature of the Eucharistic sacrifice to be a representation of the past, not a mactation in the present."[2]

Since the Christ who is sacramentally presented in the Eucharist under the mode of death is, in his own proper being, risen and glorified, the doctrine of concomitance follows as a matter of course. The whole Christ is present under each species, soul and body, humanity and divinity; it is impossible for one element to be present in isolation from the rest. The separation of blood from body, which is the essential feature in a sacrificial immolation, must be reproduced in the sacramental mode if the Eucharist is to be in truth a re-presentation of Christ's death; hence Christ instituted the Eucharist under the two species of bread and wine. There is, however, no real immolation in the natural, as distinct from the sacramental, order; there is no "desition" of the ascended Christ. Hence the whole living Christ is present in each species. As St. Thomas says, using the terminology of transubstantiation:

> "By the power of the sacrament, there is under the species of this sacrament that into which the pre-existing substance of the

---

[1] *Key to the Doctrine of the Eucharist.* p. 95.   [2] *Ibid.*, p. 122.

bread and wine is changed, as expressed by the words of the form, which are effective in this as in the other sacraments; for instance, by the words—*This is my body*, or, *This is my blood*. But from natural concomitance there is also in this sacrament that which is really united with that thing wherein the aforesaid conversion is terminated."[1]

And not only is the whole Christ present in the Sacrament as a whole; he is present under either species:

"The whole Christ is under each sacramental species yet not alike in each. For the body of Christ is indeed present under the species of bread by the power of the sacrament, while the blood is there from real concomitance, as stated above in regard to the soul and Godhead of Christ; and under the species of wine the blood is present by the power of the sacrament, and his body by real concomitance, as is also his soul and Godhead: because now Christ's blood is not separated from his body, as it was at the time of his passion and death."[2]

It is no doubt true that the doctrine of concomitance provided medieval theologians with a very useful argument in support of the legitimacy of communion in one kind, but the doctrine itself arises simply out of the fact that there is in the Eucharist no repetition in the natural order of the death of Christ. And an Anglican, at least, can hardly complain at this.[3]

A difficulty may perhaps be felt in the suggestion that "now Christ's Blood is not separated from his Body." Does this mean, it may be asked, that in the ascended Christ the earthly condition of his physical organism remains to the extent that blood is still being pumped by his heart through his arteries and veins? And if so, is not this incompatible with the transformation and the liberation from spatial and physical restrictions that we believe the Ascension to have conferred? The objection is not, I think, really valid. For the identification of the Eucharistic bread and wine with Christ's Body and Blood does not involve a direct reference to Christ's

[1] *S. Theol.*, III, lxxvi, 1c.
[2] *Ibid.*, III, lxxvi, 2c. Cf. St. Thomas's hymn:
Caro cibus, sanguis potus   "Flesh for food, and blood for wine,
Manet tamen Christus totus   Yet is Christ, in either sign,
Sub utraque specie.   All entire unchangeably."
[3] It must be added that, whatever is the proper manner of reception in the course of the Liturgy, communion in one kind can, on historical as well as on theological grounds, hardly be insufficient, since we find it as the normal mode in which the faithful communicated themselves in their homes as early as round about A.D. 180; cf. the *Apostolic Tradition* of Hippolytus.

manhood as it now is in its glorified state; it involves a reference, by the mode of sacramental re-presentation, to the chronologically *past* event of Calvary and to the manhood as it was then, and in that the separation of the Blood from the crucified Body was most patently evident. The matter is entirely unaffected by the question as to whether in Christ's glorified human nature as it is *now* in the heavenly realm the components of flesh and blood can be distinguished. It must be repeated that in the Eucharist Christ who, in the natural mode of existence, is glorified and triumphant, is made present, in the sacramental mode of existence (which is altogether different from the natural mode and is maintained not by physical subsistence but by effective signification), as he was in his death on the Cross.

IV

A few words may be added on the significance of the fact that the Eucharist is constituted in the two elements of Bread, which becomes the Body, and Wine, which becomes the Blood. I have already commented on the importance of the elements as being the joint product of the activity of the earth and of man. It will be plain also that, if the Eucharist is to be the food of the Church and its members, it is highly appropriate, if not indeed necessary, that it should consist of things that the human body can assimilate. And we have just seen how appropriate are the two separate elements, one liquid and the other solid, for the re-presentation of the separation of Christ's Body and Blood on Calvary. To follow up in detail the precise significance of Body and Blood separately would require a detailed examination of the whole of the Jewish sacrificial system which Christ fulfilled in his person; that task has been performed by Old-Testament scholars and I shall not try to repeat it here. I will only remark on the fact that the burning of the whole or part of the body of the victim on the altar fittingly typifies the wholeness of the offering made to God, as it ascends in smoke to the sky; while the pouring of the blood on the altar (whether it represents, as Dr. Hicks thought, the giving to God of the life set free or, as Dr. Farrer maintains, the death of the sacrifice and the ratification of the covenant between God and man thereby) emphasizes the cost at which that offering is made. Dr. Farrer's actual words in this connection are as follows:

"Certainly Blood was not added to Body because these two are complementary constituents of one substance; that would have required Flesh rather than Body. Rather, the two suggest different trains of thought about the one substance—Body the wholeness and the reality of the person, and its continuity here and hereafter: Blood the sacrificial death, that which is poured out, given, and not recovered, the discontinuity and the break—for the death remains death, in itself real passion and loss, however happy its consequence: as we see by comparing the possibility that man had not sinned, and Christ could have led him to like glory and Kingdom not through death. And, in suggesting the death of the Sacrifice, blood suggested also the covenant."[1]

Dr. Farrer remarks that in the Fourth Gospel, in the Eucharistic discourse, the couple Flesh-and-Blood actually occurs. But here, he points out, the emphasis is on the feeding of the soul, not on the sacrifice. "He that eateth my flesh and drinketh my blood hath eternal life." "To bread and wine (= complete sustenance), flesh and blood (= complete Person) naturally correspond."[2] We may add to this Sir Edwyn Hoskyns's point, that the crudest physical language is employed in a way that prevents all possibility of allegorizing or explaining away: in John vi. 54, he remarks, "the Greek word substituted for *eat* means literally *munch*, i.e. eat so as to be heard—it was originally used to describe animals eating."[3] And to the Jews the drinking of blood was expressly forbidden by the Levitical law.[4] Here is what Hoskyns says:

"No room is left for any 'spiritualizing' interpretation. The eating and drinking of the Flesh and Blood of the Son of man involve a real physical eating and drinking, although the Flesh and Blood are altogether misconceived if they be thought of, as the Jews are determined to think of them, as the mere material of the human Body of Jesus, instead of being rigorously defined in terms of the significance wrought out and manifested in his sacrificial death. The apparent contradiction . . . is resolved and explained only if the conscious reference to the Eucharist is perceived. The Eucharistic food and drink are physically bread and wine, spiritually the Flesh and Blood of the Son of Man; together they constitute the true food and drink of the faithful: the true food and drink because they effect the sacred union of the Son of God with those who believe on him, and thus communicate eternal life and guarantee immortality."[5]

---

[1] *The Parish Communion*, art. cit. sup., p. 88.   [2] John vi. 54. Farrer, footnote ad loc.
[3] *The Fourth Gospel*, I, p. 337.   [4] Lev. xvii. 10-14.
[5] *The Fourth Gospel*, I, p. 336. It is, however, possible that Hoskyns over-emphasized the crudity of the word *trogo*.

We may add that body, as the whole physical organism, includes in a certain sense, the blood which is a part of it. Hence the Body-Blood contrast is the contrast of the physical organism of Christ considered as a whole with that part of it which flowed out from it on the Cross.

Ave, verum corpus, natum	"Hail, true Body, born of Mary,
Ex Maria virgine,	Spotless Virgin's virgin birth,
Vere passum, immolatum	Thou who truly hangest weary
In cruce pro homine,	On the Cross for sons of earth,
Cujus latus perforatum	Thou whose sacred side was riven,
Fluxit unda sanguine . . .	Whence the water flowed and blood . . ."

The Flesh-Blood contrast, on the other hand, is the contrast between the two components which go to make up man as a physical being. Together they signify the completeness of a human nature; they mean just "man," as when our Lord said to St. Peter, "Flesh and blood hath not revealed it unto thee, but my Father which is in heaven."[1] But in separation they display the victim in the condition of death. One ought not perhaps to distinguish too sharply, but the suggestion would be that Body-Blood fastens the attention primarily upon the *act of dying*, in which the body pours out from itself the blood which is its own life-stream, while Flesh-Blood exhibits the *state of death*, in which the two components of man's material part have been already severed from each other. Flesh is what Body becomes when it has been drained of its Blood.

[1] Matt. xvi. 17.

CHAPTER XI

THE SACRAMENT OF UNITY—III

I

WE shall now consider more fully, in special relation to the Anglican formularies, the character of the Eucharistic sacrifice, and I must first point out that much confusion has been caused in Anglicanism, as indeed, I venture to think, in the rest of Christendom, by neglect to observe a peculiar ambiguity in the very definition of the word "sacrament." In two successive questions and answers of the Prayer-Book Catechism we read:

"What meanest thou by this word *Sacrament*?
—I mean an outward and visible sign of an inward and spiritual grace . . .
"How many parts are there in a Sacrament?
—Two; the outward visible sign, and the inward spiritual grace."

That is to say, a Sacrament is first of all defined as an outward sign *of* an inward grace, and then is immediately asserted to consist of the outward sign *and* the inward grace. This transition is quite understandable, because, *so far as sacramental re-presentation is concerned*, the sole function of the outward element is to signify the inward one. In somewhat the same way as, in the Thomist doctrine of perception, the sensible species is not the *quod* in which the act of perception terminates but is merely the *quo* through which the mind perceives its true *quod* (namely, a being existing in the external world), so here, in the order of sacramental re-presentation,[1] the outward part is not the *quod* of the act of faith in which the sacrament is apprehended and appropriated, but is the *quo* through which is grasped the true *quod*, namely the

---

[1] The words "in the order of sacramental re-presentation" are important. In the order of sensible perception, of course, the outward part is the precise terminus of the mental act. What I perceive by the senses of sight and touch is not the Body of Christ but the properties of bread. It is only by understanding that here is a sacrament that I apprehend the presence of the Body; and this is a matter "of faith, not of sight."

"inward part." But, if this duplicity of nuance is inevitable and indeed legitimate, it is none the less necessary to take account of it. Otherwise we shall find ourselves involved in lamentable and inextricable misunderstandings.

We must next observe that the Eucharist differs from all the other six ordinances that are "commonly called sacraments" (and in particular from the other great "Sacrament of the Gospel," namely, baptism) in that in it there is a designation of a particular limited portion of a material element for the sacramental re-pre-sentation of another concrete being; Christ said of a particular loaf of bread, "This is my Body," and of the contents of a particular cup of wine, "This is my Blood." This is, of course, the basis of the prohibition in the Prayer-Book of the removal of any of the consecrated, as distinct from the unconsecrated, elements from the Church after the Eucharist,[1] and it is in marked contrast to what obtains in the Sacrament of Baptism, in which it is not a designated portion of water, but water as such, that, in the phrase of the Baptism Office, Christ did "sanctify to the mystical washing away of sin."[2] And, as the Office for Private Baptism makes plain, the blessing of water for baptism, however edifying it may be, is not necessary to the performance of the sacrament: a fact which is confirmed by the common primitive practice, which is frequently observed to-day in the mission-field, of baptizing in a running stream, where obviously there can be no material identity between the portion of water over which the blessing, if any, is said and that in which the candidate is actually immersed. This considera-tion is at the basis of St. Thomas's remark that the Eucharist differs from other sacraments in that "this sacrament is accom-plished by the consecration of the matter, while the rest are perfected in the use of the consecrated matter,"[3] and of Sir Will Spens's statement that in the Eucharist "our Lord instituted an

---

[1] Sixth rubric at the end of the Order of Holy Communion.

[2] This is seen very clearly in the Latin formula for the blessing of the baptismal water on Holy Saturday, where the water that is blessed is the water which Moses brought forth from the rock, which Christ turned into wine at Cana, which flowed from his side on the Cross, and so forth; see p. 118 *supra*. In Holy Unction there is indeed a blessing of a particular portion of oil, but it does not sacramentally signify any concrete designated object but only the impartation of a certain effect.

[3] *S. Theol.*, III, lxxviii, 1c. Incidentally, this doctrine does not seem to be the reason for the infrequency of communion by the laity in the Middle Ages. Communion was very infrequent among Anglicans in the Hanoverian period and has become very frequent in certain Roman Catholic circles to-day. The reasons lie deeper. See Dom Gregory Dix on "The 'Clericalization' of the Eucharist" in *The Parish Communion*, p. 131 f.

effectual symbolism . . . of object, rather than directly of action."[1]
R. I. Wilberforce expounds this most lucidly as follows:

> "Our Lord does not speak of bread at large, or wine in general,
> but of *This*, i.e., of that which was consecrated or set apart. It was
> the bread which he had blessed, over which he had given thanks,
> and which he had broken; and the cup over which he had given
> thanks; which were the subject-matter of his declaration. The con-
> secration, therefore, by which these elements were separated from
> all co-ordinate specimens of the same material, is that circum-
> stance which gives them the peculiar character which his words
> express. And so we may learn also from the only other passage
> of Holy Scripture in which this subject is formally treated. When
> St. Paul explains the nature of the Holy Eucharist to the Corin-
> thians, he refers to the consecration of the elements as its distin-
> guishing characteristic. 'The *cup of blessing which we bless*, is it not
> the communion of the Blood of Christ? The *bread which we break*,
> is it not the communion of the Body of Christ?' We may infer,
> therefore, that the elements, as consecrated, are the subject spoken
> of: Our Lord's awful words do not refer to bread and wine at
> large, but to that which he held in his hands, and which he had
> blessed."[2]

Thus in the Eucharist, in contrast to the other sacraments, the
inward part has a certain double nature; what is sacramentally
re-presented by the species of bread and wine is not only the
application of the merits of Christ's Passion to the soul for its
strengthening, but also the concrete realities which are the Body
and Blood of Christ. Thus the terms, *res sacramenti* (that is, "thing
signified") and *virtus sacramenti* (that is, "effect of the sacrament"),
which in all other sacraments are for most purposes synonymous,
stand in the case of the Eucharist for two distinct objects. In
St. Augustine, as Wilberforce[3] and, following him, Dr. B. J. Kidd,[4]
have pointed out, the distinction between the two, though
recognizable, is not entirely explicit. It is clearer in St. Thomas,

---

[1] *Belief and Practice*, p. 167; cf. the article on "The Sacraments of the Church," in
Theology, Sept. 1931, p. 125. It is the neglect of this distinction that seems to me to be
the main defect in the discussion of the Eucharist in Dr. O. C. Quick's book, *The
Christian Sacraments*. It must be added that Spens's own discussion becomes unsatisfactory through his definition of *object* as a "complex of opportunities of experience,"
the logical result of which, though Spens has tried to avoid this (see his articles in
Theology, Vol. xviii, 1929), seems to be to make the Eucharistic presence (and every
other presence) exist only *quoad nos* and *propter nos*.
[2] *Doctrine of the Holy Eucharist*, p. 9 f. Wilberforce goes on (p. 16 f.) to draw out the
contrast with baptism: "In one case the medium is an *act*, in the other an *element*.'
(p. 25).
[3] *Doctrine of the Holy Eucharist*, p. 291 f.   [4] In *Laudate*, Dec. 1941, p. 69 f.

to whom is attributed the well-known prayer before communion in which the communicant begs that he may receive "not only the *sacramentum* of the Lord's Body and Blood, but also the *res* and *virtus* of the sacrament." (Even here the distinction is not entirely unambiguous, for every thirteenth-century Catholic was quite sure that, whether he was in a state of grace or not, he would certainly receive the Body of Christ, either to salvation or damnation; he might therefore be expected to pray to receive "not only the *sacramentum* and *res*, but also the *virtus*.") In the final section of the Prayer-Book Catechism, contributed by Overall in 1604, the distinction is perfectly plain. Having told us that there are two parts in a sacrament, namely, the outward sign and the inward grace, and then that the "outward part or sign" of the Lord's Supper is bread and wine, he does not go on to speak of an "inward *grace*" at all, but of an "inward *part, or thing signified*," and finally of certain "benefits."

"What is the outward part or sign of the Lord's Supper?
—Bread and Wine, which the Lord hath commanded to be received.
"What is the inward part, or thing signified?
—The Body and Blood of Christ, which are verily and indeed taken and received by the faithful[1] in the Lord's Supper.
"What are the benefits whereof we are partakers thereby?
—The strengthening and refreshing of our souls by the Body and Blood of Christ, as our bodies are by the Bread and Wine."

To summarize, then, we have now:

A. The *sacramentum* (in the restricted sense) or sign, i.e., the species of bread and wine.
B. The *res sacramenti* or thing signified, i.e., the Body and Blood of Christ.
C. The *virtus sacramenti*, the benefits received through worthy communion.

[1] It should hardly need argument to prove that "faithful" here, as in Article xix, which declares that the Church of Christ is a "congregation of faithful men" (*visibilis coetus fidelium*), is a technical term for those who have been admitted to "the Faith" in baptism, and does not necessarily imply the possession of that "lively faith" which the last answer of the Catechism affirms to be "*required* of them who come to the Lord's Supper."

II

The recognition of these three constituents in the Eucharist will lead us to see that there are two stages and not one in the Eucharistic symbolism:

  ✓ I. The species of bread and wine symbolize or signify the Body and Blood of Christ.
  ✓ II. The Body and Blood of Christ symbolize or signify the benefits of worthy reception.

Thus we can also characterize the three components of the Eucharist as follows:

  ✓ A. *Sacramentum tantum*, that which is "only a sign,"[1] namely the species of bread and wine (*mere significativum*).
  ✓ B. *Res et sacramentum*, that which is both a thing signified and also a sign of something else : the Body and Blood (*significatum et significativum*).
  ✓ C. *Res tantum*, that which is a thing signified but is not itself a sign of anything further, the "benefits" (*mere significatum*).[2]

---

[1] "Only a sign," not as meaning that the species are unreal, but that they are a sign without being themselves symbolized.

[2] It may be of interest to give three instances of this classification from medieval theologians:

Peter Lombard, in *Sent.*, L. IV, d. 8, after distinguishing in baptism between *sacramentum* and *res*, remarks that in the Eucharist the *res* is duplicated, one being contained in the sacrament and signified, the other signified but not contained. "Three things must thus be here distinguished: one which is only a *sacramentum*, another which is a *sacramentum* and a *res*, and a third which is a *res* and not a *sacramentum*. The *sacramentum* which is not a *res* is the visible species of bread and wine; the *sacramentum* and *res* is Christ's own Flesh and Blood; the *res* which is not a *sacramentum* is his Mystical Body (*mystica ejus caro*). Moreover, the visible species is the sign of both *res*, because it signifies each *res* and bears the express likeness of each. For as bread more than other foods renews and sustains the body . . . so the Flesh of Christ more than other graces spiritually renews and fattens the inner man." I shall comment later on on the description of the *res tantum* as the Mystical Body rather than as individual sanctification.

In the *Summa Sententiarum* we find:

"Three things ought to be considered: one which is only a *sacramentum*, another which is a *sacramentum* and a *res sacramenti*, a third which is only a *res*. . . . The *sacramentum* and *res* is the Body of Christ itself, and the Blood. It is a *res* in relation to those species by which it is signified, and this *res* is in turn a *sacramentum* of something else, namely the unity of the Head and the members." And this unity is later called "the spiritual flesh of Christ" (Hugh of Mauretania, tr. 6, c. 3, quoted by de la Taille, *Mysterium Fidei*, p. 509).

And Innocent III writes:

"We must carefully distinguish between three things which are distinct in this sacrament, namely the visible form (*forma*), the reality (*veritas*) of the Body, and the spiritual effect (*virtus*). The form is of bread and wine; the reality is of Body and Blood; and the effect is of unity and charity. The first is a *sacramentum* and not a *res*; the second is a *sacramentum* and a *res*; the third, a *res* and not a *sacramentum*. But the

In Stage I, B is signified by A; in Stage II, C is signified by B.

It may be added that both stages of the symbolization are effective and not merely declaratory, though the effect of the second depends upon the dispositions of the recipient. The former is purely *ex opere operato*; the second is *ex opere operantis*, that is to say, *ex opere recipientis*, for, in the words of Article xxvi, the unworthiness of the *ministers* hinders not the effect of the Sacrament.

The recognition of the double sense of the word "sacrament" will avoid much misunderstanding. When in the Latin rite of Benediction there is sung the antiphon, *Adoremus in aeternum sanctissimum sacramentum*, the word is presumably being used in the second sense, of the outward sign together with the thing signified, for it would be plain idolatry to adore the mere outward sign. On the other hand, the Anglican Article xxix uses it avowedly to mean nothing but the sign:

> "The Wicked," it says, "and such as be void of a lively faith, although they do carnally and visibly press with their teeth (as Saint *Augustine* saith) the Sacrament of the Body and Blood of Christ, yet in no wise are they partakers of Christ: but rather, to their condemnation, do eat and drink the sign or Sacrament of so great a thing (*tantae rei Sacramentum, seu symbolum*)."

It must be added that the phrase, "partaking of Christ," is itself ambiguous. It obviously refers here to the receiving of Christ into the soul, the question of physical reception of Christ's Body being skilfully ignored. We may observe that, while Article xxviii says that worthy recipients partake of the *Body and Blood* of Christ Article xxix does not deny that unworthy recipients receive the Body and Blood, but only that they "receive Christ."[1] It is the reception of the *virtus* that is denied; nothing is said about the *res* (that is, the *res et sacramentum*, the Body and Blood). We may

---

first is the *sacramentum* of both *res*, while the third is the *res* of both *sacramenta*. But the second is seen to be the *sacramentum* of the one and the *res* of the other." (*Epist. ad Joannem*, quoted by de la Taille, op. cit., p. 510.)

St. Thomas follows the Lombard quite closely: *S. Theol.*, III, lxxiii, 3c; lxxx, 4c.

De la Taille makes use of this threefold division, only substituting *signum* for *sacramentum*, no doubt to avoid the ambiguity of this latter word; see *Mysterium Fidei*, p. 501 f.

It is perhaps worth emphasizing, to avoid confusion, that *res et sacramentum* does not, of course, mean a complex made up of two entities, one of which is a *res* and the other a *sacramentum*, but one entity which is itself both *res* and *sacramentum* at the same time.

[1] See the article by Lord Hugh Cecil (now Lord Quickswood) in *Theology*, Dec. 1931, p. 307. It must, however, be admitted that the title of Article xxix shows less subtlety, like the prayer of St. Thomas quoted above.

compare the words of Peter Lombard: "As there are two *res* of this *sacramentum*, so there are two modes of eating: namely, a sacramental way, in which both good and evil men eat, and a spiritual way, in which only the good eat."[1] His point is that good and evil alike receive the *res et sacramentum*, but the *res tantum* or *virtus* is received only by the good.[2] Both, we may say, receive the Body, but only the good receive Christ.

III

We must now consider more fully the precise nature of the *virtus* or benefit of the Eucharist. The Prayer-Book Catechism defines it in a rather individualistic way: "the strengthening and refreshing of our souls by the Body and Blood of Christ, as our bodies are by the Bread and Wine."[3] But the Eucharistic Office not only thanks God for assuring us by the Sacrament of his favour and goodness towards us, but also that we are very members incorporate in the Mystical Body of his Son, which is the blessed company of all faithful people, the *coetus fidelium*, and prays for grace that we may continue in that holy fellowship. The medieval writers lay great stress upon the notion that the true *res tantum* or *virtus* of the Sacrament is the unity of the Mystical Body which is the Church of Christ, and in this they are following the consistent teaching of the fathers.[4] As Dom Gregory Dix has remarked, the Eucharist is not so much the *expression* of the Church's unity as its *cause*: "*Because* the Bread is one, we being many are one body, for we all partake of the one Bread."[5]

For the truth is that there are not three bodies of Christ but one Body, which exists in three forms, a *corpus triforme*, for Christ has only one human nature, that which he took from the Virgin Mary by the operation of the Holy Ghost and which is now glori-

---

[1] *Sent.*, L. IV, d. 9. Cf. *S. Theol.*, III, lxxx, 1–3.

[2] For a discussion of the compatibility of Anglican and Roman teaching on the Eucharist reference may be made to H. E. Symonds, *The Council of Trent and Anglican Formularies*, chs. v, vi, and A. H. Rees, *Eucharistic Doctrine and Reunion*.

[3] We may also remark on the rather unfortunate limitation of the benefit to our souls, which is paralleled by the form of administration in the Latin secular rite: *Corpus D.N.J.C. custodiat animam tuam in vitam aeternam.* The Prayer-Book form and that used by the Dominicans (*custodiat te*) are much better, as is also in this respect the "Prayer of Humble Access," in spite of its regrettable allocation of the cleansing of body and soul to the Body and Blood of Christ respectively. (Cf. *S. Theol.*, III, lxxiv, 1c.)

[4] See, e.g., de Lubac, *Catholicisme*, p. 56 f.; de la Taille, *Mysterium Fidei*, p. 475 f.; A. M. Ramsey, *The Gospel and the Catholic Church*, ch. viii.

[5] *The Parish Communion*, p. 122. Cf. 1 Cor. x. 17.

fied in heaven. As I said before, in the Eucharist the struggling, imperfect Mystical Body is repeatedly brought into union with its heavenly archetype, the glorified natural Body, through its reception of the Sacramental Body. There is therefore no contradiction between the strengthening of the individual and of the Church through the Sacrament. In it the Christian receives Christ, he is received into Christ, he is received into the glorified Body by partaking of the Sacramental Body and so is built up into the Mystical Body. And for this very reason, in the Eucharist the Mystical Body is itself receiving and being received into its exalted Head. It is the Church itself that is the true communicant. Thus we find in the sermons of St. Augustine such expressions as the following:

"If you then are the body and members of Christ, the mystery of yourselves is laid upon the table of the Lord, the mystery of yourselves ye receive. To that which you are, answer, Amen."[1]

"If you have received well, you are what you receive."[2]

"You are on the table, you are in the chalice."[3]

Wilberforce eloquently writes:

"When we speak of Christ, then, as giving his Body for our food, and of the building up of the Body of Christ as the consequence, it is obvious that the process is exactly the reverse of that which happens in the case of ordinary nourishment. Since it is *Christ's* body which is built up; in *him*, and not in *us* must be the informing Spirit. It must be the life which has its source in him, from which 'all the Body by joints and bands having nourishment ministered, increaseth unto the increase of God.' 'My body lives by my spirit; yours by your spirit. The Body of Christ cannot live save by the Spirit of Christ.'[4] So that though Christ's Body is orally received, yet *it* does not become part of *us*, but *we* become part of *him*; *he* is not resolved, as it were, into the structure of our minds, but *we* pass, on the contrary, into his divine organization. The *sacramentum* indeed, or outward part, is assimilated, like other food, to the body which receives it: but the *res sacramenti* is an energizing principle, which takes up and quickens that upon which it is bestowed."[5]

---

[1] *Serm.* 272.   [2] *Serm.* 227.   [3] *Serm.* 229.   [4] Aug. *In Joan.* Trac. xxvi, 13.
[5] *Doctrine of the Holy Eucharist*, p. 409. With the last sentence we may compare the "King's Book": "This heavenly meat is not turned into our substance, as other corporal meat is; but by the godly operation thereof we be turned towards the nature of it." (Ed. of 1932, p. 55.)

And he quotes from St. Leo and St. Augustine:

"The effect of participating of the Body and Blood of Christ is nothing else than that we pass into that which we receive."[1]

"Since the Church is his own Body, she learns to offer up herself through him."[2]

Peter Lombard is thus in the direct line of the patristic teaching when, having asserted that the *res et sacramentum* of the Eucharist is "Christ's mystical flesh," he goes on to say that the species of bread

"has a likeness to the mystical *res*, which is the unity of the faithful, for as from many grains there is made one loaf and from many grapes the wine flows into one, so from the many persons of the faithful the unity of the Church is set up. Hence the Apostle writes (1 Cor. x): We being many are one bread and one body, etc. And Augustine (*De Blasph. Spir. Sanc.*): The Church is called one bread and one body, because as one loaf is composed of many grains and one body of many limbs, so the Church is fastened together by the bond of charity from the multitude of the faithful.[3] Christ has in his table consecrated this mystery of our peace and unity. The man who receives this mystery of unity and does not hold the bond of peace receives this mystery not *for*, but *against* himself. And its sign (*sacramentum*) is the very Body of Christ, taken from the Virgin Mary; for as the Body of Christ is made up of many most pure and immaculate members, so the society of the Church consists of many persons who have been freed from the stain of guilt."[4]

And St. Thomas says that "the *res* of this sacrament is the unity of the Mystical Body."[5]

"It is to be remembered," says the so-called "King's Book," which was published by the authority of Convocation in 1543,

"that as in the receiving of this sacrament we have most entire communion with Christ, so be we also joined by the same in most perfect unity with his Church, and all the members thereof. And for that cause amongst other this sacrament was instituted of our Saviour Christ, in the form of bread, to signify the unity, concord, and charity that is between Christ our head, and his mystical body the church, and every part and member thereof one with another.

[1] *Serm.* lxiii, 7.   [2] *De Civ.*, x, 20.
[3] This thought goes back as far as to the *Didache*: "As this broken bread was scattered upon the mountains, gathered together, became one, so let thy Church be gathered together from the ends of the earth into thy Kingdom" (IX, 4).
[4] *Sent.*, L. IV, d. 8.   [5] *S. Theol.*, III, lxxiii, 3c.

o

For as bread is made of many grains or corns, which all make but one loaf, so should all true Christian people, being many in number, yet be all one in faith and charity."[1]

IV

In the course of this discussion I have made more than one digression. It may therefore be well, in conclusion, to summarize the main results which we have reached.

Christ's *actual condition* on the altar must, we saw, be as he is *now*, namely glorified. But in the Eucharist he is *sacramentally presented* as dead, the Body and Blood being sacramentally separated. The presence is thus real, but the immolation is sacramental or "mystical." And the mystical immolation is effected through the twofold consecration, which *sacramentally* separates the Body and the Blood, though in their proper and natural mode of existence they are inseparable. So in the Host the Body is present *vi consecrationis* and the Blood *vi concomitantiae*; while in the chalice the Blood is present *vi consecrationis* and the Body *vi concomitantiae*.

But if we left the matter here the Eucharist would represent heaven rather than Calvary, in contradiction to the teaching of Scripture. So we must add:

Because the elements are identified with the glorified humanity of Christ, and this is in turn hypostatically united to his divine Person,

And because, by his Godhead, this divine Person is above and transcends the temporal separation of events,

Therefore there can be an immolation which is both "mystical" and "real"; that is to say, real not as a new immolation but as a sacramental re-presentation (*anamnesis*) of the immolation (chronologically past) of Calvary.

So the Eucharist is the bringing-into-the-present of all the temporally separated events of Christ's human life—Bethlehem, Calvary, the Heavenly Session, the Second Coming.

But it is primarily the re-presentation of Calvary, because of the twofold consecration, mystically separating Body and Blood, first made in the setting of the Passover on the eve of the Passion.

It should, I think, be possible along these lines to reconcile the essential points of what we may call the "de la Taille" and

[1] *The Necessary Erudition of any Christian Man*, ed. of 1932, p. 55.

"Vonier" schools of thought. And if it be asked whether the Eucharist is related primarily to the Heavenly Session or to Calvary, the answer is, to both; to the Session if we consider the *present condition* of the divine victim; to Calvary and the Cross if we consider his mode of *sacramental re-presentation*. In the Eucharist these two great realities, Heaven and Calvary, are made present to the members of the Mystical Body who live under the conditions of multiplicity inherent in bodily existence, separated by space and time. There is therefore, I would suggest, no need for misgiving at the tendency, which became prominent in the Middle Ages and has continued since then, to multiply celebrations of the Eucharist; in each of them the Heavenly Session and the Cross of Calvary are embodied in their fullness, and in each of them the Mystical Body of Christ is the earthly instrument of the divine and human Lord, the "elect race, the royal priesthood, the holy nation, the peculiar people" of God, whose members "as living stones are built up as a spiritual house, to be a holy priesthood to offer up spiritual sacrifices, acceptable to God through Jesus Christ."[1] It is indeed good that, at the celebration of the Divine Liturgy, the faithful should be present in number, each one taking his or her part intelligently in the great Eucharistic action, and the Liturgical Movement has done a great work in furthering this aim. But it must not be forgotten—as I am afraid in certain "liturgical" circles it has been—that the Liturgy is corporate not because of the numbers or enthusiasm of the congregation in a particular building at a particular time, but because, whether the faithful who are physically present be many or few, it is the act of the great High Priest, acting through and in and for his Mystical Body, the *Corpus Mysticum Christi*. And if it be asked how it is possible for this, that and the other portion of bread and wine to become the Body and Blood of Christ, how it is possible for the divine Victim to be simultaneously present on many altars, we may indeed rightly answer in scholastic language that the Body is present, not circumscriptively as having extended dimension but through and only through its sacramental signification by the consecrated elements, but we should also add that the truth is not so much that Christ comes down in this place and that, as that the various portions of the Eucharistic elements are themselves taken up into the supernatural order and identified with the Holy Things which they contain; and that this identification is, as

[1] 1 Pet. ii. 9, 5.

regards the mode of proper existence, related to the Heavenly Session and, as regards the mode of sacramental re-presentation, related to the death on the Cross. Just as, in the case of the Incarnation, it is right to say that Christ "came down from heaven" to Bethlehem, so long as we remember that this took place "not by conversion of Godhead into flesh but by taking up of manhood into God," so, in the case of the Eucharist, it is right to say that Christ "comes down from heaven" on to our altars, so long as we remember that the manner of this descent is not a conversion of Christ into bread but a taking up of bread into Christ.[1] And just as, through his incorporation into Christ, the Christian, while remaining on earth in the temporal and spatial order as regards his natural life, is nevertheless, by his adoption into Christ, given a real participation in the timeless realities of the divine life, by which his whole natural existence is transformed and sanctified, so in the Eucharist the Church, while, on her human and creaturely side, remaining in the changing and temporal world in which her life has to be lived and her battles to be fought, is, in her inner and supernatural character as the Body and Bride of Christ, caught up with her members into the perfection and immutability of the glorified body of her triumphant Head. Thus in the Eucharist earth and heaven meet, and Christians stand with the angels and saints of heaven, united with them in their ceaseless act of homage to the Father.

"It may be seen," writes Wilberforce,

"on what principle, and in what degree, the *devotion* of Christians makes part of the sacrifice of the Holy Eucharist. . . . Considered in itself, it does not answer to those conditions which are to be looked for in the Eucharistic Sacrifice. For there is nothing sacramental in its character; there is no *sacramentum* or *res sacramenti*; the prayers which are offered at the Holy Communion do not differ from those which accompany any other act of worship. But there is one view in which the worshippers may be regarded, which connects them with that which has been shown to be the true oblation in the Holy Eucharist; and this circumstance it is

---

[1] See p. 161 *supra*. I am not, of course, suggesting that what happens to the manhood of Christ in relation to the Word in the Incarnation is in all respects the same as what happens to the bread and wine in relation to Christ in the Eucharist, still less that in the Eucharist there is an "impanation" of the divine Word. The Eucharistic change is not the same thing as the hypostatic union. Here, as with all comparisons, the differences are not less important than the similarities.

which enables themselves to 'present themselves, their souls and bodies, a reasonable, holy, and lively sacrifice.' For 'the Christian Sacrifice,' says St. Augustine is 'the many who make up one body in Christ.' So that 'the whole congregation and society of the saints is offered to God as an universal sacrifice by its great High Priest, who also offered up himself in his Passion for us, that we might be the Body of so great a Head.'[1] On this principle did the Apostle speak of the oblation, of which he was the minister, as 'the offering up of the Gentiles'; inasmuch as in this sense the Christian Church itself constitutes the sacrifice which is presented to God. Thus it is in some sort the *res sacramenti*, which is aptly symbolized by the many grains, which have been kneaded together into its outward part or earthly emblem. For 'we being many, are one bread and one body.' So that, regarded in this manner in its collective character, the Christian Church fulfils the conditions of a sacramental offering. But nothing can show more clearly than this very circumstance, that the true *res sacramenti*, Christ's Body in its Real Presence, is not excluded from the sacrifice. . . . For is it not the perfection of his Body natural, by which his Body mystical is sanctified? . . . If the Body mystical therefore of Christ be a fit sacrifice to offer to God, it is by reason of the influence and presence of that Body natural by which it is ennobled. So that when she is herself offered up 'a living sacrifice, holy, acceptable unto God,' we may not exclude that, by which alone this is rendered a grateful sacrifice to the Father. The Church, which is the mystical Body of Christ, is accepted through the perpetual pleading of his Body natural. . . .

"The Eucharistic Sacrifice . . . is the offering up of the collective Church, Christ's mystical Body, but it is also the offering up of Christ himself, by whom that Body is sanctified. . . . He who has been consecrated a Priest for ever after the order of Melchisedek, chooses this medium for giving effect to his perpetual intercession. That acceptance which he purchased by the sacrifice of the cross, he applies through the sacrifice of the altar. He himself it is, who through the voice of his ministers consecrates these earthly gifts, and thus bestows the mystery of his Real Presence. By himself, again, is the precious Victim presented before the Father's throne; and the intervention of their Heavenly Head gives reality to the actions of his earthly ministers."[2]

"Having therefore, brethren, boldness to enter into the Holy Place by the Blood of Jesus, by the way which he dedicated for us, a new and living way, through the veil, that is to say, his Flesh,

[1] *De Civ.*, x, 6. [2] *Doctrine of the Holy Eucharist*, pp. 390–3.

and having a great Priest over the House of God, let us draw near with a true heart in fullness of faith, having our hearts sprinkled from an evil conscience and our body washed with pure water."[1]

*Praeceptis salutaribus moniti et divina institutione
formati, audemus dicere:*
PATER NOSTER.

[1] Heb. x. 19–22.

CHAPTER XII

PRAYER IN THE MYSTICAL BODY

I

" CHRIST," writes Richard Hooker,

"is whole with the whole Church, and whole with every part of the Church, as touching his Person, which can no way divide itself, or be possessed by degrees and portions. But the participation of Christ importeth, besides the presence of Christ's Person, and besides the mystical copulation thereof with the parts and members of his whole Church, a true actual influence of grace whereby the life which we live according to godliness is his, and from him we receive those perfections wherein our eternal happiness consisteth."[1]

In the last three chapters we have been considering the Holy Eucharist as the supreme expression of the Church's life and worship and the means of the Church's unification and sanctification. This must not, however, be taken as derogating in the least degree from the necessity of personal conversion and personal self-dedication. What it does imply is that Christian discipleship is a corporate activity, an activity of the whole Body of Christ. As I have already maintained,[2] the ultimate end for which man was created is to share in the enjoyment of the Beatific Vision by the Mystical Body. And this means not a diminution, but an affirmation and an unimaginable enrichment of the life of the individual person, for man is essentially a social being and can attain his full development only in union with his fellows.[3] This is as true on the natural as on the supernatural level; in a properly functioning society there is no contradiction between the good of the individual and that of society as a whole. The individual finds his fulfilment through his membership of the community, while the community is built up and fortified by the interweaving initiatives of its members. M. Maritain has inspiringly expounded this theme in

---

[1] *Eccl. Pol.*, V, lvi, 10: ed. of 1888, II, p. 253. [2] See p. 146 f. *supra*.
[3] See the chapter on "Personne et Société," in de Lubac, *Catholicisme*.

his essay on "The Human Person and Society."[1] "The end of society," he writes, "is its *common good*, the good of the body politic," but he adds that "the good of the body politic is a common good of *human persons*," and that if this latter truth is forgotten we shall be faced with some kind of collectivism or totalitarianism. As a mere *individual* a man is rightly subordinated to the community as a whole, but as a *person* he has an end that is transcendent to the whole material order, and "in regard to the eternal destiny of the soul, and its supra-temporal goods, society exists for each person and is subordinated to it."[2]

We are not concerned here with the detailed relation of the person to human society. But I must emphasize that while man, as a being with a supernatural end, has rights and functions superior to those of the human community on the natural level, this supernatural end, no less (and indeed far more) than his natural end, is a social one. It is with this truth in view that I shall develop the discussion of the supernatural life which immediately follows, but I shall start farther back by considering the character of created existence as such.

Ontologically considered, created existence is itself worship, for, by the very fact of existing, finite beings declare their utter dependence upon the loving will of the God who is infinite and self-existent.[3] He is their first cause and their last end. Without his never-failing creative activity they would collapse into non-existence; and, by existing in all their finitude, in dependence upon him, they declare, by their very limitations and their ontological frailty, the perfection and power of their Maker. By the Word of the Lord were the heavens made, and they declare the glory of God, not only by their splendour but even more by their insufficiency. For every finite being, *esse* is *esse ad Deum*: the very act of existence is a leaning towards God, it is an implicit act of worship.

When we pass from sub-rational to rational beings worship becomes both articulate and voluntary. It becomes a free and "rational worship"—a λογικὴ λατρεία. As such, it is of an immeasurably higher order than is the dumb worship of the lower creation, but it is exposed to a grave danger of failure, for, being

---

[1] *Scholasticism and Politics*, ch. iii.

[2] *Ibid.*, pp. 69, 73. Cf. Thornton's discussions in *The Incarnate Lord*, pp. 59. f., 407 f.

[3] Reference may be made to the exposition of this theme in my book, *He Who Is*, ch. vi.

the exercise of a free will, it can be withheld. A rational creature can offer to God a worship beyond price, but it can also refuse to offer it. Therein lie both the greatness and the wretchedness of man.

I have dealt in detail in a previous chapter with the essential inability of man to offer, through his finite powers, a worship adequate to the infinite worthiness of the God to whom it is due, and we have seen that the answer to the problem which this raises is to be found in the twin doctrines of the assumption of human nature by Christ and of our adoptive incorporation into him.[1] In Christ we are caught up into, and made part of, an offering of filial homage which is altogether perfect and adequate. Man has by his very nature a desire for God and a tendency towards him, however much these may have become obscured and perverted by sin; and the history of natural religion is the history of man's attempt to achieve the fulfilment of this desire. In so far as he has tried to achieve it by his own power he has been fore-doomed to failure; he is, in consequence, constantly tempted to substitute for God some finite being which is within his compass, and thus it is that natural religion continually tends to degenerate into idolatry: "they changed the glory of the incorruptible God for the likeness of an image of corruptible man, and of birds, and four-footed beasts, and creeping things."[2] Man is torn between his sense that he can only be satisfied by worship of, and union with, an infinite Good which lies beyond his grasp, and his power to comprehend finite beings which are incapable of giving him full and lasting satisfaction. Only if God comes to the aid of man can this agonizing dilemma be solved. As I have already said, we cannot set limits to the power of God or to the sphere within which it may seem good to him to exercise it; nor can we restrict the operation of the saving grace of Christ to the visible boundaries of the Christian Church. We can, however, affirm that visible sacramental union with Christ is the normal and divinely appointed means by which man is enabled to offer to God a homage which is both adequate to the majesty of him to whom it is offered and also capable of satisfying the aspirations and needs of the man who offers it. To sum this up in the words of Mersch:

"Because we are finite beings, we are, by our very essence, relative and striving. And this character is shown not just in

---

[1] Ch. ix, *supra*.   [2] Rom. i. 23.

occasional manifestations. . . . The aspiration of religion, that law of our very being which relates our own reality to the one thing that is necessary, perforce underlies all our other aspirations. It is *the* aspiration, the unique and ceaseless striving. Religion, in man, is everything.

".But not everything in his religion is man. . . .

"The soul of natural religion, if we may use the term, is *striving towards God*. And this it is that is realized, though in a supernaturally perfect way, in the religion of the God-Man. And this perfecting of natural religion is not a kind of superadded dignity, but is rather an interior fulfilment, which intensifies in a transcendent way the very essence of natural religion. Between this latter and the Christian religion there is no division, for it is assumed and raised up by Christianity, as our nature is assumed in Christ. To despise it would be to blaspheme Christ. But to be content with it after Christ has appeared would be to commit a crime against it. . . .

"The Unity of Christians, the unity of the Mystical Body, has its source and its pattern in the unity of the divine Persons alone. It is indeed a unity by participation; and by a very imperfect participation, which comes to us only in the degree to which everything is common to the Head and the members. But it is a real participation nevertheless, and one which constrains the love of the Father to descend even to the least of the faithful, since Christ himself reaches thus far: 'that the love wherewith thou didst love me may be in them, and I in them.' "[1]

II

Now just as the Christian life is a participation in the life of Christ through our adoptive union with him, so the Christian virtues are a participation in the virtues of Christ, the communication of Christ's virtues to us. In the ontological sphere, union with Christ was given to us in our baptism; in the moral sphere, it is the fruit of obedience to God's will under the assistance of supernatural grace; but the two are not unconnected. On the contrary, the production and manifestation of the Christian character is, as it were, the overflowing of union with Christ from the ontological to the moral sphere. In progressing in virtue, we are becoming, morally, that which, ontologically, we already are. The Christian life thus does not consist of an external imitation of the character

[1] *Morale et Corps Mystique*, pp. 35, 50, 55. I would draw attention here to the remarks on p. 152 f. *supra*.

and actions of Jesus of Nazareth or of an external obedience to his commands; those are its fruits, not its roots. In its essence, it is the reproduction of Christ in us, or, viewing it from the opposite aspect, it is our continual and progressive fashioning into him. The Christian virtues are nothing less than the manifestation of Christ in his members, and because their incorporation into him is, as we have seen,[1] their incorporation into the Church which is his Body and his Bride, there can be no contradiction between life in Christ and life in the Church. Personal sanctification is an intensely corporate and *churchly* act; being built up in Christ is being built up in the Church.

It is thus most regrettable that there has been visible in some quarters a tendency to contrast individual progress and sanctification with the liturgical life of the Church, as though the two were, if not altogether opposed to each other, at least divergent in tendency. But it is only if sanctification is misconceived as the attainment of an individualistic and exclusive beatitude that the liturgical life can appear to be in opposition to it; for "private" prayer, as we misleadingly call it, is itself an activity of the Mystical Body, since the Christian who prays is one of the Body's members. Indeed, it is only as a member of the Body that the Christian can pray *Christian* prayer at all; for Christian prayer is Christ's own prayer communicated to us. It is our participation in the prayer of the glorified Christ "who is at the right hand of God, who also maketh intercession for us,"[2] and our union with Christ was set up by our baptism, which also made us members of his Church. "In the days when an integrated society could be assumed," writes Mr. Michael Bruce,

"it was not necessary at every stage in our private devotions to underline the fact that our religion is corporate. In our present situation it is a desperate necessity, for if we attempt to worship God in isolation we shall not worship 'the God and Father of our Lord Jesus Christ' but the mirror image of ourselves. Father Andrew, S.D.C., has written: 'There is really only one prayer to God and that is the one prayer of the one Son to the Father; our prayer is only real prayer inasmuch as it is taken into that prayer.' But we can only be in Christ by being in his Body the Church. We can only join in the one prayer if we pray as members of the Church. In the secrecy of the inner chamber, when we have closed the door, we still pray '*Our* Father,' not '*My* Father.' We

---

[1] Ch. vii *supra*.   [2] Rom. viii. 34. Cf. Heb. vii. 25.

never stand before God alone. We do indeed stand before him in
the uniqueness of our vocation, but not in the loneliness of isolation.
Uniqueness is, in fact, only possible within an organic relationship. . . . So we shall preserve the piercingly personal demands
the mystics make upon us, only in so far as we gain a sense that our
private prayer is to be thoroughly corporate."[1]

Now just as it has frequently been forgotten that prayer is an
activity of the Mystical Body, so, by an opposite divagation, the
modern Liturgical Movement, both Roman and Anglican, has
sometimes given the impression that the essence of Liturgy consists
in the celebration of the Holy Mysteries in a way that makes the
corporate character of the liturgical action strikingly evident to
the eye. This may be, of course, of great didactic and apologetic
value, but it must never be forgotten that the corporate character
of the Liturgy consists primarily not in its being celebrated by a
large number of Christians but in the fact that it is, by its very
nature, the act of the Body of Christ, even though at a particular
Eucharist the Body may be represented by the merest handful of
people. Carefully executed ceremonial, preaching and hymnody
may do a great deal to *express* this fact, but they can do nothing
whatever to *cause* it. "The one necessary thing," writes a Roman
Catholic who has had this point well in mind,

"is that before 'doing something,' before 'acting,' we should concern ourselves about *being*; before you think of Catholic action, *be*
a Catholic; before you think of the liturgical movement, *be* fully
liturgical yourself."[2]

Both Liturgy and sanctification thus arise out of the ontological
fact of incorporation into Christ; they are the overflowing of that
incorporation into the practical realm. To quote the last-
mentioned writer again:

"The whole supernatural structure of Christian life, theological
virtues included, rests upon this basic fact that, to be able to
accomplish any supernatural actions at all man must first *be*
supernatural: psychology comes after ontology, *operari sequitur esse*.
To *be* supernatural is to share in Divine Life, and this communion
in the Divine life which we call sanctifying grace lies embedded
in the normal and necessary channels of this grace, and these
channels are the Sacraments, principally the Eucharist."[3]

[1] "The Corporate Element in Private Prayer," in *Theology*, Feb. 1940, p. 115.
[2] Theodore Wesseling, O.S.B., *Liturgy and Life*, p. 119.
[3] "Liturgy and the Love of God." (Review of Dom Aelred Graham's *Love of God*,
in *Eastern Churches Quarterly*, July 1940, p. 108.)

The Christian is thus the "liturgical man," the man whose whole life is set in the context of the perpetual prayer which Christ for ever offers in heaven. The use which has been made of this truth by the French priest Fr. Couturier in organizing prayer for Christian unity is too well known to need more than passing mention. It is, however, a truth which, both in Catholic and in Protestant circles, was allowed to fall sadly into the background in the individualistic atmosphere of post-Reformation Christianity. Nevertheless, even at the worst of times the best spiritual writers have seen its importance. The spirituality of the great figures of the French School of the seventeenth century—Bérulle, de Condren and Olier—shows it in a marked degree,[1] even if in a somewhat baroque dress, with their doctrine of adherence to Christ in his "states" as the basis of Christian life, though in them it is somewhat marred, as Mersch remarks,[2] by a negative and rigorist tone which is untrue to its real nature. "From all eternity," writes the Cardinal Pierre de Bérulle,

"there has been a God infinitely adorable, but there had not yet been an infinite Adorer; there had in truth been a God, worthy of being infinitely loved and served, but there had been no man nor infinite servant, fit to render infinite service and love. Now art thou, O Jesus, this Adorer, this man and infinite servitor, fit in quality and dignity and might to satisfy fully this duty and render this divine homage."[3]

And the doctrine of prayer as an "adherence" to the Incarnate Word and an "appropriation" of his "states" arises precisely out of the truth that we can pray a truly *Christian* prayer only if Christ's own prayer is being prayed in us. It is true that, expounded as a *method* of praying, this doctrine may seem to be nothing more than a psychological technique, an imaginative union with the virtues of Christ as they were manifested nineteen hundred years ago in his humiliated earthly life, rather than a real union with the ascended Christ in his present glorified manhood. But this method is quite clearly shown to have as its end nothing less than the manifestation in the moral sphere of the ontological union with Christ which the Christian already possesses in virtue of his baptismal

---

[1] The best modern account of the French School is to be found in Henri Bremond's *Literary History of Religious Thought in France*, Vol. III.   [2] *The Whole Christ*, p. 542.
[3] *Œuvres*, pp. 183–4; quoted by Bremond, p. 53. It will be noticed that Bérulle does not use the word "adoration" to describe the filial homage rendered by the Son to the Father within the life of the Trinity. I do not think this is more than a verbal point.

incorporation. For Bérulle the Incarnation is by no means to be thought of as merely a past event.

"The Incarnation," he writes, "is a permanent state, permanent for all eternity. Unceasingly the Father bestows his Son upon man; unceasingly this Son who is the Gift of God bestows himself upon our humanity; unceasingly the Eternal Father begets his Son in a new nature. . . .

"He is ours by eternal state."[1]

As Bremond says,

"St. Ignatius insists on our contemplating especially the 'actions' of Jesus, Bérulle, his 'states'; where the former dwells upon Jesus obeying his mother at such a time in such a way, the latter dwells upon Jesus 'inclining towards Mary'; the first beholds what passes, the second, what is prolonged, what abides, what finally, since it is concerned with a Divine Person, has the stamp of eternity."[2]

Christ, writes Bérulle,

"alone can adore by his state the Divine Persons and Emanations, whom the angels truly adore in heaven by the *actions* of their comprehension and goodwill, but not by this species of adoration of which we speak, which is very different. For we speak of an adoration that is by state and not by action, an adoration not simply emanating from the faculties of the intellect and depending on its thoughts, but concrete, permanent and independent of powers and actions, imprinted in the depths of the created being and in the condition of its state."[3]

Christian prayer is thus the articulation and vocalization of what it is to be a member of the New Creation, as human prayer in general is an articulation and vocalization of what it is to be a member of the old. If, with the Apostle, the Christian can say, "I live, yet it is not I that live, but Christ liveth in me," he can also say, "I pray, yet it is not I that pray, but Christ prayeth in me." Christian prayer is, from one standpoint, the prayer of Christ, prayed by him in his members; from another, it is the prayer of Christians, taken up into the prayer of Christ. And for this reason Christian prayer is no more an act of individuals in separation than is the Christian Liturgy. It is the act of the

---

[1] *Œuvres*, pp. 921, 967; Bremond, p. 58.

[2] *Literary History of Religious Thought in France*, p. 55.

[3] *Œuvres*, p. 363; Bremond, p. 55. "The created being" here means, of course, the human nature of Christ.

Mystical Body, Head and members, in indissoluble union. It is the act of the Whole Christ.

Whatever may be the variety manifested on the psychological and phenomenological level in the prayer-life of Christians—and to this variety the treatises on ascetical and mystical theology bear abundant witness—all Christian prayer has the same essential character. It is the prayer of Christ operating in and through his members, and the personal effort for which it calls from each of them, and the struggle against distraction, aridity and self-love that it involves, have no other end than the removal of the obstacles that sin has interposed to the free operation of Christ's own prayer in the human soul, an operation which does not, as the quietists supposed, destroy or suppress the soul's own life, but, even (or perhaps it would be truer to say, especially) in the highest grades of "passive" contemplation, energizes it to the most intense degree.[1] The discussions of the spiritual writers about the various types and modes of prayer are far from unimportant, but they concern the methodology and phenomenology of prayer more than its ontology; they are concerned with the way it goes, rather than with what it is. In its essence, all Christian prayer is one; for it is all the prayer of Christ.

III

In the light of what has been said, it should be easy to see that there can be no fundamental contradiction between the ancient, simple, "liturgical" tradition of prayer, which is so beautifully exemplified in the Benedictine ideal of Christian life, and the elaborate modern discussions of which the great Spanish Carmelites of the sixteenth century provide the finest instances. For, in spite of the contentions of certain recent writers who have seen in St. John of the Cross nothing but a Buddhist who had the misfortune to be born in counter-Reformation Spain, the Carmelite spirituality is incarnational through and through. St. Teresa, it is well known, insists that even one who has reached the higher stages of mystical prayer must not neglect to meditate on the manhood of Christ,[2] and, while on this point St. John of the

---

[1] It might, from this point of view, seem better to use the word "receptive" than "passive."

[2] *Interior Castle*, Man. VI, ch. vii; *Life*, ch. xxii, 9–11. Cf. the quotations from the Spanish Carmelite Mother Cecilia of the Nativity given in E. I. Watkin's *Philosophy of Mysticism*, p. 73 f.

Cross appears to differ from her,[1] the reason is certainly not that he is concerned with a type of mysticism in which specifically Christian dogma is irrelevant or unnecessary. For his writings abound in references to the Incarnation; nothing could be more explicitly Christian than his "Prayer of the Soul enkindled with Love": "Thou wilt not take from me, my God, that which once thou gavest me in thine only Son Jesus Christ, in whom thou gavest me all that I desire. . . . God himself is mine and for me, for Christ is mine and all for me. . . ."[2] And when he comes to write about the supreme heights of mystical union, he describes it in explicitly trinitarian terms. The Living Flame of Love is the triune God, and in particular the Holy Spirit:

> "The movements of this Divine Flame . . . are not made only by the soul that is transformed in the flames of the Holy Spirit, neither are they made by him alone; but by the Spirit and the soul together, the Spirit moving the soul, even as the fire moves the air that is enkindled."[3]

And, as we have seen,[4] there is no pantheistic absorption of the soul into God; for all the privileges that are conferred upon it, it is still a creature:

> "Even as God is giving himself to the soul with free and gracious will, even so likewise the soul, having a will that is the freer and the more generous in proportion as it has a greater degree of union with God, is giving God in God to God himself, and thus the gift of the soul to God is true and entire. For in this state the soul sees that God truly belongs to it, and that it possesses him with hereditary possession, with rightful ownership, as an adopted child of God, through the grace that God gave to it, and it sees that, since he belongs to it, it may give and communicate him to whomsoever it desires of its own will; and thus it gives him to its beloved, who is the very God that gave himself to it."[5]

> "The soul now loves God, not through itself, but through himself; which is a wondrous brightness, since it loves through the Holy Spirit, even as the Father and the Son love one another."[6]

> "The soul is now able to see that [created] things are distinct

---

[1] According to the best texts; see the footnote in Peers's translation of the *Works*, I, p. 232. Abbot Chapman's discussion of the differences between St. Teresa and St. John (*Spiritual Letters*, pp. 78, 269 f.) are very illuminating, but it needs to be remembered that he was thinking aloud and also had a very marked sense of humour.
[2] *Works*, trans. by Peers, III, p. 243.
[3] *Living Flame*, 2nd red., st. III, 10; Peers, III, p. 166.   [4] p. 97 f. *supra.*
[5] *Living Flame*, 2nd red., st. III, 78; Peers, III, p. 204.
[6] *Ibid.*, 2nd red., st. III, 82; Peers, III, p. 206.

from God, inasmuch as they have a created being, and it sees them
in him, with their force, root and strength [and] it knows equally
that God, in his own being, is all these things, in an infinite and
pre-eminent way,[1] to such a point that it understands them better
in his Being than in themselves. And this is the great delight of
this awakening: to know the creatures through God and not God
through the creatures; to know the effects through their cause and
not the cause through the effects; for the latter knowledge is
secondary and this other is essential."[2]

The soul can even be described as "God by participation in
God"; nevertheless, "the substance of this soul . . . is not the
Substance of God, for into this it cannot be substantially changed."[3]
We are concerned all along with that elevation of the soul into the
life of the triune Godhead which it enjoys through its adoptive
union with the humanity of Christ, which in turn is hypostatically
united to the Person of the Eternal Word.[4] The essential point is
not that the Christian must be consciously occupied with the
consideration of our Lord's human nature—as regards this there
is ample room for difference, as we saw above in relation to
St. Teresa and St. John of the Cross—but that, whether he is
consciously so occupied or not, his prayer is a participation in the
prayer of Christ. And we have seen already that for the great
Carmelite doctor the Beatific Vision itself is the possession not of
the individual Christian in isolation but of the whole Mystical
Body as the Spouse of Christ.[5] It is true that in St. John's works
there is singularly little reference to the Liturgy, but that is surely
because it is taken for granted rather than because it is ignored or
belittled.[6] Everything that he says presupposes the context within
which he writes and within which he lives, and which is the source
from which his spiritual life is derived even when he himself is least
conscious of it.

In asserting, as I have, that all Christian prayer is a participation in the prayer of Christ, I am not in the least intending to deny
the general teaching of the mystical theologians that there is a real

---

[1] That is, as St. Thomas says, "in the divine wisdom are the types of all things."
(*S. Theol.*, I, xliv, 3c.)   [2] *Living Flame*, 2nd red., st. IV, 5; Peers, III, p. 209.
[3] *Ibid.*, 2nd red., st. II, 34; Peers, III, p. 158.
[4] See ch. iii *supra*.   [5] See p. 147 *supra*.
[6] It has been remarked that the same characteristic marks the spiritual letters of
Dom John Chapman, in spite of the fact that he was Abbot of one of the great liturgical
centres of English Roman Catholicism. His predecessor, Abbot Butler, remarks that
the singing of the Office, as well as other vocal prayer, can be truly contemplative.
(*Western Mysticism*, 2nd ed., p. 316.)

P

and most important distinction to be drawn between the two great divisions of the ordinary or ascetical and the extraordinary or mystical degrees of prayer. I shall therefore devote a little space to consideration of Christian mysticism, and in doing this I shall begin by outlining the discussion which is to be found in Fr. Gardeil's brilliant work, *La Structure de l'Ame et l'Expérience Mystique*, though I shall later on suggest that it needs supplementing in one important particular.[1]

Gardeil begins by considering the essential structure of the human soul. It is a mind, a *mens*, a special kind of created spirit, and as spirit it bears upon itself the image of the supreme Spirit, God its creator. As spirit it has a natural desire for God, but as finite spirit it can tend to him only according to the idea which it can form of him, and it is totally incapable of raising itself to this infinite object of its desire. Nevertheless, what it cannot do for itself God can do for it, for, leaving out of account sin, which is a distortion of the soul and not an element in its true nature, there is nothing in the soul that is *repugnant* to the vision of God. The soul is merely helpless to attain it by its own powers.

Now the soul is a created analogue of God, for man is made in God's image, and, by his presence of immensity, God is more present to the soul than it is to itself. Hence we may expect that the best analogue that we can find to the soul's knowledge of God is its knowledge of itself. This self-knowledge has one very remarkable characteristic: namely, that, although the soul is, ontologically considered, more immediately related to itself than to any of the beings which it apprehends (since it *is itself*, entitatively, whereas it merely *knows them*), it knows other beings before it knows itself. Indeed, it comes to know itself only as a result of those acts in which it turns towards external beings. (It may be noted that, absurd as it might seem, children learn to recognize external objects before they learn their own self-identity.) Therefore, by analogy and *a fortiori*, we may expect that the God who is more interior to the soul than it is to itself will also be known only as a result of the soul's acts.

But as a result of what acts? The act of self-reflection may indeed give us some kind of knowledge of God, if the soul which is its object is a created analogue of him. But such a knowledge will be only a knowledge of him in his effects, not a knowledge of

---

[1] The following passage is reproduced almost *verbatim* from my book, *He Who Is*, p. 144 f.

him in his own proper being. It will be of the same kind as the soul's knowledge of God through his effects in the external world, though of a vastly higher degree. Is there, we therefore ask, any kind of human act through which we may come to know God himself in a way comparable with the way in which, in self-reflection, we come to know our own selves? We know already that God is *near* enough for this, for he is present by immensity at the very heart of our being, in the most intimate way conceivable. But is there any way by which we can be made to see him there, any way by which our faculty of knowledge can be brought to exceed the limitations of its finitude and be raised to the apprehension of this infinite Being?

It is asserted that there is, and its name is grace. Just as, through the operation of his natural acts of knowledge directed towards the external world man can come to know not only the external world but also himself, so, by sanctifying grace, he can come to know God. And this means that, in addition to his presence of immensity, God must be made present in a new and higher mode in the soul, for only God can know God adequately, and so man can know God in a way that is analogous to God's knowledge of himself only if he is elevated into God's own act of self-knowledge. Just as by nature the soul knows itself as the principle of its natural acts, so by grace it knows God as the principle of its supernatural acts. Even so, this indwelling of God in the soul by grace, which is offered to anyone who is prepared to live by the theological virtues, is not enough to give us a knowledge of God that is parallel in all respects to the knowledge of ourselves which we have through our natural acts.

"When, by psychological knowledge, the soul reflects upon the act which it has just performed, it seizes this act in its entirety—in its term, namely the concept, in its movement or intention of knowledge, in its efficient principle, namely the soul itself in so far as it is activated by its act—for all this is in itself actually intelligible. On the other hand, in the intentional life of living faith, all that can be actually apprehended are the object of this life, constituted by the truths of the Faith (which are themselves representatives of the divine reality), and the activity of living faith itself."[1]

---

[1] *La Structure de l'Ame*, II, p. 185. It should be noted that in this extract words such as "term," "intention" and "object" are used in the technical senses suggested by their Latin derivations and not in their popular English meanings.

This is as far as the soul can get in the ordinary "ascetical" mode of Christian prayer. For anything more the *ad hoc* initiative of God is necessary, and in this the soul, whatever it may have previously done in the way of preparation, is entirely passive.[1] The soul can neither demand nor expect this; it is a pure gift from God, and it may raise the soul ultimately to the highest point of union attainable in this life, that of the Spiritual Marriage or Transforming Union. The predominant part in this is played by the virtue of charity and the gift of wisdom.

> "The Holy Spirit . . . communicates to the soul that loves God his knowledge of divine things, that is, in particular, what is deepest, most formal, *most God* (if we may venture to use the phrase), for the Holy Spirit comprehends God in his depths and in an infinite mode. . . . The human spirit, having placed itself by its use of the gift of wisdom under the rule of the Spirit who uncovers before it the depths of God, allows itself to be joined to this interior God without any concept, *tanquam ignoto et inaccessibili*, and in this attitude of absolute renunciation of seeing or of making for itself ideas of God, it lets itself be carried towards God by the Holy Spirit. . . . No doubt the soul will then contemplate nothing, but, if it truly shares in the divine wisdom, it will do better than contemplate; in so far as it has become one spirit with God, it will feel, touch and experience immediately the substantial presence of God within itself."[2]

Such an experience can come rarely, and then only transiently, in this life; and, as I have said, it is a pure gift from God. Nothing remains beyond it but the Beatific Vision, of which it is a kind of foretaste.[3]

It will be readily seen, from this description of the life of the soul in grace, how unjustified is the complaint of the neo-Protestant school that Catholic mysticism, and indeed Catholic religion in general, is just an attempt of man, in defiance of the divine transcendence and his own creatureliness, to climb up to God. On the contrary, Catholic spirituality finds place for both the transcendence and the immanence of God. God is immanent in the depths of the soul and it is there that he is to be found. But he is immanent there, not as contained in it but rather as containing it; not in the sense that he is limited and restricted by man,

---

[1] Passive, of course, as regards the soul's attainment of the state, not as regards its condition afterwards, which is one of intense activation, not by the soul itself but by God; see p. 209 *supra*.

[2] *La Structure de l'Ame*, II, pp. 258–60.   [3] Cf. p. 61 f. *supra*.

but in the sense that man, at the very root of his being, is altogether dependent upon God. God, then, is immanent, but the unveiling of this immanent God is not the work of man. All that man can do without grace is to know God as the author of certain effects, and he can know this only because God *is* the author of them; not because man can, as it were, put God under his scrutiny. Anything beyond this is the work of sanctifying grace, of the elevation of man by God to a participation in God's own life; and the very essence of grace is that it is gratuitous, a free gift of God which man has neither the right to demand nor the power to appropriate by his own efforts. Finally, in mystical experience—and it is against this that the neo-Protestants raise their strongest protests— the human soul is devoid of all activity whatever that proceeds from itself, even of the least active co-operation; it loves God, as St. John of the Cross says, "not through itself, but through himself. . . . It loves through the Holy Spirit, even as the Father and the Son love one another."[1] And the unanimous teaching of all Catholic mystical theologians is that, whatever man may do in the way of preparing himself for mystical union with God, and however large or small may be the proportion of souls that God calls to it (questions which have received much discussion in recent years[2]), the actual elevation to mystical prayer is a pure and unconditioned gift from God for which man has nothing more than an entirely passive or obediential capacity.[3]

IV

Now where, I suggest, Gardeil fails to be sufficiently explicit and where in consequence he weakens his case against the opponents of Catholic mysticism, is in his lack of emphasis upon the fact that the grace by which the soul is enabled to know God as the principle of its supernatural acts and by which it is elevated to a participation in God's own life, is—at any rate normally— the "grace of our Lord Jesus Christ," the grace by which we are incorporated into the human nature of the incarnate Word. Whatever qualifications it may be necessary to make in order to safeguard the sovereign rights of God to confer his favours where and as he sees fit, and however ready we may be to admit that the

[1] *Living Flame*, 2nd red., st. III, 82; Peers, III, p. 206.
[2] Cf., e.g., the works of Poulain, Saudreau, Farges, etc., and the balanced discussion by Garrigou-Lagrange in *Perfection Chrétienne et Contemplation*.
[3] See the Appendix to this chapter: "Nature, Grace and Mysticism."

effects of the Incarnation cannot be restricted in their scope to the visible limits of the sacramental Church,[1] the fact remains that Catholic mysticism is in no way a "flight of the alone to the alone" by which the mystic detaches himself from the fellowship of his "even-Christians" or from his adherence to the distinctive dogmas of the Faith once delivered to the saints, in order to emulate the raptures of Buddha or Plotinus; it is Christian and churchly through and through. Brunner is altogether off the point—at least as regards the Christian mystics—when he sees the essence of mysticism to consist in "feeling" and when he asserts against it the undoubted fact that faith and not ecstasy is the means by which the living God is apprehended.[2] For no genuine Christian mystic would ever assert that his mystical experiences were in themselves the means of either his ontological or his moral union with God; the former of these is the work of adoption, the latter is the work of faith, hope and charity. St. John of the Cross explicitly directs confessors to tell their penitents "how much

---

[1] See ch. viii supra.

[2] Man in Revolt, p. 252. It should be noted that words like "ecstasy" and "rapture" are very ambiguous. They often refer merely to certain psycho-physical concomitants of the higher (though not the highest) grades of mystical prayer, which are, in Maréchal's words, "a feeble adaptation of our somatic mechanisms to the excessive central supertension of high intellectual contemplation." (Studies in the Psychology of the Mystics, p. 177; cf. E. I. Watkin, Philosophy of Mysticism, p. 216 f.) St. John of the Cross refers to "the raptures and trances and dislocations of the bones which always happen when the communications are not purely spiritual." (Dark Night, II, i, 2; Peers, I, p. 399.) On the other hand, "rapture" is also used to denote the momentary earthly experiences of the Beatific Vision which some few great saints are alleged to have enjoyed. (S. Theol., II II, clxxv; Chapman, E.R.E., IX, p. 96, s.v. "Mysticism.") To St. Bonaventure "ecstasy" meant the degree of mystical union immediately beneath rapture in the sense just defined; and we may notice that for him ecstasy, so far from being conceived in intellectual terms, is a state in which the soul knows nothing, being united to God purely by love; he compares it to taste rather than to sight. (Gilson, Philosophy of St. Bonaventure, p. 459 f.) And so far is it from being unrelated to anything specifically Christian that the instance of ecstasy which for all Franciscans is most dear is that experienced by St. Francis on Mount Averno, in which the central figure was the crucified Christ. William James is typical of Protestants generally when he defines mysticism entirely in terms of its psychological characteristics without any relation to its object. (Varieties of Religious Experience, ch. xvi.)

It may be added that the neo-Protestants are opposed to Catholic mysticism quite as much on account of its emphasis upon love as for any other reason. For them, faith, not love, is the proper attitude of the soul in the presence of God; love is the property of God alone. How deeply the disastrous opposition of faith to love as mutually exclusive can vitiate an otherwise sympathetic and illuminating discussion of Christian spirituality is seen in Nygren's Agape and Eros. And whether faith itself means the same to Protestants as to Catholics may be doubted; I am not sure that Brunner would agree with St. John of the Cross in defining faith as "a habit of the soul, certain and obscure" which "makes us believe truths revealed by God himself, which transcend all natural light, and exceed all human understanding, beyond all proportion." (Ascent, II, iii, 1; Peers, I, p. 70.) Confusion is often increased through the common Protestant rejection of the distinction between fides informis (bare intellectual assent supernaturally motivated) and fides caritate formata, which, in Catholic doctrine, justifies a man and unites him to God.

more precious in God's sight is one work or act of the will performed in charity than are all the visions and communications
that they may receive from heaven, since these imply neither merit
nor demerit."[1] St. Teresa has some very strong words about those
who abandon themselves to spiritual consolations: "They fancy
this is a trance and call it one, but I call it nonsense; it does
nothing but waste their time and injure their health."[2] And in
any case, so far from ecstasy being the essence of mysticism, it
almost invariably vanishes altogether in the highest stages, as
St. John himself points out.[3] Mystical experience indeed requires
a high degree of Christian faith and charity as its presupposition,
but it does not itself confer it; still less is it a substitute for it.

For mystical experience, while it is the result of an almost
incredible condescension and generosity on the part of the
Creator and while it is something altogether beyond the power of
the soul to acquire for itself, is far more a grace of the psychological
and gnoseological orders than of the ontological or moral.[4] That

---

[1] *Ascent*, II, xxii, 19; Peers, I, p. 184.   [2] *Interior Castle*, Mans. IV, ch. iii, 11.
[3] *Dark Night*, II, i, 2; Peers, I, p. 399.

[4] I am not intending to deny that mystical union is a most profound experience,
which penetrates to the very depths of the soul's being. If knowledge consists in the
knower becoming in a mysterious manner the object that is known (*mens quodammodo
fit omnia*), the knowledge of God, who is the soul's creator and its end, must transform
it through and through. But it has to be added that the knower becomes the object
known not *entitatively* but *intentionally*; there is a difference between seeing a block of
salt and undergoing the experience of Lot's wife, and to see the purple cow of a famous
verse is not the same as to "be one." Furthermore, all mystical theologians agree that
the knowledge of God that is conferred in mystical union is extremely obscure and
perplexing: the soul is united to God *tanquam ignoto et inaccessibili* (see the quotation
from Gardeil, p. 214 *supra*). For, except perhaps in exceedingly rare instances of
rapture, which are a momentary earthly enjoyment of the Beatific Vision (and for
the possibility and nature of this reference may be made to St. Thomas, *S. Theol.*, I,
xii, 11, and II II, clxxv; St. John of the Cross, *Ascent*, II, xxiv: Peers, I, p. 187;
Chapman, *E.R.E.*, IX, p. 96; Butler, *Christian Mysticism, passim*; Maréchal, *Études sur
la Psychologie des Mystiques*, II, *passim*), the soul in mystical union is united to God not
by intentional being of *knowledge* but by intentional being of *love*; in this, as Maritain
points out, the lover does not so much become the beloved, but rather the beloved
becomes for the lover another self. (*Degrees of Knowledge*, p. 453, n. 4.)   In matters
such as this it is, of course, wise to tread with the utmost caution, but it may be suggested
that, although one can set no limits to the graces that God may successively confer
upon the soul (short of an actual entitative conversion of the substance of the soul
into the substance of God, or the hypostatic union of its human nature to one of the
Persons of the Trinity), and although conceivably two degrees of grace successively
conferred upon the soul may differ *quantitatively* (if the term may be allowed) from
each other more than either of them differs from the purely natural condition, yet the
really decisive *qualitative* change in the soul occurs in its incorporation into Christ, the
normal instrument of which is baptism and the necessary development of which is not
mystical experience but the life of the supernatural virtues of faith, hope and charity. It
would, I think, be difficult on this point to improve on the words of Mr. E. I. Watkin:
"Since mystical experience is an increase and manifestation of sanctifying grace, it
does not differ essentially from the hidden life of grace in the souls of all the just.
Throughout the entire process from grace to glory no new principle is introduced.
Hence the mystical union-intuition involves no such introduction of a new principle.
It is but a development and unfolding of a principle already present. Whereas the

is to say, it does not so much bring about a change in the soul's character, as created and redeemed, as give it a unique and pre-eminent insight into the condition in which it already stands. As, in the "acquired contemplation" which is the highest stage of ordinary ascetical prayer, the mind has ceased to have any clear thoughts about God because it has turned away from the sensible images in terms of which it formerly pictured him, so, in the "infused contemplation" of mystical prayer, it is conscious of him again, but this time "in his light" and not in its own. As Garrigou-Lagrange says, "the mystical life is the Christian life which has become in some way conscious of itself."[1] And the extent and the manner in which the mystic is conscious of the grace that he has received depends very largely upon his temperament and circumstances. "Though the union and its degree are the work of grace," writes Mr. E. I. Watkin, "the apprehension of them depends on natural conditions. Inasmuch as mystical experience is the awareness of the union of charity at a given degree of its growth it is the gift of grace. That this degree of union is consciously apprehended by its subject is due to natural causes."[2]

---

infusion of sanctifying grace in our regeneration is a new creation, the mystical way is but the growth of that new creature, mystical experience a concomitant manifestation of the new life thus growing." (*Philosophy of Mysticism*, p. 241.) And again: "*The way from sanctifying grace to beatific glory is one continuous road of increasing supernatural union between the soul and God.*" (*Ibid.*, p. 129.)

[1] *Perfection chrétienne et Contemplation*, I, p. 149.

[2] *Theism, Agnosticism and Atheism*, p. 149. In his *Philosophy of Mysticism*, in which he discusses this question very fully, Mr. Watkin distinguishes very clearly between the mystical union, which, as he uses the term, is the effect of the complete purgation of the soul by God, and the consciousness of this union by the soul itself. It is, of course, the latter that is usually understood by the terms "mysticism," "mystical prayer" and "mystical experience." He is thus able to assert with Père Poulain that almost all the canonized saints have enjoyed the mystical union, in spite of the fact that many of them have not been, in the obviously recognizable sense, "mystics." "There is," he writes, "but one and the same way by which all the saved must reach the Fullness of Divine Union . . . , a union which when it has reached a certain stage is the mystical union, normally revealed to consciousness in mystical intuition. . . . It is clear that the essential and indispensable element of mystical union, as the way to beatific vision, is not the consciousness of God as the object of union but the union itself. This union, when it reaches a certain stage, is usually conscious when fully actualized, although not directly so in the desolations. . . . This consciousness, however, is not the essential part of the mystical union and, even if he has not actually done so, God could dispense with it" (pp. 130,138). Whether one restricts the adjective "mystical" to the consciousness of union (as I have for the most part in the text) or whether, with Mr. Watkin, one applies it to the underlying union itself is mainly a matter of words. I should add that the most thorough and comprehensive account known to me of the very important discussions by Roman Catholic theologians of the first quarter of the present century concerning the many controversial points relating to contemplation and mysticism is to be found in the "Afterthoughts" in the second edition of Abbot Butler's *Western Mysticism*. Cf. also the difficult but suggestive article by W. Bardon, O.P., "The Platonic Tradition and St. Thomas Aquinas," in *Eastern Churches Quarterly*, July–Oct. 1941.

Even before it receives the special graces of mysticism, the soul, in so far as it is in faith and charity, is looking upon the face of God in virtue of its baptismal union with Christ, who is the eternal and perfect adorer of the heavenly Father, but it is so dazzled by the splendour that confronts it that it cannot be conscious that it is looking upon him, even while it knows this by faith; it cannot realize in the psychological realm what it already enjoys in the ontological. But if and when it receives the special graces of mysticism, this consciousness is conferred upon it, in a mode which depends partly upon its own peculiar characteristics and partly upon the all-wise and compassionate will of God. The true human contemplative is the incarnate Word himself, and the contemplation of Christians is their participation in his. And like everything else that Christians receive through their incorporation into him, this contemplation belongs to them not as separate individuals but as members of the Mystical Body, the *Totus Christus*. It is this Whole Christ, the Head and his members, Jesus united to his Bride, that is the complete contemplative. The Church's whole life is thus, as it were, a contemplation by her of the Father through the eyes of her glorified Head, and her Liturgy, her social action and the prayers of her members—whether they individually ascend to the mystical heights or remain on the lower levels of ascetical prayer—are the various modes in which it is manifested and the various components that go to make it up. What belongs to one belongs to all, and the peculiar graces of the mystic—his illuminations, and his sufferings as well—are given to him not merely for his own sake but for the sake of all his brethren. And he in his turn is aided by every act that they perform in faith, hope and love.[1]

[1] It should be noted that I have said that in mystical experience the soul is conscious of the fact that it is looking upon God, whereas it previously knew this only by faith, but I have not said that it "sees" God; that can take place only in the Beatific Vision (and perhaps in moments of rapture). We have to consider the following degrees of knowledge of God:
1. Looking at God "through our own eyes" and representing him in images derived from the senses. Discursive meditation.
2. Looking at God "through the eyes of Christ," by incorporation into him. This has three grades, in which respectively:
    (a) We know that this is so "by faith." Acquired or non-mystical contemplation.
    (b) We are "conscious" that this is so, although we cannot "see" God. Infused or mystical contemplation.
    (c) We know that this is so, because we can "see" God. Rapture and the Beatific Vision.
It must be added:
    (i) That any scheme such as this is bound to be an over-simplification, and that in any particular case there may be overlapping.

V

A few further remarks must be made. In the first place, it is clear that the contemplation of the Christian differs *toto coelo* from the "philosophical contemplation of eternal truths" which the ancient world conceived to be the noblest pursuit of the leisured and cultured aristocrat. The Christian mystics are concerned not with truths but with the Truth, the Truth which is also Life and Love, the triune God. As Maritain writes:

> "Christian contemplation is distinguished from the contemplation of the philosophers by the three following characteristics: instead of having for its sole end the perfection of him who contemplates, it is for the love of him who is contemplated; it does not come to rest in the intellect as its terminus, but passes over into affection through love; it is not opposed to action so as to exclude it, but on the contrary it allows action to issue from its superabundance."[1]

And, in the words of Dom Bede Griffith:

> "The Platonic way is ascetic, whereas the Christian is sacramental; the Platonist seeks for God by means of liberation from the body, the Christian by means of union with the body of Christ; the Platonist's heaven is a solitary state of ecstasy with an incomprehensible being, the Christian heaven is a communion of saints in the Mystical Body of Christ."[2]

Secondly, the antithesis sometimes alleged between Christocentric and theocentric spirituality can be seen to have no validity outside the psychological and phenomenological sphere. From

---

(ii) That God is perfectly free, when he sees fit, to give to souls of good will who have never received visible incorporation into the Body of Christ graces that normally are mediated only in virtue of it. (For a Christian assessment of non-Christian mysticism and an attempt to disentangle the various factors involved, see Maritain on "The Natural Mystical Experience and the Void," in *Redeeming the Time*, p. 225 f.

(iii) That, while there is a real continuity (and, according to many mystical theologians, an identity of essence) between mystical union and the Beatific Vision, mystical union is knowledge of God by faith, not by sight. The mystic, like the ordinary Christian, is *in via*, not *in patria*.

[1] *Théonas*, p. 44. Cf. *Scholasticism and Politics*, ch. vii, "Action and Contemplation." Maritain most significantly asserts that no purely intellectual mystical experience can rise above the natural order; all supernatural experiences must be the work of charity. (*Redeeming the Time*, p. 251.) He insists that in this view he is expressing the authentic teaching of St. John of the Cross; cf. *Degrees of Knowledge*, ch. vii ff., especially p. 453.

[2] "The Platonic Tradition and the Liturgy," in *Eastern Churches Quarterly*, Jan. 1940, p. 7. The word "ascetic" in this passage is not, of course, used in the technical sense which it bears in Christian spirituality, as contrasted with "mystical."

the point of view of method, there is of course a distinction between prayer that is explicitly offered to the Incarnate Lord and prayer that is explicitly offered to the transcendent Godhead, between conscious colloquy with Christ and conscious colloquy with God. And we have seen that there is a certain difference of opinion among mystical writers as to whether, as the soul advances towards the higher regions of prayer, meditation upon the human nature of Christ is to be encouraged or not. But in the ontological sphere the distinction is of very minor importance, and this for two reasons. First, because, whatever psychological form it takes, the prayer of the Christian is a participation by him in the prayer of Christ and Christ is the eternal adorer of the Father, so that no prayer can merely terminate in Christ's manhood and fall short of the end to which Christ's own prayer is directed. Secondly, because Christ is the perfect image of the Father, and in him the Father is perfectly manifested. "Have I been so long time with you, and dost thou not know me, Philip? he that hath seen me hath seen the Father. . . . Believest thou not that I am in the Father, and the Father in me?"[1]

In the third place, and arising out of this last question, it may be inquired whether it is the Person of God the Father or the Triune God in whom Christian prayer ultimately finds its end. This is a more difficult question, and it inevitably reminds one of the difference between the approaches made by the Christian traditions of East and West to the doctrine of the Holy Trinity itself, the Eastern tradition tending to start from the Father as the source or *aitia* of the Godhead and to see the Son and the Spirit as eternally deriving their being from him, while the Western tends to start from the unity of the divine Essence and see the three Persons as eternal differentiations within it. But again, the antithesis seems to affect mainly the psychological sphere. It is true that during his earthly life the Incarnate Word habitually addressed his prayer to the Father and that the classical pattern of Christian Liturgy has been directed to the Father through the

---

[1] John xiv. 9, 10. Cf. this passage from St. Gregory the Great:
"Whereas every man that apprehends something of the eternal One by contemplation beholds the same through his coeternal likeness, it is rightly added: *An image was before mine eyes.* For the Image of the Father is the Son. . . . When therefore his eternity is perceived, as far as the capacity of our weakness allows, his image is set before the eyes of our mind; for when we truly strain towards the Father, in so far as we receive him we see him through his image, that is, through the Son. And through that likeness which was born of him without beginning we strive in a certain way to perceive him who has neither beginning nor ending." (*Morals*, V, 63, 64.)

Son in the unity of the Holy Spirit, as witness most of the ancient Eucharistic canons. And if Christian prayer is a participation in the prayer of Christ its concentration upon the Person of the Father might seem to follow as a matter of course. Nevertheless, we must remember that, according to Christian doctrine, the whole essence of the Godhead is possessed in its fullness by each of the divine Persons, and the three Persons mutually coinhere and interpenetrate one another. It is therefore impossible to adore the Father without at the same time adoring the triune God. And certainly no Christian would admit that in addressing the Father he was excluding the Son and the Spirit from his prayer. Like the previous one, this question loses most of its point in the light of orthodox dogma.

APPENDIX TO CHAPTER XII

NATURE, GRACE AND MYSTICISM

WITHIN the last few years the two distinguished Protestant theologians, Dr. Brunner and Dr. Niebuhr, have both vigorously criticized the traditional Catholic doctrine concerning the relation of nature and supernature in man.[1] This doctrine, which is based upon St. Irenaeus's exegesis of Genesis i. 26 (though, of course, no one maintains that it necessarily expresses the original meaning of the Hebrew text), distinguishes between the divine image ($\epsilon i \kappa \acute{\omega} \nu$, *imago*) in man, which it alleges to be indestructible, and the divine likeness ($\delta \mu o \acute{\iota} \omega \sigma \iota s$, *similitudo*), which, it asserts, was lost through the Fall, though it can be progressively restored by grace in those who are regenerate. Furthermore, it equates the image with man's natural endowments, and the likeness with a *donum superadditum*, which is supernatural both *quoad modum* and *quoad essentiam*, and which exceeds anything that man's nature can either demand or obtain for itself. The strictures of Brunner and Niebuhr are the more important since neither of them is extreme in his view of human corruption. Brunner explicitly repudiates the Lutheran teaching that the image of God

---

[1] Brunner, *Man in Revolt*, chap. v (c) and Appendix I; Niebuhr, *The Nature and Destiny of Man*, Vol. I, ch. x.

in man is so completely wrecked that nothing but a "relic" of it remains, and he even more decisively rejects Barth's view, which apparently denies the survival of even a relic. Niebuhr, again, is prepared to accept the distinction between image and likeness as representing respectively "man's character as a creature embedded in the natural order" and "the freedom of his spirit, his transcendence over natural process and finally his self-transcendence," and he considers that "Protestantism . . . was wrong in asserting that man's essential nature had been destroyed."[1] Where, however, both of them disagree with the Catholic doctrine is in their assertion that it introduces into man an unnatural dualism, which sees man's highest activities as merely an accidental and, as it were, superfluous addition to a nature which could perfectly well find its fulfilment in the things of this world; and that, moreover, it belittles the evil of sin by affirming that the Fall leaves man's nature essentially unimpaired. Both of them maintain that man's spiritual endowments are rooted in his very nature, and they consider the effect of sin to be neither the loss of the "likeness," as in Catholic doctrine, nor the destruction of the "image," as in Lutheran and Barthian doctrine, but rather the perversion and distortion of the image.

Now it may be readily admitted that Catholic theologians have sometimes written as if man's supernatural endowments had no organic relation to his nature and as if the Fall merely caused him to lose something superfluous which he could in any case have quite well done without. But at its best the Catholic tradition has held no such view. St. Thomas Aquinas, for instance, insists that fallen man is not only *spoliatus gratuitis* but also *vulneratus in naturalibus*.[2] The point is, of course, that to lose something which you once possessed is not the same as never to have possessed it— in this sense, it is far *worse* to have loved and lost than never to have loved at all—even while it is also true that man, when restored by grace, can be raised above his unfallen condition.

There is doubtless room for a far fuller investigation than has yet been made of the implications of the doctrine that man had by nature only a *potentia obedientialis*, a purely passive capacity, for receiving grace. It does not mean that, in the concrete, there has ever existed a purely and merely natural man. What it does mean is that, if we define man as a "rational animal," God might perfectly well have created such a being on the level of pure

---

[1] *The Nature and Destiny of Man,* Vol. I, pp. 286, 292.   [2] *S. Theol.,* II I, cix.

nature, and that a purely natural existence is all that the possession of rationality in itself demands. If we consider successively the various levels of material beings—lifeless matter, vegetable life, animal life, rational life—it is clear that the appearance on earth of a rational being does not of necessity involve for it any kind of union with God or participation in his life. Man might have exercised his reason simply upon the beings of the created world and in reflection upon his own nature; indeed many people actually try to do so to-day. He might have been led to the conviction of a Supreme Being as the ground of the universe and to construct for himself something like the Aristotelian arguments for the existence of God. He might well have longed to know more about this God than he had managed to find out for himself. But he could not have conceived the possibility—still less could he have achieved the actualization—of a real elevation into and participation in the life of God. He would have had to be content with a merely natural beatitude, in which any regret at the absence of anything higher would be compensated by the reflection that what he already had was all that a finite being had any right to expect. He would have had no more reason for resentment at not being raised to the supernatural order than we have for resentment at not being angels instead of men.

If, however, a finite rational being can neither expect nor effect his elevation into the life of God, there is nothing to prevent God, if he sees fit, from conferring it upon him. As a *rational* being man is constitutionally adapted for knowing whatever is knowable, even while as a *finite* being he can by his own powers know only what is finite. Hence if he is to know that which is supremely knowable—namely, God—he must have a power conferred upon him which by nature he cannot have. Man's *potentia obedientialis* for the supernatural is not a mere nothing; were that so, a cow would be as fit for elevation to life in God as man is. Grace is thus not merely something added to nature, but something that completes and perfects it. Nature is not only accompanied by grace but elevated by it. Supernature is neither contrary to nature nor indifferent to it; rather it is nature's fulfilment.

With such considerations in mind, Fr. Charlier has written as follows:

"What is first in the divine intention and willed therein defines a being better, in the eyes of the theologian, in its concrete existence (*donné*) than does its metaphysical constitution. I am

first of all a child of God, before I am a rational animal. . . .
There is, indeed, a radical distinction between the orders of nature
and grace. The supernatural order is, indeed, above the powers
and requirements of nature. Furthermore, when we interpret the
gifts of grace in philosophical language, we must say that they are
accidents, and indeed contingent accidents in relation to nature.
But the theologian must not put the stress primarily on this. Seen
in God, our sonship by adoption is the essential element in what
God has willed to make of us. Hence, grace does not appear to
the theologian as an inherently indifferent *superadditum* to our
nature. Is it not God's primary design to make us, his creatures,
into his children, and to create for this a nature capable of receiving
such a gift and altogether directed towards this sublime end?"[1]

When the Catholic doctrine is expounded in this way, it is clear
that it differs from the teaching of Brunner and Niebuhr far less
than might appear at first sight. It must not be assumed, however,
that the difference is negligible. Brunner and Niebuhr from their
standpoint, like their complete opposite, Berdyaev, from his,
reject quite definitely the idea that God ever confers upon his
creatures anything that the nature which he has initially given to
them does not, in some form or other, include; for them, all that
man can ever become is somehow contained in his primary constitution. In contrast, Catholicism leaves the way open for a whole
succession of gifts which depend upon the sheer bounty of God,
none of which can be demanded by man's nature, though all of
them are compatible with it. In consequence, for the Catholic the
spiritual life becomes an adventure filled with the most glorious
surprises, and the soul constantly finds itself exclaiming, like the
Queen of Sheba when confronted with the splendour of King
Solomon, that the half had not been told it.[2] And it may be
suggested that in this contrast is to be found the explanation of the
flat repudiation of mysticism, upon which I have already remarked[3] as being common to the neo-Protestant theologians, and

---

[1] *Essai sur le Problème théologique*, p. 157.
[2] It is most important that this point should be made clear. Any participation in
his nature that God grants us will be altogether satisfying and will leave no ground
for discontent or resentment. Nevertheless, it will always leave open the possibility of
the conferment of an even deeper participation, should God see fit to grant this.
For a finite being can participate in God only in a finite mode—*quidquid recipitur
recipitur ad modum recipientis*—and one of the properties of finitude is that there is no
"greatest finite quantity"; given any finite quantity, *however great*, we can always
conceive a greater. (For the bearing of this truth on the doctrine of creation, see my
He Who Is, p. 105.) Thus theologians have held that even in the Beatific Vision "one
star differeth from another in glory." (*S. Theol.*, I, xii, 6.)   [3] See p. 214 *supra*.

which is found in Barth and Nygren[1] no less than in Brunner and Niebuhr.

For, as soon as we forget or deny the teaching of the great Catholic mystical theologians that mystical union with God, in all its degrees and forms, is a pure gift conferred by God, from which the soul can indeed, with the help of grace, remove obstacles but which all its own personal efforts are powerless to achieve, we shall either conceive the mystical union as the soul's elevation of itself to the level of the transcendent deity, in which case we shall virtually deny the creatureliness of man, or we shall set forward a technique for the identification of the human personality with a purely immanent deity, in which case we shall virtually deny the divine transcendence. Against all such types of mystical theory the remonstrances of the neo-Protestants are justified. But they are emphatically not justified against the Catholic doctrine, as it is, for example, taught by the great Spanish Carmelites, with their two fundamental principles that God is transcendent before he is immanent and that mystical union is achieved not by the exercise of any human powers but by the act of God himself. I have pointed out elsewhere[2] how much confusion has been caused by both the supporters and the opponents of mysticism through the assumption that such "pantheizing" writers as Eckhart and Angelus Silesius are typical representatives of Catholic mystical theology, and this confusion has not been lessened by the discussion in Mr. Aldous Huxley's recent book, *Grey Eminence*, in which Catholic mysticism is condemned for a quite different reason from that of the neo-Protestants. According to Mr. Huxley, the real trouble with Catholicism is that it is Christian; it has, at least in its later manifestations, postulated as its object not the super-essential—and, as he suggests, impersonal—deity, but the human nature of Jesus of Nazareth, with results that he alleges to have been disastrous for both personal and political life. Now it must be admitted, and

---

[1] Barth, *Epistle to the Romans*, p. 109, etc.; Nygren, *Agape and Eros*, II, p. 483 f., etc.

[2] *He Who Is*, p. 148 f. It is true that in his more recently published second volume of *The Nature and Destiny of Man* Niebuhr describes Eckhart as a "heretical mystic"and characterizes St. John of the Cross as one "in whom the mystical version of Christianity is expressed in the most classic form" (pp. 94–8). He then condemns St. John for deprecating the love of one's neighbour and the performance of active works. But, as is seen if the passages from which he quotes are read in full (*Ascent*, I, v; *Spir. Cant.*, 2nd red., xxviii), what St. John is attacking is the taking of pleasure in creatures instead of in God and the making of activity a substitute for contemplation. He explicitly approves of activity that issues from contemplation (*Cant.*, xxviii, 3; Peers, II, p. 347). See the full discussion of these "stumbling-blocks" in Peers's *Spirit of Flame*, Part II, chs. iv, v.

indeed emphatically asserted, that, whatever the neo-Protestants may say, Catholic mysticism is through and through Christian, as I have tried to show. But it must be added, in reply to Mr. Huxley, that, whatever may be true in individual cases, Catholic mysticism, like Catholic liturgy and Catholic religion in general, does not make the incarnate Lord the ultimate terminus of its devotion. Catholicism is Christocentric in the precise sense that Christ is its *centre*—the Christian is *in* Christ, and his approach to the Father is *through* Christ—but it is not, if we may coin a word, Christoterminal.[1] "No one cometh unto the Father but by me," "I am the way, and the truth, and the life," "Your life is hid with Christ in God," "Through him we both [Jews and Greeks] have our access in one Spirit unto the Father"[2]—these are the great texts of Catholic devotion. *Per Christum ad Patrem in Spiritu* is the pattern of Catholic life. And it is precisely by this union with and incorporation into the incarnate Lord that the Christian is raised up into that participation in the life of God whose supreme earthly manifestation is mystical union. It is thus the Catholic mystical tradition and not the anti-mysticism of neo-Protestantism that is truly Christian and Pauline. For it was the Apostle of the Gentiles who was caught up into the third heaven and heard unspeakable words which it is not lawful for man to utter.

---

[1] See p. 221 *supra*. There is an excellent discussion of the position maintained in *Grey Eminence*, by Fr. Gerald Vann, O.P., in *Blackfriars*, April 1942.
[2] John xiv. 6; Col. iii. 3; Eph. ii. 18.

Q

CHAPTER XIII

THEOLOGY IN THE MYSTICAL BODY

I

THE Christian theologian, no less than the Christian mystic or the ordinary Christian, is a member of the Body of Christ, and his theological research is an activity that takes place within the Mystical Body. It will therefore, I think, be suitable to conclude this book with some discussion of the nature of Christian theology, considered in the light of the conceptions which have been elaborated in the earlier pages of the work. This task would seem to be the more important in view of the fact that, in spite of the very large volume of theological work that has been produced in the Anglican Communion in recent years, singularly little attention has been explicitly given by Anglican writers to the question of the precise character of theology itself.[1]

Now to determine the exact nature of a science we need to answer three questions about it. They are the following: What is it ultimately about? What is the material upon which it has to work? What are the instruments which it is to use? Or, more briefly still: Where do we want to go? Where must we start? What path must we take? I shall consider these in order.

II

"Geography is about Maps,
But Biography is about Chaps,"

sang Mr. E. C. Bentley. But what is theology about? There would, I think, be general agreement in theory with the definition given by St. Thomas Aquinas that the object (strictly speaking, the material object) of theology is, primarily, God; and, secondarily,

---

[1] None of the following well-known works, for example, pays any serious attention to it: *The Thirty-nine Articles*, by E. C. S. Gibson; *Outlines of Christian Dogma*, by Darwell Stone; *Introduction to the Thirty-nine Articles*, by E. J. Bicknell; *Christian Theology*, by A. C. Headlam; *Doctrines of the Creed*, by O. C. Quick. And the long article by Dr. N. P. Williams entitled "What is Theology?" in *The Study of Theology* consists merely of a very full summary of the various divisions of the science.

created things in their relation to him.[1] In practice, however, this has been largely forgotten. "The 'theology' which is taught in the now undenominationalized faculties of modern universities," wrote Dr. N. P. Williams, "is not so much the 'science of God' as the 'science of men's thoughts about God' ";[2] and this is, I would suggest, the main reason why it is generally felt to be irrelevant to everything that goes on at the present day. It appears to the modern layman to have as little relation to concrete fact as the Ptolemaic Theory of the Solar System or the Phlogistic Theory of combustion. It is not always realized how much of what is called theology to-day is at this second remove. The history of Christian dogma, liturgy and ecclesiastical politics; the discussion of the authorship and contents of the books of the Bible; the comparative study of religions—all these sciences, which make up so large a part of theological syllabuses to-day, are of course of the highest importance; but they are not in the strict sense *theology*, but rather sciences bearing upon it. And the other subject which finds a leading place in the syllabuses—namely, the philosophy of religion—is usually admitted only on the understanding that it ignores the traditional philosophy of the Christian Church. As Prebendary Hanson has said: "Many Anglican theologians quote Aquinas (who was an orthodox Christian), with something very like apologies, grudgingly and with very limited understanding, while Kant (who was ashamed to pray) they will quote you with profound reverence, affectionately, almost as one of ourselves."[3] There is, I believe, little hope that the non-theological world will cease to look upon theology as (in the bad sense) a purely academic study until theologians themselves again believe, as there are fortunately signs in various quarters that they are beginning to believe to-day, that theology is a living science intimately in touch with reality, through the pursuit of which men may be enabled to learn more and more, not merely of what people used to think about God in the days when religion was taken seriously, but of God himself and the dealings which he has with his creatures.

[1] *S. Theol.*, I, i, 7. Cf. A. C. Headlam: "Theology is the science which teaches us about God. The term . . . is used for the science of God in the widest sense, so as to mean not only our knowledge of his being and nature, but also of his relation to the world and to man, of man's relation to him, and of the relation of men to one another as dependent upon their relation to him." (*Christian Theology*, pp. 1, 2.) And F. J. Hall: "Sacred learning, or theology in its largest sense, is the science of divine things; and treats of God and of whatever in any manner pertains to him, in so far as it does pertain to him." (*Intro. to Dogmatic Theology*, p. 10.)
[2] "The Theology of the Catholic Revival," in *Northern Catholicism*, p. 131.
[3] "Mediaeval Philosophy and Abailard," in *Laudate*, June 1933, p. 73.

Only too often theologians seem to have held much the same view of their science as the young research-student in Mr. Charles Williams's novel, *The Place of the Lion*, held of hers. She was passionately interested in the doctrines of the *eidola* and the *angeli* without having any particular belief about either. But the only justification for theology is that it tells us about God, and the first thing that the theologian must be convinced of is that it can.

III

We come closer to the general theme of this book when we approach our second question: what is the material upon which theology has to work? Traditionally it has been recognized that the raw material of theology is the supernatural revelation given by God to men in Christ and his Church, a revelation to which the unaided powers of the mind, whether exercised in the mode of "reason" or in that of "religious experience," cannot attain. This accounts for the stress which St. Paul lays on "the Revelation of the Mystery." "By revelation," he writes to the Ephesians, "was made known unto me the mystery . . . which in other generations was not made known unto the sons of men." And he speaks in almost the same words to the Colossians, the Romans and the Corinthians.[1] St. Peter and St. John teach the same truth, though in different words.[2] Christian truth, on which theology is to be based, is therefore not something discovered by man, but something revealed to man by God. But two points need stressing in this connection.

The first point is that in this revelation the Old Testament is an essential, though a preparatory, element. *Novum testamentum in vetere latet; vetus testamentum in novo patet.* Any attempt to separate the New Testament from the Old breaks down at once if we ask the question: What is the view of the Old Testament that the New Testament itself holds, the view, for example, that is implied by the use made of the Old-Testament scriptures in such books as St. Matthew's and St. John's Gospels and the Epistle to the Hebrews?

The second point is that the revelation, which is given primarily in the hypostatic union of human nature with God the Word, in him in whom dwelleth all the fulness of the Godhead bodily, needs

[1] Eph. iii. 3, 5. Cf. Col. i. 25, 26; Rom. xvi. 25, 26; 1 Cor. ii. 7, 10.
[2] 1 Pet. i. 12; 1 John i. 2.

to be formulated in terms of human speech before it can become the material of theology. Partly, of course, this formulation is given in the words of the incarnate Lord himself, but the diversity of interpretations which Christians have been able to give to the teaching of Christ, to say nothing of the questions which many of them have asked as to whether in any case we have an accurate record of that teaching in the Gospels, makes it plain that it was not the purpose of the Lord Jesus to give through his own lips a doctrine whose formulation was from the beginning fully developed and unambiguous. The further formulation falls into two clearly distinguishable parts—the inspiration of Holy Scripture and the definition of dogma. Each of these is, in its own special way, the work of the Holy Spirit.

From an *a priori* standpoint there might seem to be no need for a divinely inspired Bible at all. Why, in addition to the personal revelation of himself which God has given to man in the Incarnation of the divine Word, should there be a written revelation consisting of the most astonishingly diverse collection of documents composed over a period of many centuries? Many answers have been, and can be, given to this objection; they need not be set out here. But it is not perhaps irrelevant to remark that, when all has been said for and against the congruity of a written revelation, the ultimate reason for accepting the Bible is that it has been given us by God. "God moves in a mysterious way his wonders to perform," and, as he has seen fit to give us the Bible, we shall do better to receive it in humility from his hands and try to understand it than to spend all our time discussing whether it was really necessary and, if so, whether it fulfils its purpose as well as we might have hoped. (This does not, I need hardly say, imply a denial of the legitimacy of critical study of the Bible.) An Anglican, at any rate, need hardly apologize, in the face of Articles vi and vii, for emphasizing the fundamental importance of Holy Scripture. But it is abundantly clear that the Bible does not provide us with a neatly arranged body of theological definitions; the futility of attempting to treat it in this way is shown by the amazing variety of conflicting doctrines which have been alleged to be the clear and indisputable teaching of the Bible. The Bible is rather like a mine from which precious ore can be quarried than like the articles made out of the extracted metal. The work of quarrying, extracting, refining and moulding is again the work of the Holy Spirit, but here he acts not through inspired individual writers but through the Church, which is the Spirit-bearing Body through whose decisions, explicit or tacit, divine truth becomes formulated as dogma.

We can, as a matter of history, see in the life of the Church the process of the gradual formulation of dogma, in which the human instruments[1] are Councils, Fathers, liturgical formularies, the living traditions of the great sees, and the general consciousness of the faithful, and in which the Spirit not only makes use of these instruments to express divine truth, but also guides the body of the Church to discriminate between councils which are authoritative and those which are spurious, between fathers and heretics, and between widely held views which express the genuine insight of the Spirit-bearing Body and those which are temporary aberrations from the Church's own mind.

We must, however, be careful not to over-simplify a very intricate question by assuming that Scripture must be complete before dogma can begin to be formulated, or that the formulation of dogma must be complete before the theologian can begin to theologize. Such a suggestion would be ridiculous; in both the writing of Scripture and the formulation of dogma theologians have played their part, as witness such conspicuous examples as St. Paul, St. John, St. Athanasius and the Cappadocian Fathers. And, indeed, while the canon of Scripture is presumably closed, the formulation of dogma still goes on. It is none the less true that the Church has always appealed to Scripture in support of her teaching, and that orthodox theologians have always taken as their starting-points the already existing defined and accepted dogma of the Christian Church. I am not, therefore, forgetting the extremely elaborate interrelations between Scripture, dogma and theology if I define the material upon which the theologian has to work as being primarily the divine revelation (*revelatum, donné révélé*), which comes to him as rooted in Scripture and as to a greater or less degree formulated as dogma.

In asserting that the divine revelation is the material of theology we must not overlook the existence of what has been commonly called *natural theology*. There *is* a certain knowledge of God attainable without revelation, as St. Paul recognized in the Epistle to the Romans. It is precisely because "the invisible things

---

[1] The word "instrument" must not be taken as implying the suppression of the free-will of the human beings concerned. God uses all his instruments according to their particular natures. And, paradoxical as it may sound, the man who is most under the control of God is the man whose freedom is most fully operative.

of him since the creation of the world are clearly seen, being perceived through the things that are made" that the Gentiles who,
"knowing God, glorified him not as God" are "without excuse."[1]
This knowledge of God which is accessible to the human reason is,
however, partial and insufficient; that is, among other reasons,
why God has revealed himself in Christ. Furthermore, man's
natural powers are themselves weakened through sin, and so his
natural knowledge of God is, even in its own order, clouded and
distorted; one need not be a Calvinist to recognize that man is
not only *spoliatus gratuitis* but also *vulneratus in naturalibus*. It is this
that has caused so much attention to be given in recent years to
the problem of a Christian philosophy. If Philosophy (of which
natural theology is a part) is the work of reason and not of revelation, how can it make any difference to a man's philosophy
whether he is a Christian or not? How shall we account for the
difference between the natural theology of an Aristotle and an
Aquinas? This question has been discussed more or less independently by both M. Maritain and M. Gilson, and, in spite of
differences on minor points, the answers that they give are substantially the same.[2] It is that grace not only supplies perfections
that lie above the level of nature, but also restores nature to its
own integrity. *Gratia* is *sanans* as well as *elevans*. It follows, therefore, that, while in principle there is a certain limited knowledge
of God which is accessible to the human reason as such, in practice
it is only in the light of revelation and under the assistance of grace
that the human reason can function adequately and can obtain,
even within its own proper sphere, a knowledge of God which is
free from error. Philosophy and theology[3] are thus in the abstract
autonomous, being concerned respectively with the sphere of
reason and nature and with the sphere of revelation and grace, but
in the concrete a true philosophy can only be developed in the
light of the Christian revelation. This is the truth which St. Augustine expressed in his famous sentence, *Verus philosophus est amator
Dei*, and which lay behind the refusal of St. Bonaventure and the
Franciscans generally to draw a clear-cut line between philosophy
and theology, but it is no less involved in the position of their

---

[1] Rom. i. 20, 21.

[2] J. Maritain, *De la Philosophie chrétienne*; E. Gilson, *Christianisme et Philosophie*, also
The Spirit of Medieval Philosophy, chs. i, ii. Cf. also A. D. Sertillanges on "La Croyance
et l'Autonomie de la Philosophie," in *Le Christianisme et les Philosophies*, I, p. 21 f.

[3] "Theology" here, as generally through this chapter, means revealed theology;
natural theology is, as we have seen, a part of philosophy.

Aristotelian and Dominican opponents. It provides the explanation of the extraordinary change that came over Aristotelianism in the hands of St. Thomas, with his doctrine of a personal, conscious God and of the immortality of the individual human soul.

The distinction between natural and revealed theology was universal in traditional Anglicanism; Bishop Butler's famous *Analogy* is only one instance of it. In the Liberal period, however, a tendency grew up to consider the difference between the two as being merely one of degree, or at least to assume that they ought not to be made into two distinct sciences. Sometimes, of course, this was due to a desire to whittle away the uniqueness of the Christian revelation; it went with the view that Jesus of Nazareth, so far from being the Son of God in any metaphysical sense, was only the supreme product of human evolution. But it was present even where this heresy of the evolutionary Christ was absent, and the reason seems to lie in a curious assumption that, if two things always occur together, however different their proportions may be in different cases, they must be really identical, or that, at any rate, it is illicit to discuss them separately. Such a denial of the principle of abstraction really makes science impossible. As any physical scientist knows, it is quite futile to attempt to solve any complicated problem without having first dissected out from it certain simpler problems which do not exactly correspond to any real occurrence. In electrodynamics it is customary to discuss the properties of electric circuits with resistance but no self-induction, and of those with self-induction but no resistance, in spite of the fact that every circuit has both; in hydrodynamics the study of non-viscous liquids invariably precedes the study of viscous liquids, although every liquid found in nature has some viscosity, however small it may be in particular cases. The Report of the Archbishops' Doctrinal Commission was perfectly correct in asserting that "there is a factor in our knowledge of God due to reflection on the general nature of experience," and that "there is also a factor due to the apprehension of individual historical facts through which God reveals himself to man in a special manner or degree," but it quite missed the point when it added that "the body of Christian doctrine, however, cannot be split up into two portions assignable respectively to those two factors, as though such doctrines as those of God's unity and of his moral government of the world were assignable exclusively to the first, and the doctrines of the Trinity, Incarnation, and gift of supernatural grace to the second," and this on the ground that "the two factors which we have recognized, while distinguishable, are always interdependent."[1] It is precisely because the two factors are distinguishable that they have to be considered separately, though it is of course necessary to recognize their interrelations. After all, it is a plain fact that God's unity and moral government of the world are believed in by many non-Christians, while the doctrines of the Trinity, the Incarnation and supernatural grace (in the Christian sense of "the grace of our Lord Jesus Christ") are not. And if we refuse to make a separate study of these latter doctrines, we shall be in grave danger of confusing the "general revelation" made to all men in virtue of the fact that they are created in the image of the divine Logos who is the "Light which lighteth every man that cometh into the world,"[2] with the "special revelation" (that is, revelation in the strict and proper sense which I am giving to the word in this chapter) given "at sundry times and in divers manners"[3] to the Chosen People and culminating in the personal manifestation of the Word-made-flesh. And so doing we shall be led into a conscious or unconscious denial of the uniqueness of the Incarnation.[4]

Christian theology, then, has a twofold material on which to work—namely, the deliverances of natural knowledge, and the

---

[1] *Doctrine in the Church of England*, p. 44.   [2] John i. 9.   [3] Heb. i. 1.

[4] Dr. Leonard Hodgson has denied the legitimacy of the Thomist distinction between natural and revealed theology, on the ground, among others, that the acceptance of the Christian revelation makes a difference to one's outlook upon everything, so that there can be no sphere in which the Christian philosophizes in the same way as the non-Christian to the exclusion of all conclusions derived from the Faith. (*The Doctrine of the Trinity*, lect. i.) The premise is certainly true; it provides the justification for the work of St. Bonaventure, on which even so convinced a Thomist as M. Gilson has bestowed the highest praise. It is indeed a necessary and urgent task to interpret the whole of experience in the light of Christian truth. But it is of not less importance, in a world in which Christians and non-Christians live together, to determine whether there is a region in which, whatever may be true in any concrete case, Christians and non-Christians can at least in principle find some common ground of discourse. Fr. John-Baptist Reeves has brought out this point excellently in discussing the special vocations of the Dominican and Franciscan Orders. "The Friars Preachers," he writes, "were founded to win to Christ the minds of men whose wills were good; the Friars Minor to win to Christ the hearts of men whose morals were relaxed but whose minds were as well informed on Catholic doctrine as was that of St. Francis himself. . . . St. Thomas sang and prayed to the piping of St. Francis, but with emphasis on the part played by the mind in both song and prayer; St. Bonaventure philosophized as sedately as any Dominican, but was all the time emphatically a philosopher with a heart." (*The Dominicans*, p. 100.) As Gilson writes: "The philosophy of St. Thomas and the philosophy of St. Bonaventure are complementary, as the two most comprehensive interpretations of the universe as seen by Christians, and it is because they are complementary that they never either conflict or coincide." (*The Philosophy of St. Bonaventure*, p. 495; cf. ch. xv *in toto*.)

revelation given by God in Christ, which latter comes to the theologian through the medium of Scripture, to a very great extent formulated as dogma. The relation between these two, which is both intricate and delicate, is simply one of the many instances of the relation between nature and grace. Logically, natural knowledge is prior to revelation, for grace presupposes nature as that in which grace works: "First . . . that which is natural, and afterwards that which is spiritual."[1] But in the concrete, revelation has priority over natural knowledge, for in a fallen world grace has not only to supply what lies outside the intrinsic powers of nature, but has also to restore the powers of nature to their own integrity.

IV

We can now pass on to our third question, and this will bring us to the very heart of the theme with which this book has been concerned. What is the instrument by which theology is to work on its material?

Liberal theology would answer that it is simply the human reason. One of the most orthodox of Anglican Liberal theologians could write as follows towards the end of his life:

> "I have, ever since I was an undergraduate, been certain that I must be in the true sense a free thinker, and that either not to think freely about a disturbing subject, or to accept ecclesiastical authority in place of the best judgment of my own reason, would be for me an impossible treason against the light. I must go remorselessly where the argument leads me."[2]

It has been the boast of liberal theology that it is a purely rational study which can hold its own with any secular science. For it, the truth about religion is to be obtained by a quite dispassionate and unbiased investigation of the phenomena of the world in which man finds himself, of the psychological data of the human consciousness and unconsciousness, of the religious practices of man (preferably of backward or prehistoric races), and of the religious documents which have come down from antiquity. Theology, in the only sense in which the word can be taken seriously, is simply one, though presumably the most important one, of the exercises of the human reason.

[1] I Cor. xv. 46.   [2] *Belief in God*, Preface.

It is interesting to note that on this question of the theological instrument, if upon no others, Liberal theology seems to be in agreement with post-medieval scholasticism.[1] Fr. Charlier, O.P., in his brilliant *Essai sur le Problème théologique*,[2] has argued this in much detail. Taking as examples Cajetan, Bañez and John of St. Thomas he shows how in the later scholastic period the task of theology came to be conceived as simply the elucidation, by rational deduction, of the consequences of the fundamental revealed principles of the Christian religion. These principles have to be accepted simply by the divine virtue of supernatural faith, though reason may prepare the ground by providing preambles to faith and motives of credibility (this is the work of apologetics rather than of theology proper). The scholastic and the Liberal differ vastly in their views as to the material upon which theology should work, but they seem to be in fairly close agreement as to the instrument which should be used upon it.

In contrast with the "scholastics" and claiming in his support his master, St. Thomas, Fr. Charlier envisages theology differently. "Demonstration," he says, "in the rigid sense of the word, cannot be applied in theology."[3] The theologian is concerned not to demonstrate conclusions from premises, but to make explicit the content of the living tradition of the Church. His success or failure will not depend merely upon the acuteness of his intellectual powers, though this will of course play its part, and a very impor-

---

[1] Thus Fr. R. Garrigou-Lagrange, O.P., writes: "Theology is a wisdom of the supernatural order because it necessarily assumes infused faith as its root, since its aim is: (1) to explain or analyse conceptually the revealed truths, or truths of faith, in order fully to understand them, in contrast to the deformations of heresy; and (2) to *deduce* from them (*d'en déduire*) other truths which are virtually contained in them and which are called theological conclusions in the strict sense, being the fruit of *reasoning* which is not only explanatory but *objectively illative*." Again: "The work of *conceptual analysis* (which is the most important part of theological treatises on the Trinity, the Incarnation, the Sacraments, Grace, etc.) and that of the *deduction* of theological conclusions are *a human work performed upon the data of revelation* or *donné révélé*." (*Le Sens du mystère et le Clair-obscur intellectuel*, p. 51 f., my translation and italics.) The author rightly adds that theology occupies an intermediate place between infused faith and metaphysics, and, being rooted in the former, is superior to the latter. His book was published in 1934.
    Fr. A. Gardeil, O.P., had previously written even more strongly: "The science of the 'theologically revealable' or scholastic theology is as indispensable as the theological science of the 'formally revealed' or positive theology.... The deductive process imposes itself upon this kind of science.... Scientific theology receives, in the immediate theological datum which is for us only another name for the *donné révélé*, its whole equipment of truth (*sa fourniture totale de vérité*). Its role is to manifest to our direct intuition that which exists implicitly or virtually in a way that escapes us at first sight. *It is concerned with the syllogism.*" (*Le Donné révélé et la Théologie*, p. 224 f., my translation and italics.) This was written in 1909.
[2] Published in 1938.   [3] *Essai sur le Problème théologique*, p. 137.

tant part. It will depend primarily upon his adherence to, and his life in, the Mystical Body of Christ. He will be, as it were, an organ through which the divine Head himself may speak. "Theology," writes Charlier, "by reason of its very nature and of its end, has a method of working and a spirit of its own, which are neither those of the philosopher nor those of the historian,"[1] and he insists that, while "it uses the historic and the scholastic method as its auxiliaries,"[2] its chief needs are a sense of God and of mystery, and a supernatural sense of the Church, with which last there goes the sense of the Church's teaching authority, its *magisterium*. "To live supernaturally in the Church and with all the Church is a necessity for the theologian who wishes to be an instrument of the progress of sacred science and a true servant of divine truth."[3] M. Maritain has written to much the same effect. "Theology," he says, "is not a simple application of philosophy to revealed data— as many have thought since the time of Descartes. Were this so it would involve submitting the content of faith to human judgment and discernment. Theology is a *habitus* of wisdom rooted in faith; hence it is radically and virtually supernatural, and hence it uses philosophical knowledge as its instrument and judges it in its own light."[4] It is, of course, true that Charlier, as a modern Roman Catholic, interprets the *magisterium* of the Church in a way which few Anglicans would be ready to accept, but we shall, I hope, see that his treatment is strengthened rather than weakened when it is modified on this point.

I suggest, then, that the instrument which the theologian should use in performing his task is not just his rational faculty, as the post-Thomist scholastics and the Liberals have assumed, but his whole self in its sacramental union with Christ in his Mystical Body; in this, his rational powers, strengthened and illuminated by grace, will, of course, play an organic and prominent part. He is not concerned simply to make deductions from premises or to pass judgment upon the dogmas of the Faith, but to allow himself to be used by the divine Head of the Mystical Body as an organ through which, in accordance with the will of God for him and for his time, some tiny fraction of the truth which is in Christ may

---

[1] *Essai sur le Problème théologique*, p. 153.   [2] *Ibid.*, p. 164.   [3] *Ibid.*, p. 158.
[4] *Science and Wisdom*, p. 113; cf. *The Degrees of Knowledge*, p. 312: "Theology . . . is not the simple application of natural reasoning and philosophy to the substance of revelation, but the elucidation of the substance of revelation by a faith vitally united with reason, progressing in step with reason, armed with philosophy." (My translation.)

be expressed more clearly. Putting this in terms not of the theologian but of his science, we may say that the task of theology is to display in its fulness and bring to its blossoming the revelation which God has committed to his Church. It will be immediately clear how difficult and dangerous, and yet at the same time how noble, is the work to which the theologian is called. He will indeed need to use to the utmost whatever intellectual gifts God has endowed him with, but he will need still more the virtues of humility, faith and adherence to Christ. Because he is to express not just his own thoughts but those that the divine Head is thinking in his Mystical Body, of which the theologian is a member, the primary need of the theologian is that he should be living *in the Revelation itself*; that is to say, that he should be living *in Christ*, who is the eternal Truth and the entire self-utterance of the Father; that he should be living *in the Church*, which is Christ's Body, the organism in which Christ, who is himself the Revelation, is manifested now upon earth. A man cannot, of course, be a theologian without being equipped by God with special gifts for his special vocation, but he can exercise those gifts rightly only through adherence to Christ and Christ's Body. He must, in a word, be a *liturgical man*.[1] For since the divine revelation is not in the first place a set of propositions but is Christ himself, and since Christ abides and acts on earth in his Mystical Body, the theologian is not a spectator examining the Revelation from outside; he is actually *in the Revelation*. And he is its very partial and fallible organ. "*La théologie*," writes Charlier, "*est la foi elle-même en travail*."[2]

From what I have just written it will follow that the first fact about the theologian is his baptism, by which he was made a member of Christ. It will also follow that his theological adequacy will depend intimately upon the maintenance and nourishment of his sacramental and moral union with Christ. His theology is, for example, almost certain to suffer disastrously if he falls into mortal sin, and even venial sins will impair it. The really great theologian must be a saint as well and, on the other hand, there are few worse states for a soul to be in than that of the theologian who has fallen from grace and humility, for not only has he stumbled himself, but he may be the cause through which multi-

[1] Cf. the admirable working out of this theme in Dom Theodore Wesseling's book, *Liturgy and Life*.
[2] *Essai sur le Problème théologique*, p. 75. Cf. p. 77: "Theology must be a theology of the *donné révélé* grasped at the heart of the mystery of the Church, even before being a theology of the *magisterium*."

tudes of others may be made to stumble. It were better for him that a millstone were hanged about his neck and that he were drowned in the depth of the sea.

We shall also expect that the theology of those bodies in which the sacramental life is lived in its fulness will express the divine revelation with a completeness and a balance which will be lacking in those whose sacramental life is partly or wholly defective. It is not, for example, surprising that the Lutheran and Calvinist bodies have developed a very one-sided doctrine of sin and sanctification. On the other hand, we are very far from being committed to every detail of medieval or post-Tridentine Roman Catholicism. I have already stressed the fact that it is the duty of the theologian to be, as it were, a mouth through which the consciousness of the Mystical Body can find expression, and this simply because the essence of Christianity is incorporation into the Body of Christ. In the last three centuries, however, Romanism has almost universally defined Christianity as consisting in sub-mission to the Pope—that is, as being a jurisdictional rather than a sacramental fact. (The confusion caused in this way is well exemplified by the uncertainties raised by *Ab acatholicis nati* as to validity of marriages.) And this attitude is not less prominent in the acts and utterances of the great figures of the medieval Papacy: "The Lord Jesus Christ has set up one ruler over all things as his universal Vicar, and as all things in heaven, earth and hell bow the knee to Christ, so should all obey Christ's Vicar, that there be one flock and one shepherd"; "We declare, state, define and pronounce that for every human creature to be subject to the Roman Pope is altogether necessary for salvation."[1] It is therefore not surprising that, in the book already cited, Fr. Charlier lays what to an Anglican must seem exaggerated stress upon the *magisterium*, the teaching authority, of the Holy See. It is on the theologian's obedience to this particular embodiment of the *magis-terium*, rather than upon the maintenance of his vital and sacra-mental union with the Mystical Body, that the stress tends to fall

---

[1] Innocent III, Boniface VIII ; quoted by Deanesly, *History of the Medieval Church*, pp. 144, 180. I am indebted to my friend, Mr. T. M. Parker, for the example of the domination of medieval theology by canon law and of the medieval habit of inter-preting the *sacerdotium* almost entirely in terms of "governing" souls, the *sacerdotium* being thereby assimilated to the *regnum*, the civil power, and then put in contrast with it. He suggests as causes of this the feudalization of the Church through the necessity of endowment in land, the general Latin concentration on "catholicity" rather than "orthodoxy," and the struggle with the State which caused the Western Church to adopt to some extent the role of a "counter-state."

as Fr. Charlier develops his theme. As a consequence there is an unresolved tension in his final conclusions which is essentially the same as that between the outward and inward aspects of the Church in Fr. Congar's *Divided Christendom*. One finds oneself asking such questions as the following: Is it baptism or submission to the Pope that makes one a Catholic? Is a baptized Christian who is not in communion with the Pope a bad Catholic or not a Catholic at all? Is the baptized baby of non-Roman-Catholic parents a Catholic or not? These problems, it should be observed, are quite independent of the questions as to whether a Christian *ought* normally to be in communion with the Pope and, if so whether there are any conditions that can justify this communion being severed in a particular case.[1]

This is, however, a digression. The point that I am anxious to maintain is that the primary task of the theologian is to take his tiny share, from his place in the Mystical Body, in the great task of rendering explicit the revelation committed to the Body by its Head with whom it is united. For, while the process of revelation attained its completion in the manifestation in human flesh of him who is, simply and finally, Prophet, Priest and King, so that nothing remains to be revealed which was not given in him, the displaying of all that is involved in that revelation is one of the great works of the Holy Spirit in the Mystical Body. "Every scribe who hath been made a disciple to the Kingdom of Heaven is like unto a man that is a householder, which bringeth forth out of his treasure things new and old."[2] "I have yet many things to say unto you, but ye cannot bear them now. Howbeit when he, the Spirit of truth, is come, he shall guide you into all the truth."[3] Revelation can advance no more, but we can advance within it.[4]

This does not imply that the Church and her theology never

[1] See p. 152 *supra*, and cf. the learned discussion of "Membership in the Church," by Victor White, O.P., in *Blackfriars*, Sept. 1941.
[2] Matt. xiii. 52.　　　　　　　　[3] John xvi. 12, 13.
[4] Cf. the agreed statement in the Report of the Anglican and Rumanian Conference at Bucarest, June 1935:
"The Revelation of God is transmitted through the Holy Scriptures and the Holy Tradition. Everything necessary for salvation can be founded upon Holy Scripture, as completed, explained, interpreted and understood in the Holy Tradition, by the guidance of the Holy Spirit residing in the Church. We agree that by Holy Tradition we mean the truths which have come down from our Lord and the Apostles and have been defined by the Holy Councils or are taught by the Fathers, which are confessed unanimously and continuously in the Undivided Church and are taught by the Church under the guidance of the Holy Spirit.
"We agree that nothing contained in Tradition is contrary to the Scriptures. Though these two may be logically defined and distinguished, yet they cannot be separated from each other nor from the Church."

require reformation. Much gratitude is due to such recent Protestant writers, as Mr. D. T. Jenkins,[1] for their insistence upon the Church's constant need for "Reformation according to the Word of God." There is nothing contrary to Catholic doctrine in this idea. But where I suggest that the Protestants are wrong is in their conception of the Word of God as an extraneous principle of judgment perpetually standing "over against" the Church rather than as a divine gift committed to the Church herself to be the instrument by which the indwelling Spirit, who is both the inspirer and the interpreter of the written Word, leads the Church to reform herself by bringing herself into conformity with her true essence. There is sound theological basis for the classical Anglican appeal not merely to Scripture but to Scripture and the fathers; that is, in effect, to Scripture as the fathers interpret it. For this means that there is a permanent duty incumbent upon the Church's leaders and thinkers to rectify and verify all developments in practice and doctrine by the standard of the apostolic tradition.[2] Individual reformers may indeed accomplish much that is of value and they may be the instruments of God. But they are no more than the generality of the faithful immune from error, and there are certain forms of error to which they are especially prone. There is therefore always need that their pronouncements and proposals shall be checked by the tradition which the Church received from her Lord as her own treasure; otherwise the last state of a reformed Church may well be worse than the first.

In addition to this primary work of rendering explicit the Christian revelation, theology has a secondary, but nevertheless a most important task. This is to illuminate and fertilize the workings of the natural reason, and so to bring the sciences of the natural reason to their own fructification. The precise bearing of theology upon each science will vary from case to case, as will also the contribution that the science concerned will have to offer to theology;[3]

---

[1] See *The Nature of Catholicity*, p. 162 f.

[2] Witness is borne to this by the weight which was given by the Church, during the period of the formation of the canon of Scripture, to the assertion of apostolic authorship on behalf of any book claiming canonical status. Until the canon was more or less settled, the norm of the Church's belief and teaching was the apostolic tradition which the Church had inherited; apostolic authorship would thus be a strong extrinsic guarantee that the book in question was in accordance with the Church's faith and could be accepted as interpreting and not distorting the tradition.

[3] An excellent example of legitimate influence of a secular science upon theology is provided by the advance in knowledge of the mechanism of human procreation since the Middle Ages, which sheds light upon many previously obscure points in sexual ethics, and incidentally greatly strengthens the ethical case against contraception. See H. Doms, *The Meaning of Marriage*, especially ch. xiv.

it will increase in weight in proportion as the subject-matter of the several sciences approximates to that of theology itself. As always, grace perfects nature but does not destroy it. Theology will thus have much more to say about the sciences that deal with human beings, who are made in the image of God and are his vice-gerents on earth—such sciences, that is, as politics, psychology and the theory of education—than about those, such as physics or mathematics, which deal either with real beings in so far as they are amenable to measurement (*entia realia sub ratione quantitatis*) or with beings that are simply constructs of the reason (*entia rationis cum*, or even *sine, fundamento in re*). Its influence will be exercised both by its general stabilization and illumination of the natural reason and by its power to indicate the true ends and the mutual relations of the various sciences and their relations to theology itself.[1] And in doing this it will not suppress but will rather strengthen the legitimate autonomy which every science has within its own sphere. By so doing, theology may once again be allowed to bear its proud title of *Regina scientiarum*, and cease to be looked upon as either merely one among many human studies or a harmless diversion for religious cranks. For, while it has its own special task to perform, theology has also a reference to every speculative or practical pursuit of man.

V

Something needs to be said here about the relation of the theologian to the Episcopate, for, however different her interpretation of it may be from that of Roman curialism, the Anglican Church does presumably believe that the Church has an authority to teach, a *magisterium*, and it appears that, in common with the Church of the early centuries, she locates it primarily in the bishops, who corporately form the earthly manifestation of the Apostolic body, and each of whom in his own diocese is severally *vicarius Christi*.[2] Clearly the proper fulfilment of the office of either bishop or theologian will depend upon the degree to which the individual, by his moral and sacramental union with the Mystical

---

[1] There is great need for someone to do for the present day what Newman tried to do for his day in his lectures *On the Scope and Nature of University Education*. The mere titles of the first three lectures are illuminating: Theology a Branch of Knowledge; The Bearing of Theology on Other Branches of Knowledge; The Bearing of Other Branches of Knowledge on Theology. But Newman wrote in 1852, and much water has flowed down both the Liffey and the Cam since then. [2] See p. 120 f. *supra*.

Body, is actually, and not merely virtually, the organ and instrument of the Body and its Head. Just as there have been theologians who have misconceived their task as being the use of their own superior intellects to correct the Faith of the Church, so there have been bishops who have misconceived *their* task as lording it over the flock of Christ, and whose exercise of the *magisterium*, like that of their other functions, has suffered in consequence. But, as Fr. Charlier reminds us, "the *magisterium* is not to be conceived as a mere external norm of faith, which imposes upon the faithful the beliefs that they are to hold; it is an organic function of the Church and emanates from it as one of its vital faculties."[1] It is obvious that as regards the necessity of a devout and humble relation to the Body of Christ there can be no difference between the bishop and the theologian. There can be only one Gospel for the *pastor fidelium* and the *doctor theologiae*, but, whereas the theologian's work is the investigation of the content of divine revelation, the function of the bishop as teacher (the only aspect of his work with which we are concerned here) is the proclamation of the Faith to the Church and the world and its defence against strange and erroneous teachings. It is not the theologian's place to usurp the *magisterium* of the Episcopate, and the bishop is not fulfilling his duty if he offers, as has sometimes been the case in the Church's history, an undue deference to theologians who have viewed their task as being the correction and improvement of the Faith once delivered to the saints. Both bishop and theologian must act as organs of the Body of Christ, and the very close links that should exist between them cannot annul their difference of status. For the bishop's relation to the Christian revelation arises out of his special position as pastor of the flock of Christ, a position to which the theologian *qua* theologian has no claim. But this will by no means exonerate the theologian from responsibility for the evil effects that intellectual pride or rashness on his part may have upon the souls of Christian people.

VI

Such a view of the nature of theological science as I have outlined here will, no doubt, appear to many as obscurantist and reactionary. I am afraid that cannot be helped. What I would claim for it is that it is capable of defending theology from the

[1] *Essai sur le Problème théologique*, p. 65.

frequent charge of being both irrelevant and, in the bad sense of
the term, academic, that it is what is implied in the traditional
Anglican appeal to Scripture ánd the Fathers, and that it grounds
theology in the very life of the Christian and the Church. And,
since it may be broadly described as an "anti-Liberal" position,
it may be well in conclusion to see how it stands in relation to that
theological Liberalism which has for long been the prevailing
influence in Anglican theology and which is by no means yet
extinct.

Liberalism may be defined as the attempt to insert Christianity
into an intellectual framework derived from some contemporary
understanding of reality which is secular (that is, non-religious) in
origin.[1] The obvious advantage which it offers is that of presenting
the Christian religion in a dress which will be familiar and attractive to some, at least, of one's contemporaries; its hope is that it
will be able to beat the unbelievers on their own ground—it is
always satisfactory to win an away match. Its great drawback is
that the ground may be unsuitable for the contest; more explicitly,
it suffers from three grave defects. There is, first of all, the danger
that it will deform Christian truth in trying to fit it into the setting
of contemporary categories. In the second place, it must ignore,
or at least sadly understress, the claim which is part of the very
essence of Christianity, to be a God-given revelation outstripping
all schemes of purely secular origin. And, thirdly, it will have
constantly to change its ground, for there will be as many "Liberal
theologies" as there are schemes of contemporary thought.[2]

In actual fact, theological Liberalism has broken down mainly
on account of the fact last mentioned. The chief bases which it
assumed were a philosophical tradition deriving ultimately from
Kant, and an evolutionary theory of the development of religion
from less perfect to more perfect forms (animism—polytheism—
monolatry—monotheism), neither of which is by any means
undisputed to-day. But a still more important factor has been the
impasse reached in the critical study of the Bible. The new school

---

[1] It will doubtless be objected that this is precisely what St. Thomas Aquinas did
in synthetizing Christianity and Aristotelianism. But it must be replied: (1) that, so
far from Christian theology being brought into line with Aristotelianism, it was
Aristotelianism that was very drastically brought into line with Christian theology;
(2) that one of the tasks to which St. Thomas deliberately addressed himself was that
of clearly delimiting the respective spheres and methods of theology and philosophy,
a task in the performance of which modern Liberal theology has been remarkably
deficient.

[2] I feel bound to draw attention to Dr. V. A. Demant's remarkably penetrating discussion of the whole liberal movement of thought in his book, *The Religious Prospect*.

of Biblical scholars, represented by such scholars as the late Sir Edwyn Hoskyns and Professor Dodd, has shown that the critical method itself, when applied to the Bible, in spite of its many important results, fails to answer the questions with which the Bible itself is mainly interested and that in consequence there must be a revival of that type of Biblical study that is primarily exegetical and, in the fullest sense, theological.

It is therefore hardly surprising that a tendency has appeared in some quarters to repudiate any rational approach to theology, and to confine theology to the proclamation of the bare Word of God, as that in the presence of which all human faculties must be paralysed and no flesh may glory. The extreme example of this is, of course, Karl Barth, but he has many more or less wholehearted disciples. Such a tendency is by no means unique in the history of Christian thought. M. Gilson has called attention to its existence in the thirteenth century; he gives it the name "theologism," and he shows how it existed side by side with rationalism until (and even after) the Thomist synthesis had established an organic relation between revelation and reason. The position of the theologists, he tells us, "is very simple; since God has spoken to us, it is no longer necessary for us to think";[1] and he remarks that, "despite their radical opposition, the Theologism and the Rationalism of the thirteenth century had at least one common feature, their one-sidedness."[2]

The main stream of Christian theology has been neither rationalistic nor irrationalist. It is ready to give full weight to the truth for which Liberalism has contended—namely, that the human reason is a God-given faculty having full rights in its own proper sphere and under proper control, but it is free from the subjectivism and ephemerality to which Liberalism is exposed. It refuses to agree with Liberalism that the terrain of theology must be cleared of the accumulated work of nearly two millennia in order that, on the bare earth of natural reason, there may be erected an entirely new theological edifice to twentieth-century specifications. On the contrary, it views the task of the theologian as the addition of at most perhaps a new wing, at least a few more bricks, to the building which has been slowly constructed, not without mistaken enthusiasms and unsuccessful experiments, by the labours of the great doctors and theologians of the past. For

---

[1] *Reason and Revelation in the Middle Ages*, p. 6.
[2] *Ibid.*, p. 69. Cf. *The Unity of Philosophical Experience*, ch. ii.

its material and its inspiration it turns not merely to the deliverances of the human mind, weakened and wounded by the Fall of man, but to the revelation which God has committed to his Church and which, as the centuries have rolled by, has become more and more explicit under the guidance of the indwelling Spirit. This does not mean that the human reason has no part to play in theology; quite the contrary. As nature is healed and strengthened by grace, so is the human reason by divine revelation. Indeed, only in the Body of Christ can the natural infirmities of the human mind be progressively overcome and the theological intellect rescued from its own partiality and error. Only as he lives in union with Christ in the Mystical Body can the theologian without peril of presumption and damnation speak about God and the things of God. For if the highest activity of which the human mind is capable is the contemplation of the Ever-blessed Trinity, its true home is the Spirit-bearing Body of Christ. It is, as St. Augustine so well knew, in his mind above all else that man bears the beauty of the image of God, and

> ". . . in the Land of Beauty
> All things of beauty meet."

Bone Pastor, Panis vere,
Jesu, nostri miserere;
Tu nos pasce, nos tuere,
Tu nos bona fac videre
  In terra viventium.
Tu qui cuncta scis et vales,
Qui nos pascis hic mortales,
Tuos ibi commensales
Coheredes et sodales
  Fac sanctorum civium.

BIBLIOGRAPHY

(In each case the edition mentioned is the one that has been made use of in this book. The dates given are normally those on the title-pages. Collective works are indexed under their titles.)

Anglican Orders (English), London: S.P.C.K. 1932.

ARENDZEN, J. P. *Whom Do You Say——? A Study in the Doctrine of the Incarnation.* London: Sands. 1927.

ARSENIEV, N. *Mysticism and the Eastern Church.* E.T. by A. Chambers. London: S.C.M. 1926.

AULÉN, G. *Christus Victor. An Historical Study of the Three Main Types of the Idea of the Atonement.* E.T. by A. G. Hebert. London: S.P.C.K. 1931.

BARTH, K. *The Epistle to the Romans.* E.T. by E. C. Hoskyns. Oxford Univ. Press. 1933.

BERDYAEV, N. *Freedom and the Spirit.* E.T. by O. F. Clarke. London: Bles. 1935.

BICKNELL, E. J. *A Theological Introduction to the Thirty-nine Articles of the Church of England.* London: Longmans. 2nd ed., 1925.

BINDLEY, T. H. *The Oecumenical Documents of the Faith.* London: Methuen. 3rd ed., 1925.

BORN, M. *Experiment and Theory in Physics.* Cambridge Univ. Press. 1943.

BREMOND, H. *A Literary History of Religious Thought in France.* Vol. III. The Triumph of Mysticism. E.T. London: S.P.C.K. 1936.

BRIGHT, W. *Select Sermons of S. Leo the Great on the Incarnation, with his twenty-eighth Epistle, called the "Tome."* London: Masters. 2nd ed., 1886.

BRUNNER, E., *Man in Revolt. A Christian Anthropology.* E.T. by O. Wyon. London: Lutterworth Press. 1939.

BULGAKOV, S. *The Orthodox Church.* E.T. by E. S. Cram. London: Bles. 1935.

BUTLER, C. *Western Mysticism. The Teaching of SS. Augustine, Gregory and Bernard on Contemplation and the Contemplative Life. Neglected Chapters in the History of Religion.* London: Constable. 2nd ed. 1927.

CHAPMAN, H. J. *The Spiritual Letters of Dom John Chapman.* Edited by R. Hudleston. London: Sheed & Ward. 2nd ed., 1935.

CHARLIER, L. *Essai sur le Problème théologique.* Thuillies: Ramgal. 1938.

CHAVASSE, C. *The Bride of Christ. An Enquiry into the Nuptial Element in Early Christianity.* London: Faber. 1940.

The Church of God. An Anglo-Russian Symposium. Edited by E. L. Mascall. London: S.P.C.K. 1934.

CONGAR, J.-M. *Divided Christendom.* E.T. by M. A. Bousfield. London: Bles. 1939.

CROSS, F. L. *Darwell Stone, Churchman and Counsellor.* London: Dacre Press. 1943.

DEANESLY, M. *A History of the Medieval Church, 590–1500.* London: Methuen. 1925.

DE LA TAILLE, M. *Mysterium Fidei de Augustissimo Corporis et Sanguinis Christi Sacrificio atque Sacramento.* Paris: Beauchesne. 2nd ed., 1924. (E.T. of first book: *The Mystery of Faith.* London: Sheed & Ward. 1941.) *The Mystery of Faith and Human Opinion contrasted and defined.* E.T. by J. B. Schimpf. London: Sheed & Ward. 1930.

DE LUBAC, H. *Catholicisme. Les Aspects sociaux du dogme.* Paris: Ed. du Cerf. 1938.

DEMANT, V. A. *The Religious Prospect.* London: Muller. 1939.

DENZINGER, H. *Enchiridion Symbolorum Definitionum et Declarationum de rebus fidei et morum.* 11th ed., edited by C. Bannwart. Friburgi Brisgoviae: Herder. 1911.

Doctrine in the Church of England. The Report of the Commission on Christian Doctrine appointed by the Archbishops of Canterbury and York in 1922. London: S.P.C.K. 1938.

DODD, C. H. *The Apostolic Preaching and its Developments.* London: Hodder & Stoughton. 1936.

History and the Gospel. London: Nisbet. 1938.

DOMS, H. *The Meaning of Marriage.* E.T. by G. Sayer. London: Sheed & Ward. 1939.

Encyclopaedia of Religion and Ethics. Edited by J. Hastings. Edinburgh: T. & T. Clark. Vol. VII, 1914. Vol. IX, 1917.

Essays Catholic and Critical. By Members of the Anglican Communion. Edited by E. G. Selwyn. London: S.P.C.K. 3rd ed., 1929.

FANFANI, A. *Catholicism, Protestantism and Capitalism.* E.T. London: Sheed & Ward. 1935.

Foundations. A Statement of Christian Belief in terms of Modern Thought. By Seven Oxford men. London: Macmillan. 1912.

GARDEIL, A. *Le Donné révélé et la Théologie.* Paris: Ed. du Cerf. 1932. (Reprint of ed. of 1909.) *La Structure de l'Ame et l'Expérience mystique.* Paris: Gabalda. 3rd ed. 2 vols. 1927.

GARRIGOU-LAGRANGE, R. *Perfection chrétienne et Contemplation, selon S. Thomas d'Aquin et S. Jean de la Croix.* Paris: Desclée. 7th ed. 2 vols. 1923. *Le Sens du Mystère et le Clair-obscur intellectuel.* Paris: Desclée. 1934.

GAVIN, F. *Some Aspects of Contemporary Greek Orthodox Thought.* Milwaukee: Morehouse. London: S.P.C.K. 1923.

GIBSON, E. C. S. *The Thirty-nine Articles of the Church of England.* London: Methuen. 2nd ed., 1898.

GIFFORD, E. H. *The Incarnation. A Study of Philippians II.* 5–11. London: Hodder & Stoughton. 1897.

GILL, E. *The Necessity of Belief.* London: Faber. 1936.

GILSON, E. *God and Philosophy.* New Haven: Yale Univ. Press. London: Milford. 1941.

The Mystical Theology of St. Bernard. E.T. by A. H. C. Downes. London: Sheed & Ward. 1940.

The Philosophy of St. Bonaventure. E.T. by I. Trethowan and F. J. Sheed. London: Sheed & Ward. 1938.

Reason and Revelation in the Middle Ages. New York and London: Scribner. 1939.

The Spirit of Medieval Philosophy. E.T. by A. H. C. Downes. London: Sheed & Ward. 1936.

The Unity of Philosophical Experience. London: Sheed & Ward. 1938.

Christianisme et Philosophie. Paris: Vrin. 1936.

GONSETH, F. *Les Fondements des Mathématiques.* Paris: Blanchard. 1926.

GORE, C. *Belief in Christ.* London: Murray. 1922.

Belief in God. London: Murray. 1921.

Dissertations on Subjects connected with the Incarnation. London: Murray. 2nd ed., 1896.

HALL, F. J. *Evolution and the Fall.* New York: Longmans. 1910.

Introduction to Dogmatic Theology. New York: Longmans. 2nd ed., 1912.

The Kenotic Theory, considered with particular reference to its Anglican Forms and Arguments. New York: Longmans. 1898.

HEADLAM, A. C. *Christian Theology. The Doctrine of God.* Oxford: Clarendon Press. 1934.

HEBERT, A. G. *The Form of the Church.* London: Faber. 1944.

HICKS, F. C. N. *The Fullness of Sacrifice. An Essay in Reconciliation.* London: Macmillan. 1930.

HIPPOLYTUS, ST. *The Treatise on the Apostolic Tradition of St. Hippolytus of Rome, Bishop and Martyr.* Edited by G. Dix. London: S.P.C.K. Vol. I. 1937.

HODGSON, L. *And Was Made Man. An Introduction to the Study of the Gospels.* London: Longmans. 1928.

The Doctrine of the Trinity. London: Nisbet. 1943.

HOOKER, R. *The Works of that Learned and Judicious Divine, Mr. Richard Hooker.* Arranged by J. Keble. 7th ed., revised by R. W. Church and F. Paget. Oxford: Clarendon Press. 1888.

HOSKYNS, E. C. *Cambridge Sermons.* London: S.P.C.K. 1938.

The Fourth Gospel. Edited by F. N. Davey. London: Faber. 1940.

HUGON, E. *The Mystery of the Incarnation.* E.T. edited by A. Whitacre. London: Faith Press. n.d.

HUSAIN, I. *The Dogmatic and Mystical Theology of John Donne.* London: S.P.C.K. 1938.

HUXLEY, A. *Grey Eminence. A Study in Religion and Politics.* London: Chatto & Windus. 1941.

JALLAND, T. G. *The Church and the Papacy. A Historical Study.* London: S.P.C.K. 1944.

The Life and Times of St. Leo the Great. London: S.P.C.K. 1941.

JAMES, W. *The Varieties of Religious Experience. A Study in Human Nature.* London: Longmans. 2nd ed., 1902.

JENKINS, D. T. *The Nature of Catholicity.* London: Faber. 1942.

JOHN OF THE CROSS, ST. *The Complete Works of St. John of the Cross, Doctor of the Church.* Translated from the critical edition of P. Silverio de Santa Teresa, C.D., and edited by E. Allison Peers. London: Burns, Oates. 1934–5.

JONES, MAURICE. *The Epistle to the Philippians.* (Westminster Commentaries.) London: Methuen. 1918.

KARRER, O. *Religions of Mankind.* E.T. by E. I. Watkin. London: Sheed & Ward. 1936.

KIRK, K. E. *Ignorance, Faith and Conformity. Studies in Moral Theology.* London: Longmans. 1925.

KNOWLES, D. *The English Mystics.* London: Burns, Oates. 1927.

KNOX, W. L., and VIDLER, A. R. *The Development of Modern Catholicism.* London: Philip Allan. 1933.

KRAEMER, H. *The Christian Message in a non-Christian World.* New York: Harper. 1938.

LEWIS, C. S. *Out of the Silent Planet.* London: John Lane. 1938.

Perelandra. London: John Lane. 1943.

A Preface to Paradise Lost. Oxford Univ. Press. 1942.

The Problem of Pain. London: Bles. 1940.

The Screwtape Letters. London: Bles. 1942.

MACDONALD, A. *The Sacrifice of the Mass in the light of Scripture and Tradition.* London: Kegan Paul. 1924.

MANNING, B. L. *Essays in Orthodox Dissent.* London: Independent Press. 1939.

MARÉCHAL, J. *Studies in the Psychology of the Mystics.* E.T. by A. Thorold. London: Burns, Oates. 1927.

MARITAIN, J. *The Degrees of Knowledge.* E.T. by B. Wall and M. R. Adamson. London: Bles. 1937.

Redeeming the Time. London: Bles. 1943.

Science and Wisdom. E.T. by B. Wall. London: Sheed & Ward. 1940.

Scholasticism and Politics. E.T. edited by M. J. Adler. London: Bles. 1940.

True Humanism. E.T. by M. R. Adamson. London: Bles. 1938.

De la Philosophie chrétienne. Paris: Desclée. 1933.

Théonas, ou les Entretiens d'un Sage et de deux philosophes sur diverses matières inégalement actuelles. Paris: Nouvelle Librairie Nationale. 2nd ed., 1925.

MASCALL, E. L. *He Who Is. A Study in Traditional Theism.* London: Longmans. 1943.

MATTHEWS, W. R. *God in Christian Thought and Experience.* London: Nisbet. 1930.

MERSCH, E., *The Whole Christ. The Historical Development of the Doctrine of the Mystical Body in Scripture and Tradition.* E.T. by J. R. Kelly. Milwaukee: Bruce. 1938.

Le Corps mystique du Christ. Étude de Théologie historique (original of the above). Louvain: Museum Lessianum. 2 vols. 1933.

Morale et Corps mystique. Paris: Desclée. 1937.

MICHAEL, J. H. *The Epistle of Paul to the Philippians.* (Moffat Commentary.) London: Hodder & Stoughton. n.d.

MOZLEY, J. K. *The Impassibility of God. A Survey of Christian Thought.* Cambridge Univ. Press. 1926.

A Necessary Doctrine and Erudition for any Christian Man, 1543. (" The King's Book.") London: S.P.C.K. 1932.

NEWMAN, J. H. *On the Scope and Nature of University Education.* London: Dent. Everyman's Library. n.d.

NIEBUHR, R. *The Nature and Destiny of Man.* London: Nisbet. Vol. I: *Human Nature.* 1941. Vol. II: *Human Destiny.* 1943.

Moral Man and Immoral Society. A Study in Ethics and Politics. New York: Scribner. 1934.

Northern Catholicism. Centenary Studies in the Oxford and parallel Movements. Edited by N. P. Williams and C. Harris. London: S.P.C.K. 1933.

NYGREN, A. *Agape and Eros. A Study of the Christian Idea of Love.* Part I. E.T. by A. G. Hebert. London: S.P.C.K. 1932. Part II. E.T. by P. S. Watson. London: S.P.C.K. 2 vols. 1938–9.

The Parish Communion. A Book of Essays. Edited by A. G. Hebert. London: S.P.C.K. 1937.

PARKER, T. M. *The Re-creation of Man.* London: Dacre Press. 1940.

PEERS, E. ALLISON. *Spirit of Flame. A Study of St. John of the Cross.* London: S.C.M. 1943.

PIUS XII, Pope. *The Mystical Body of Jesus Christ.* E.T., by G. D. Smith, of the Encyclical Letter *Mystici Corporis Christi.* London: Catholic Truth Society. 1944.

POULAIN, A. *The Graces of Interior Prayer.* E.T. by L. L. Yorke Smith. London: Kegan Paul. 1921.

PRESTIGE, G. L. *Fathers and Heretics. Six Studies in Dogmatic Faith with Prologue and Epilogue.* London: S.P.C.K. 1940.

God in Patristic Thought. London: Heinemann. 1936.

QUICK, O. C. *The Christian Sacraments.* London: Nisbet. 1927.
Doctrines of the Creed. Their Basis in Scripture and their Meaning to-day. London: Nisbet. 1938.

RAMSEY, A. M. *The Gospel and the Catholic Church.* London: Longmans. 1936.

RAVEN, C. E. *Apollinarianism. An Essay on the Christology of the Early Church.* Cambridge Univ. Press. 1923.

REES, A. H. *The Doctrine of Justification in the Anglican Reformers.* London: S.P.C.K. 1939.
Eucharistic Doctrine and Reunion. London: S.P.C.K. 1936.

REEVES, J. B. *The Dominicans.* London: Sheed & Ward. 1939.

RELTON, H. M. *A Study in Christology.* London: S.P.C.K. 1917.

RUSSELL, B. *The Principles of Mathematics.* London: Allen & Unwin. 2nd ed., 1937.

Russia and the English Church. Containing a Correspondence between Mr. Palmer, Fellow of Magdalen College, Oxford, and M. Khomiakoff in the years 1844–1854. Edited by W. J. Birkbeck. London: Rivington. 1895. S.P.C.K. 1917.

RUYSBROECK, J. VAN. *The Seven Steps of the Ladder of Spiritual Love.* E.T. by F. Sherwood Taylor. London: Dacre Press. n.d. (1944).

SELLERS, R. V. *Two Ancient Christologies.* London: S.P.C.K. 1940.
The Council of Chalcedon, London : S.P.C.K. 1953.

SERTILLANGES, A. D. *Le Christianisme et les Philosophies.* Paris: Aubier. n.d.

SMYTH, F. H. *Manhood into God.* New York: Round Table Press. 1940.

SOLOVYEV, V. *God, Man and the Church. The Spiritual Foundations of Life.* E.T. by D. Attwater, from the French version of G. Tsebrikov and A. Martin. London: James Clarke. n.d.

SPENS, W. *Belief and Practice.* London: Longmans. 2nd ed., 1917.

STONE, D. *A History of the Doctrine of the Holy Eucharist.* London: Longmans. 2 vols. 1909.
Outlines of Christian Dogma. London: Longmans. 4th ed., 1907.

The Study of Theology. Prepared under the direction of K. E. Kirk. London: Hodder & Stoughton. 1939.

SYMONDS, H. E. *The Council of Trent and Anglican Formularies.* Oxford Univ. Press. 1933.

TANQUEREY, A. *Brevior Synopsis Theologiae Dogmaticae.* Paris: Desclée. 1931.

TAWNEY, R. H. *Religion and the Rise of Capitalism. A Historical Study.* London: Murray. 1926.

TEMPLE, W. *Christus Veritas.* London: Macmillan. 1924.

TERESA OF JESUS, ST. *The Interior Castle.* E.T. by a Benedictine of Stanbrook. London: Thomas Baker. 4th ed., 1930.

THOMAS AQUINAS, ST. *Summa contra Gentiles.* E.T. by the English Dominican Fathers. London: Burns, Oates. 1924–9.
Summa Theologica. E.T. by the English Dominican Fathers. London: Burns, Oates. 1920–5.

THORNTON, L. S. *The Common Life in the Body of Christ.* London: Dacre Press. n.d. (1942).

The Incarnate Lord. An Essay concerning the Doctrine of the Incarnation in its relation to Organic Conceptions. London: Longmans. 1928.

Thy Household the Church. Proposals for Government and Order in the Church of England. By a Group of the Clergy. London: Dacre Press. 1943.

TILLICH, P. *The Interpretation of History.* E.T. by N. A. Rasetzki and E. L. Talmey. New York: Scribner. 1936.

Twelve Sermons preached at the Consecration of the Cathedral Church of Truro. Truro: Heard. London: Wells Gardner; Masters. 1888.

TUCKWELL, W. *Reminiscences of Oxford.* London: Cassell. 1900.

USHENKO, A. P. *The Problems of Logic.* London: Allen & Unwin. 1941.

VERRIÈLE, A. *Le Surnaturel en nous et le Péché originel.* Paris: Bloud et Gay. New ed. 1934.

VIDLER, A. R. See KNOX, W. L.

VINCENT, MARVIN. *A Critical and Exegetical Commentary on the Epistles to the Philippians and to Philemon.* (International Critical Commentary.) Edinburgh: T. & T. Clark. 1897.

VONIER, A. *A Key to the Doctrine of the Eucharist.* London: Burns, Oates. 1925.

WATKIN, E. I. *Theism, Agnosticism and Atheism.* London: Heritage. 1936.

The Philosophy of Mysticism. London: Grant Richards. 1920.

WESSELING, T. *Liturgy and Life.* London: Longmans. 1938.

WESTON, F. *The Christ and His Critics. An open Pastoral Letter to the European Missionaries of his Diocese.* London: Mowbray. 1919.

The One Christ. An Enquiry into the Manner of the Incarnation. London: Longmans. 1907.

WHALE, J. S. *Christian Doctrine.* Cambridge Univ. Press. 1941.

WHITEHEAD, A. N. *Process and Reality. An Essay in Cosmology.* Cambridge Univ. Press. 1929.

WILBERFORCE, R. I. *The Doctrine of the Holy Eucharist.* London: Mozley. 1853.

The Doctrine of the Incarnation of our Lord Jesus Christ in its Relation to Mankind and to the Church. London: Mozley. New ed. 1875.

WILLIAMS, N. P. *The Ideas of the Fall and of Original Sin. A Historical and Critical Study.* London: Longmans. 1927.

WORDSWORTH, C. *A Church History to the Council of Nicaea.* London: Rivingtons. 1881.

The Holy Bible with Notes and Introductions. London: Rivingtons. 3rd ed. Commentary on the Pentateuch. 1880. Commentary on the Song of Songs. 1876.

ZANKOV, S. *The Eastern Orthodox Church.* E.T. by D. A. Lowrie. London: S.C.M. 1929.

ZERNOV, N. *Three Russian Prophets. Khomiakov, Dostoevsky, Soloviev.* London: S.C.M. 1944.

INDEX OF PROPER NAMES

(Asterisks refer to footnotes. The more important references are in heavy type. Biblical names have not been included.)